metaphors be with you

Also by Dr. Mardy Grothe

Neverisms

Ifferisms

I Never Metaphor I Didn't Like

Viva la Repartee

Oxymoronica

Never Let a Kiss Fool You or a Fool Kiss You

metaphors be with you

an a-to-z dictionary of history's greatest metaphorical quotations

Dr. Mardy Grothe

HARPER

NEW YORK · LONDON · TORONTO · SYDNEY

HarperCollins books may be purchased for educational, business, or sales promotional use. For information, please email the Special Markets Department at SPsales@harpercollins.com.

FIRST HARPER PAPERBACK EDITION PUBLISHED 2017.

Designed by Bonni Leon-Berman

Library of Congress Cataloging-in-Publication Data
Names: Grothe, Mardy, compiler.
Title: Metaphors be with you : an A to Z dictionary of history's greatest
  metaphorical quotations / Dr. Mardy Grothe.
Description: First edition. | New York, NY : HarperCollins Publishers, [2017]
  | Includes index.
Identifiers: LCCN 2016044709 (print) | LCCN 2017005907 (ebook) | ISBN
  9780062445339 (hardcover) | ISBN 9780062445353 (eBook)
Subjects: LCSH: Metaphor--Dictionaries. | Metaphor--Usage. | Quotations,
  English. | Semantics (Philosophy)
Classification: LCC P301.5.M48 G76 2017 (print) | LCC P301.5.M48 (ebook) |
  DDC 808/.032--dc23
LC record available at https://lccn.loc.gov/2016044709

ISBN 978-0-06-244534-6 (pbk.)

HB 12.28.2023

To my Wombmate,
and our Big Sister,
who remind me of the truth of an Ann Hood observation:

"A sibling is the lens through which you see your childhood."

contents

introduction *xi*

navigation guide *xxxvii*

the ten best things ever said on 250 topics

Contents { *viii* }

Contents { *ix* }

Contents   { *x* }

introduction

More than fifty years ago, my life was turned around by one of history's most famous metaphorical passages:

> **If a man does not keep pace with his companions,**
> **perhaps it is because he hears a different drummer.**
> **Let him step to the music which he hears,**
> **however measured or far away.**
>
> —HENRY DAVID THOREAU

I was in the middle of what is now called an *identity crisis*, and Thoreau's words were a lifeline. I didn't even know what a metaphor was at the time, but one of the best things about metaphors is that you don't have to know what they are to be moved by them.

You've probably experienced something similar in your life, for "we are lost, and then we're found" is one of history's great themes. And when we *are* found, it's often because of soul-stirring words from writers whose thoughts have lived on in their works.

Over the years, I've often wondered how life might have turned out differently had I never come across that *Walden* passage. More recently, that thought spawned another: What if Thoreau had expressed his observation literally, not metaphorically? Writing instead something like:

**Certain individuals are different from most other people,
and it is good that this is the way things are.**

The core of Thoreau's message is the same, but had it been phrased this way, I don't believe I would've been moved. And that prospect stimulated another thought: What if the device of metaphor had not even been available to Thoreau?

A WORLD WITHOUT METAPHOR

People rarely think about electricity when they flick on a light switch, and something similar occurs with metaphorical language. In everyday communication, people rarely think about the powerful role metaphor plays in their lives. With electricity, though, an occasional power outage jars our attention and reveals our dependence. What if we experienced a metaphor outage?

What *would* life be like in a world without metaphor? Your first thought might be that life would be bleak, or maybe barren. Sadly, though, you can't say things like that during a metaphor outage. In a world without metaphor, you can legitimately describe a physical terrain—like a desert or a coastline—as bleak or barren, but life is not a tangible thing. "Life" cannot be seen or touched or felt; it is a *concept* that exists only in our minds. When we take terms that are literally appropriate for physical objects and apply them to concepts and ideas, we are engaging in an act of metaphor.

Describing life as empty or impoverished would also be disallowed in a world without metaphor for the same reason. While one can literally describe a container as full or empty, or a person as wealthy or impoverished, a concept like *life* can be described in those ways only when we make the move from literal to figurative language.

When we say that people are "speaking figuratively," we mean they are using figures of speech to describe things and convey ideas. A defining characteristic of all metaphorical language is that it is literally false. When we employ the metaphor "time is money," for example, we know it's not truly the case, but it so perfectly captures our experience of time that we say it is figuratively—as opposed to literally—true.

"Time is money" is also relevant to our discussion of a world without metaphor. Not long after Ben Franklin first introduced it ("Remember that time is money") in *Advice to a Young Tradesman* (1748), the metaphor burrowed so deeply into the nation's consciousness that aspects of it began showing up in everyday phrases and expressions. The notion that money can be wasted resulted in sayings like "You're wasting my time" or "He wasted his life away." The fact that money can be spent resulted in sayings like "He spent a ton of time on that project" or "Come, spend a little time with me."

While none of these sayings would be described by the average person as metaphorical, they all derive from the original "time is money" saying—a metaphor that forms the foundation of hundreds of other expressions, including saving time, investing time, budgeting time, running out of time, and even living on borrowed time. None of these sayings, of course, would be possible in a world without metaphor. In *More Than Cool Reason: A Field Guide to Poetic Metaphor* (1989), George Lakoff and Mark Turner remind us:

WHAT IS A METAPHOR?

The *American Heritage Dictionary* defines metaphor this way:

A figure of speech in which a word or phrase that ordinarily designates one thing is used to designate another, thus making an implicit comparison, as in "a sea of troubles" or "All the world's a stage."

The word *metaphor* derives from two ancient Greek roots: *meta*, meaning "over, across, beyond," and *pheiren*, meaning "to carry, transfer." The root sense of the word is "to carry something across" from one conceptual domain to another.

Metaphor is an intellectual tool that allows us to make imaginative leaps. We know, for example, that the world is not literally a stage, but we give it such a name to make it more comprehensible. Aristotle had a lovely way of describing this process: "Metaphor consists in giving the thing a name that belongs to something else."

The *American Heritage Dictionary* definition says a metaphor is "an implicit comparison." This unusual term is used for one reason, and one reason only: to distinguish it from a simile, which makes an explicit—or direct—comparison.

We'll come back to similes a bit later, but I bring this up now because "implied comparison" is the *least* important thing to be said about metaphor. To describe a metaphor as "an implicit comparison" is like saying a dog is a four-legged mammal. Technically true, yes, but it is a bland and boring description. It also fails completely to capture the essence of the thing it attempts to describe. To get a better grasp of metaphor, forget dictionary definitions and choose from any one of the following metaphorical descriptions:

An idea is a feat of association,
and the height of it is a good metaphor.

—ROBERT FROST

Metaphor is the energy charge that leaps between images,
revealing their connections.

—ROBIN MORGAN

Effective metaphor does more than shed light
on the two things being compared.
It actually brings to the mind's eye
something that has never before been seen.
It's not just the marriage ceremony linking two things;
it's the child born from the union.

—REBECCA MCCLANAHAN

McClanahan makes a critical point here. It is not the *act* of comparing, but the *result* of the comparison that makes metaphor so special. Nowhere is this more apparent than in one of literature's most famous passages. When Shakespeare wrote, "All the world's a stage," he wedded two separate domains. But this was only the beginning. Once the linkage was made, all the attributes of what is called the *source domain* (the stage) could then be applied to the *target domain* (the world). Look at the first four lines:

All the world's a stage
And all the men and women merely players.
They have their exits and their entrances,
And one man in his time plays many parts.

True to the root sense of the word, Shakespeare "carries" or "transfers" attributes from *the stage* to *the world*. He describes inhabitants of the world as actors, refers to their exits and entrances, and points out the many roles they play in a lifetime. As readers, we could pick up the mantle and, as the saying goes, "pursue the metaphor" even further. We might contrast people who are well suited for their roles with those who are miscast. We could compare lead actors with those who play supporting roles. We could go on to describe human life in terms of the quality of the player's performances, much as the Latin writer Lucius Annaeus Seneca (Seneca the Younger) did sixteen hundred years before Shakespeare:

**Life is like a play: it's not the length,
but the excellence of the acting that matters.**

Picking up on Seneca's observation, we might contrast excellent performances with mediocre, forgettable, or disastrous ones. Applying the metaphor to ourselves, we might contemplate the importance of occasionally going off-script, improvising, or even abandoning lines that were written by others for us. To recall the earlier McClanahan observation, the "children" born from the union of *world* and *stage* are many, and they are varied. It was this attribute of metaphor that José Ortega y Gasset was thinking about when he wrote in *The Dehumanization of Art* (1925):

The metaphor is probably the most fertile power possessed by man.

Bernard Malamud expressed a similar idea in a 1975 *Paris Review* interview:

I love metaphor.
It provides two loaves where there seems to be one.
Sometimes it throws in a load of fish.

In many metaphorical observations, the *A is B* assertion is not explicitly stated. For example, when Margaret Atwood writes, "Potential has a shelf life," we must use our reasoning powers to deduce the precise underlying metaphor (*potential is a perishable commodity*). The same is true with an observation widely attributed to Pablo Picasso, but in fact written by the nineteenth-century German writer Berthold Auerbach:

Music washes away from the soul the dust of everyday life.[*]

While no formal *A is B* assertion appears in this observation, one is clearly suggested: *music is a cleansing liquid*. The quotation also nicely illustrates the difference between literal and figurative truth. In real life, music cannot wash anything. And a soul doesn't literally accumulate dust. But by imbuing music with the cleansing properties of water, Auerbach offers a timeless metaphor.

METAPHOR: A FIGURE OF SPEECH OR AN ACT OF THOUGHT?

While we generally associate metaphor with words and language, it is a misconception to view metaphor as simply a figure of speech. Indeed, one could make the case that metaphor has more to do with thoughts and thinking than with words and language.

---

[*] In the Picasso attributions, the observation is about art, and not music.

Aristotle recognized this aspect of metaphor in *Poetics* (322 BC). In singing the praises of gifted writers and orators, Aristotle described them as "masters of metaphor." Their special gift, he said, was a keen "eye for resemblance." By this, he meant they were unusually adept at discerning a relationship between things that appeared to have little in common. In his discussion of the ability to detect "the similarity in dissimilars," Aristotle was describing a *thinking* function, not a writing or a speaking one.

The very first step in metaphorical language, then, is an act of thought: perceiving a relationship between apparently unrelated things. Once the relationship is established, a second step enables the maker of a metaphor to express it in words. James Geary put it nicely in his book on the secret life of metaphor, *I Is an Other* (2011):

Metaphor is a way of thought long before it is a way with words.

The notion that metaphor is as much about ideas as it is language is now widely accepted, in part because of *Metaphors We Live By* (1980), a groundbreaking work by George Lakoff and Mark Johnson. In their book, which focuses on the conceptual rather than the linguistic aspects of metaphor, a key passage argues:

The essence of metaphor is understanding and experiencing one kind of thing in terms of another.

Keep this observation in mind as we examine a keen insight about metaphor offered more than five hundred years ago by one of history's most influential thinkers.

Desiderius Erasmus was a Dutch Catholic priest who grew gravely concerned over the corruption in his beloved church in the late fifteenth century. He ultimately presented his critique in the 1509 essay *In Praise of Folly*, which paved the way for the Protestant Reformation by satirizing ecclesiastical abuses. Erasmus was also one of the world's first great quotation collectors, compiling thousands of them in *Adagia* (Latin for "adages"), first published in 1500. In that book, he wrote:

An idea launched like a javelin in proverbial form strikes with sharper point on the hearer's mind and leaves implanted barbs for meditation.

Here Erasmus describes a core function of thought and thinking: the transmission of an *idea*. He likens it to a javelin throw—a wonderful example of finding a "similarity in dissimilars"—and pays homage to proverbial wisdom in the process. He continues with this remarkable observation:

It will make far less impression on the mind if you say "Fleeting and brief is the life of man" than if you quote the proverb "Man is but a bubble."

In arguing that a metaphor is more likely to penetrate the minds of people than a declarative statement, Erasmus offers an intriguing insight. When people hear "Brief is the life of man," the statement is processed cognitively. And it pretty much ends there. By contrast, when people hear "Man is but a bubble," the phrase compels them to imagine their own lives as a fragile entity that might burst and disappear in an instant. The contemplation of this striking visual image takes people beyond simple cognitive understanding and into the realm of the intuitive mind.

For many, the *word picture* created by "Man is but a bubble" also has an emotional—even an existential—component. This is pretty much what happened when I first encountered Thoreau's "different drummer" observation, and I believe something similar happens to everyone who's ever been moved by a metaphor. As noted in the Lakoff and Johnson observation earlier, people in the grip of a metaphor are truly understanding and experiencing one kind of thing in terms of another.

METAPHOR'S LESS ASSERTIVE COUSIN: THE SIMILE

So far, I've discussed only metaphor, but in the family of figurative language, there are several other important relatives. The simile is one of them. *Webster's New World Dictionary* defines *simile* this way:

A figure of speech in which one thing is likened to another dissimilar thing by the use of "like," "as," etc. ("a heart as big as a whale," "her tears flowed like wine").

Viewed structurally, a metaphor says that *A is B*, while a simile says *A is like B*. If we were to take the earlier Shakespeare passage and express it as a simile, only one word would need to be added: "All the world's *like* a stage."

The simile might be described as the less assertive first cousin of the metaphor. Not willing to boldly declare that A *is* B, the simile simply suggests that A is *similar* to B. A simile makes an *explicit* comparison; a metaphor, as discussed earlier, makes an *implicit* one.

The simile is far more common than the metaphor, employed in thousands of expressions we use every day without ever thinking we're speaking metaphorically, including "hard as a rock," "soft as a pillow," "light as a feather," "selling like hotcakes," and "shaking like a leaf." In his syndicated column on the art of writing, James J. Kilpatrick wrote of the simile:

> **It's the most familiar of all literary embellishments,**
> **in a class with a wedge of lemon or a sprig of parsley.**
> **It can raise a cupcake to the level of a** *petit four.*

In addition to *like* or *as*, a host of other words and expressions indicate the presence of a simile. They include *A may be likened to B*, *A is a kind of B*, and *A is not dissimilar to B*. After *like* or *as*, though, the most common simile indicator is *than*, as in "cuter than a button," "higher than a kite," "faster than a speeding bullet," or this thought from the title character in *King Lear*:

> **How sharper than a serpent's tooth**
> **It is to have a thankless child.**

While metaphor is the preferred vehicle of people offering a big idea, simile is the figure of choice for people who are trying to make a compelling point—as in this saying widely attributed to the nineteenth-century German chancellor Otto von Bismarck:

Laws are like sausages.
It's better not to see them being made. *

The best similes are not unlike a one-two combination in boxing. The first portion jabs at us in an arresting way; the second delivers the major blow. Two similes about life nicely illustrate the point:

Life is like a game of cards.
The hand that is dealt you represents determinism.
The way you play it is free will.

—JAWAHARLAL NEHRU

Life is like a ten-speed bicycle.
Most of us have gears we never use.

—CHARLES M. SCHULZ

Similes with a similar structure are also often found in the setup and punch lines of comedians and humorists:

Life is like a dog-sled team.
If you ain't the lead dog, the scenery never changes.

—LEWIS GRIZZARD

---

* Bismarck never said anything like this, though. In *The Quote Verifier* (2006), Ralph Keyes calls this an *orphan quotation*, a saying authored anonymously and then attributed to a famous person to give it cachet or credibility.

A bikini is like a barbed-wire fence.
It protects the property without obstructing the view.

—JOEY ADAMS

These examples are not to suggest, however, that similes are intellectual lightweights when compared with metaphors. Many are quite robust on their own. And when similes and metaphors are blended into the same observation, a potent combination can result:

We can think of history as a kind of layer cake
in which a number of different layers run side by side through time,
each with a dynamic of its own, and yet each from time to time
profoundly penetrating and interacting with others.

—KENNETH E. BOULDING

METAPHOR'S MORE CEREBRAL
COUSIN: THE ANALOGY

If a metaphor says *A is B* and a simile says *A is like B*, then an analogy says *A is to B as C is to D*. Shakespeare's famous passage expressed as an analogy might go something like this: "People are to the world as actors are to the stage."

It's actually a fun mental exercise to transform popular metaphorical observations into analogies. Take the classic Rudyard Kipling quotation: "Words are, of course, the most powerful drug used by mankind." The essential metaphor here is *a word is a drug*. Expressed as a simile, one would say,

"A word is like a drug." To analogize it, one might say, "Words are to the mind as drugs are to the body."

The Oxford Dictionary of Literary Terms (2008) defines *analogy* this way:

Illustration of an idea by means of a more familiar idea that is similar or parallel to it in some significant features, and thus said to be analogous to it. Analogies are often presented in the form of an extended simile.

Compared with metaphors and similes, analogies are slightly more complex, because *two sets of parallel ideas* are being considered simultaneously. Since the ability to think in this way has long been considered a sign of high mental functioning by psychologists, analogies have been a staple of intelligence tests for over a century (many of you will recall the analogy items from your high school SATs, or the Miller Analogies Test you took when applying to grad school).

Analogies are easy to spot because they're all phrased similarly. The most common form is *A is to B as C is to D*:

Reading is to the mind what exercise is to the body.

—JOSEPH ADDISON

Poetry is to prose as dancing is to walking.

—JOHN WAIN

Another common form is *as A is to B, so C is to D*:

As cold waters to a thirsty soul, so is good news from a far country.

—THE BIBLE, PROVERBS 25:25

As smoking is to the lungs, so is resentment to the soul.

—ELIZABETH GILBERT

Analogies phrased in this distinctive manner have been traced to the earliest days of civilization. By the classical Greek era, philosophers commonly used analogies to dispense ethical principles and moral lessons. In the fourth century BC, for example, the philosopher Antisthenes offered a powerful warning about envy:

As iron is eaten away by rust,
so the envious are consumed by their own passion.

Antisthenes could have simply declared that envy was a destructive passion, but he wasn't interested in transmitting an abstract thought. No, he wanted to create an image that had the potential to penetrate deeply. And he succeeded, for few images are as compelling as the slow, corrosive process whereby one thing eats away at—and eventually destroys—something else.

Analogies are often without peer when it comes to expressing important ideas. In 2006, the *New York Times* did a profile on Harry Whittington, a Texas lawyer who, a few days earlier, had been shot in the face by Vice President Dick Cheney in a hunting accident. In addition to his career as a lawyer and real estate investor, Whittington had served for a time on the Texas Board of Corrections. After a few years in that role, he came to an unsettling conclusion: while prisons did get criminals off the streets, they failed at rehabilitation and even fostered further criminal behavior. He began to express his view this way:

Prisons are to crime what greenhouses are to plants.

When well crafted, analogies can be an extremely economical way to express profound ideas. Henry David Thoreau loved them so much that he wrote:

All perception of truth is the perception of an analogy.

Admittedly, Thoreau may have gone a little overboard in his gushing tribute, but he was hardly alone in harboring a deep affection for this special mode of communication:

**Apt analogies are among the most
formidable weapons of the rhetorician.**
—WINSTON CHURCHILL

**Analogies, it is true, decide nothing,
but they can make one feel more at home.**
—SIGMUND FREUD

THE CULMINATION OF
A LIFE'S PASSION

Quotations—especially those of a metaphorical nature—have had a place in my life that was aptly described by Robert Burns in a 1792 letter:

I pick up favorite quotations, and store them in my mind as ready armor, offensive or defensive, amid the struggle of this turbulent existence.

They've lifted me up when I've been down, clarified things when I was confused, and helped me achieve a fresh perspective when old ways of looking at things were no longer working. In my career as a psychologist, I also used quotations in my therapy practice. I always knew I'd hit the bull's-eye when, after I proffered a quotation, a client would say, "Wait a minute; I want to write that down." That very thing happened a number of times with the following quotation:

Alcoholism isn't a spectator sport.
Eventually the whole family gets to play.

This comes from a writer you've likely never heard of, Joyce Rebeta-Burditt. She offered it in a little-known 1977 novel *The Cracker Factory* that is primarily remembered these days only by Natalie Wood fans (the novel was made into an ABC-TV movie of the week in 1979, with Wood in the starring role).

I was first drawn to the quotation because it so dramatically captured the essence of my own growing-up years. My siblings and our mother didn't sit around all day and simply watch Dad's alcoholism play out. No, we were intimately involved in—and deeply affected by—the drama. Over the years, I've shared the observation with hundreds of people who grew up in families affected by alcoholism. Many were so touched by the powerful and poignant phrasing that it immediately became their favorite quotation on the subject.

Metaphorical quotations also figured prominently in my three-decade speaking career. In my talks on leadership, for example, I sprinkled my presentations with dozens of them, almost always to the delight of those in the audience. One quotation in particular was routinely hailed as the single best thing people had ever heard on the subject:

A leader is a dealer in hope.

—NAPOLEON BONAPARTE

As my career as a psychologist and speaker began to wind down in 2008, I even wrote a book celebrating my love of metaphorical quotations: *I Never Metaphor I Didn't Like: A Comprehensive Compilation of History's Greatest Analogies, Metaphors, and Similes.*

That book—which featured two thousand quotations organized into chapters like "Wit & Humor," "Stage & Screen," and "The Literary Life"—was published when I was sixty-seven years old. While working on the book, I thought it might represent the culmination of a lifelong passion. But it didn't. If anything, it further whetted my interest, and my collecting efforts continued. It wasn't long before I was sitting atop a mountain of quotations.

Then, after a friend passed away unexpectedly in 2011, I had a sobering thought: if I died that day, my entire quotation collection would vanish. The thought of a lifetime's work disappearing *just like that* was painful to imagine. In that moment, I decided to do something that might be considered unusual—even risky—for a seventy-one-year-old man with a cancer history: I embarked on a ten-year plan to create a permanent online database of metaphorical quotations. Here's how I described it in an April 2013 e-newsletter:

> My goal is to put together the largest collection of metaphorical quotations ever assembled and make the entire collection freely available to people around the world. I'm envisioning a compilation of over 100,000 quotations (that's about the size of five *Bartlett's* quotation books), organized into an A-to-Z format. So, for anyone who wants to see the greatest metaphorical quotations ever authored on adversity, aging, or art (or life, love, and laughter; or science, sex, and success; or several hundred other topics), the information will be available instantaneously. And unlike the error-plagued quotations found on most websites, the ones I feature will be authenticated and fully sourced.

On January 1, 2014, I formally launched the project. Called *Dr. Mardy's Dictionary of Metaphorical Quotations* (*DMDMQ*), it's available for your perusal at www.drmardy.com/dmdmq. You can also access it by scanning this QR Code:

Now, nearly three years after its launch, *DMDMQ* is the world's largest online database of metaphorical quotations, with more than 25,000 quotations organized into over 1,000 A to Z categories. Will I make it to 100,000 quotations? At age seventy-four, who knows? But I'm having the time of my life. And, unlike almost all people my age, I know exactly what I'll be doing the day I shuffle off this mortal coil.

HOW THIS BOOK CAME ABOUT

From the beginning, my work on the online database was a labor of love, but I wasn't prepared for the extent of the labor involved. Finding quotations is easy, but the amount of sleuthing required to authenticate them and track down original sources is staggering. Two years into the project, I was consumed. I even began to wonder if I would ever again publish a traditional book. Then, one day while taking a nap, I had a dream.

Strolling through a neighborhood on Manhattan's Upper West Side, I accidentally happened upon a Museum of Quotations. Intrigued about the prospect of what might be found inside, I entered the building. A lobby billboard had a picture of the museum's curator, a guy I'd never heard of. I felt a tinge of envy, thinking, "I could've done this."

I soon found myself in the museum's Courage Gallery, where the walls were hung with beautifully framed works of art that blended words and images—all on the theme of courage. The works of art were all illuminated from above, and small groups of patrons were gathered in front of a number of them, engaged in conversation about elegant phrasing and striking imagery. A sign near the far exit directed people to other galleries, on such themes as love, life, sex, politics, and so forth. I then woke up. My first thought was, "Why didn't I think of that?" And the idea for this book was born.

What you hold in your hands is a museum of quotations disguised as a book—but not just *any* book. This is a new kind of quotation anthology, with some features never before seen in a popular reference work. First, though, a few words about its traditional aspects.

Metaphors Be With You is an anthology of 2,500 quotations fashioned from the three superstars of metaphorical language: metaphors, similes, and analogies. The book follows the format of a standard dictionary of quotations, which means it is organized by topic rather than by author. After this introductory chapter and an upcoming navigation guide, the remainder of the book consists of quotations only. No commentary or further text will be provided, except for an occasional footnote.[*]

THE TEN BEST THINGS EVER SAID ON 250 TOPICS

The heart of *Metaphors Be With You* is my selection of *the ten best things ever said* on 250 topics of deep human interest (a total of 2,500 quotations). The complete list of topics begins on page vii.

While many previous quotation anthologies—including some of my own—have purported to present "history's greatest sayings" or "the best things ever said," no previous book has taken on the challenge of selecting *the* ten best things ever said on such a large number of subjects. And while choosing the top ten of *anything* is always a challenging task, it's more fun

---

[*]   Footnotes often get a bad rap (William James called them "little dogs yapping at the heels of the text"), but when used judiciously, they can enhance understanding *and* enjoyment. I also like the word *footnote* because, like *insight* and *skyscraper*, it's a one-word metaphor (a page is like a body, with a head—ergo, *headline*—and a foot).

than it is difficult when you're selecting, say, the ten greatest Broadway musicals or the ten best rock groups.

The challenge of compiling a ten-best list becomes more daunting, however, when the universe of possibilities is significantly enlarged. And that is exactly the case when you consider the tens of thousands of things that have been said over the centuries on such timeless subjects as beauty, courage, life, and love. Lists from a number of people on *the* best quotations on subjects like these will be widely divergent, often reflecting the personal—even idiosyncratic—tastes of the compilers.

An ancient Latin saying says, "In matters of taste, there can be no disputes." But the truth of the matter is that I fully expect—and even fervently hope—that readers *will* dispute my selections. Spirited debate over *the* best quotations should not be dismissed, but welcomed. In fact, the celebration of such differences of opinion is built into the very heart of this project.

Let's say your favorite quotation on a topic didn't make my ten-best list. Not a problem. Each of the 250 major topics in this book is digitally linked by a QR Code to its corresponding section of *Dr. Mardy's Dictionary of Metaphorical Quotations*, mentioned a moment ago. If your favorite does not appear in these pages, you will likely find it there. If you also fail to find your favorite in the online database, I'll rectify the error as soon as you alert me to it (my contact information appears on page xxxvi).

FROM COLLECTOR TO CURATOR

I officially became a *quotation lover* when, as a college undergraduate, I was so moved by the wisdom of Henry David Thoreau that I copied a dozen quotations from *Walden* onto three-by-five-inch Oxford index cards and tacked them to a bulletin board above my desk.

As the decades passed, I evolved into a serious *quotation collector,* filling scores of spiral notebooks with hand-copied quotations (with the advent of the digital era, the spiral notebooks were replaced by computer files). My personal library contains *every* major quotation compilation published in the past century, along with close to five hundred other "quote" books. I've also published six books of quotations, which formally makes me a *quotation anthologist.*

In this project, my role has shifted to *quotation curator.* Instead of simply compiling quotations, my challenge has been to assess merit, judge quality, and select the very best. In compiling the 2,500 quotations that appear here, I estimate that I've examined more than five million quotations.

You will find many of history's most famous sayings in these pages, some from celebrated figures, others from people who deserve to be better known, and more than you might expect from people whose identities will never be known. A surprisingly large number go back to the classical era of Greece and Rome, serving as a reminder of how little the essential human condition has changed over the ages.

This is not simply a celebration of the ghosts of quotations past, though. Creations from all the modern masters of metaphor—male and female— are also honored. Be aware, though, that it is the quality of the observation and not the fame of the author that resulted in a quotation's inclusion. Many quotations are quite modern, with the most recent coming from a 2016 American broadcast of *Downton Abbey* (and no, for you fans of the show, it doesn't come from the Dowager Countess). More than five hundred of the quotations featured here have never before appeared in a published anthology of quotations.

I'm a stickler for accuracy, but I'm sure I've made some mistakes. If you spot one or would like to write for any other reason, you can e-mail me at drmgrothe@aol.com

I also have a website, where you can delve into the topic much further, learn about my other books, or sign up for my free weekly e-newsletter, *Dr. Mardy's Quotes of the Week*. Come visit sometime: www.drmardy.com.

navigation guide

*M*etaphors Be With You breaks new ground by using QR Codes to seamlessly link each of the book's 250 topics to its corresponding section of *Dr. Mardy's Dictionary of Metaphorical Quotations (DMDMQ)*, the world's largest online database of metaphorical quotations.

A QR ("quick response") Code is a small dot-matrix barcode 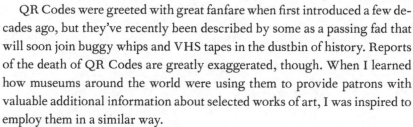 that can link the page of a book to a website. By scanning the QR Code on the right with your smartphone or tablet computer, you will be taken to the *DMDMQ* home page. You can also access the site directly on your computer (www.drmardy.com/dmdmq/).

QR Codes were greeted with great fanfare when first introduced a few decades ago, but they've recently been described by some as a passing fad that will soon join buggy whips and VHS tapes in the dustbin of history. Reports of the death of QR Codes are greatly exaggerated, though. When I learned how museums around the world were using them to provide patrons with valuable additional information about selected works of art, I was inspired to employ them in a similar way.

QR Codes have been used before in books, but never as extensively as

I use them here—or with such a singular motivation to serve the interests of curious readers. In this navigation guide, I demonstrate how, when used properly, QR Codes can connect the offline and online worlds in remarkable ways.

The following pages reproduce a typical *Metaphors Be With You* section—this one on the topic of Courage. All 250 topics in the book will be laid out similarly.

The topic name appears at the very top, along with a QR Code that will take readers to a corresponding section of COURAGE quotations in the online database (every major topic in the book has its own individual code, meaning there are 250 QR Codes in all). Just below the topic name are a number of *see also* cross references, should you wish to explore any related topics. The remainder of the section presents my selection of the ten best things ever said on the subject of courage.

Please note that I am presenting a "ten best" as opposed to a "top ten" list. This means that the quotations are arranged alphabetically by author, and *not* in a descending one to ten order. You will also notice that no source information for the quotations is provided. Detailed citations for all 2,500 quotations—and much more—can be found in the online database.

COURAGE

(see also COWARDICE and FEAR and HEROES &
HEROISM and RISK & RISK-TAKING)

**Courage and perseverance have a magical talisman,
before which difficulties disappear and obstacles vanish into air.**

—JOHN QUINCY ADAMS

**Courage is Fear
That has said its prayers.**

—KARLE WILSON BAKER

**Courage is the price that
Life exacts for granting peace.
The soul that knows it not, knows no release
From little things.**

—AMELIA EARHART

What a new face courage puts on everything!

—RALPH WALDO EMERSON

**Courage has need of reason, but it is not reason's child;
it springs from deeper strata.**

—HERMANN HESSE

Courage is reckoned the greatest of all virtues;
because, unless a man has that virtue,
he has no security for preserving any other.

—SAMUEL JOHNSON

It isn't for the moment you are struck that you need courage
but for the long uphill climb back to sanity and faith and security.

—ANNE MORROW LINDBERGH

Courage cannot be counterfeited.
It is one virtue that escapes hypocrisy.

—NAPOLEON BONAPARTE

Life shrinks or expands in proportion to one's courage.

—ANAÏS NIN

What is more mortifying
than to feel that you have missed the plum
for want of courage to shake the tree?

—LOGAN PEARSALL SMITH

After examining these "ten best" selections, you may be tempted to
quibble with my choices. Perhaps you were disappointed that your favorite
quotation didn't even make the list. You may have wondered, for example,
"What? Nothing from Churchill? I seem to recall a great courage quotation
from him."

Or perhaps you found yourself thinking, "Didn't Atticus Finch say something pretty memorable on the topic of courage in *To Kill a Mockingbird*?"

You may have thought, "Didn't Andrew Jackson offer a quotable observation about one man with courage making a majority?"

And finally, you may have wondered, "Doesn't a great book title—like Stephen Crane's *The Red Badge of Courage*—deserve inclusion in a list of the best metaphorical quotations?"

All good questions. And they take us to a feature of *Metaphors Be With You* that makes it different from all—and I do mean all—previously published quotation anthologies. By scanning the QR Code at the top of the COURAGE quotations page, you will be taken directly to the COURAGE section of *DMDMQ*, where more than one hundred additional quotations on the subject can be found, including all of those you might have wondered about.

In the online database, you will find the Churchill quotation you vaguely recalled. But you will also discover that the sentiment was not originally his, even though almost every Internet site attributes the quotation directly to him. Here's the full *DMDMQ* entry, which includes the quotation, source information, and an explanatory note from me:

Courage is rightly esteemed the first of human qualities, because, as has been said, it is the quality which guarantees all others.
WINSTON CHURCHILL, "ALFONSO THE UNLUCKY,"
IN *STRAND* MAGAZINE (JULY 1931)

QUOTE NOTE: This has become one of Churchill's most popular quotations, commonly with the "as has been said" portion omitted.

That phrase, however, indicates that Churchill was not claiming the sentiment as his own. He was clearly thinking about a 1775 remark Samuel Johnson made to James Boswell: "Courage is reckoned the greatest of all virtues; because, unless a man has that virtue, he has no security for preserving any other."

In the *DMDMQ* compilation, you'll also find the Atticus Finch quotation, but it's not exactly phrased in the most quotable way. You may also be surprised to discover that Finch offered the thought to his son, Jem, and not to his daughter, Scout, as many Harper Lee fans mistakenly believe. Here's the full entry:

I wanted you to see what real courage is,
instead of getting the idea that courage is a man with a gun in his hand.
It's when you know you're licked before you begin
but you begin anyway and you see it through no matter what.

HARPER LEE, ATTICUS FINCH SPEAKING TO HIS SON JEM, IN
TO KILL A MOCKINGBIRD (1960)

You will also discover that the popular Andrew Jackson quotation about one man with courage making a majority is apocryphal:

One man with courage makes a majority.

ANDREW JACKSON, QUOTED BY ROBERT F. KENNEDY IN THE FOREWORD TO
A 1964 RE-ISSUE OF JOHN F. KENNEDY'S *PROFILES IN COURAGE* (1956)

ERROR ALERT: This saying became very popular after it was offered—without a source—by Robert Kennedy (he found the quotation in a WWII notebook kept by older brother John). Ronald Reagan famously repeated the quotation when he nominated Robert Bork to the Supreme Court in 1987. An 1860 biography indicated that Jackson might have said, "Desperate courage makes one a majority," but there is no evidence he expressed his thought in the manner recalled by JFK. The phrasing of the apocryphal quotation might have been borrowed from a saying long attributed to Scottish clergyman John Knox (1505–72): "A man with God is always in the majority."

And finally, you will also find *The Red Badge of Courage* title, along with an explanatory note where you will see—possibly for the first time—the original passage that inspired the title of the book. Here's the complete entry:

The Red Badge of Courage.

STEPHEN CRANE, TITLE OF 1895 NOVEL

QUOTE NOTE: Since the publication of Crane's literary classic, a wartime wound or injury has been described as *a red badge of courage*. The novel's protagonist is Henry Fielding, a Union soldier who feels deep shame after fleeing from a Civil War battle. The narrator says of him: "At times he regarded the wounded soldiers in an envious way. He conceived persons with torn bodies to be peculiarly happy. He wished that he, too, had a wound, a red badge of courage."

These four illustrations demonstrate the kind of synergy that is possible between a book and a website. No published anthology of quotations has ever been linked to an online database in this manner. It's not unlike having an oceanfront property with a swimming pool in your backyard. Sometimes a dip in the pool is all you desire; it's convenient, refreshing, and thoroughly enjoyable. But sometimes you want—or need—something more, and the ocean provides a universe of possibilities (windsurfing, kayaking, scuba diving, snorkeling, surfing, fishing) that are simply not available in the limited environment of your backyard.

As a book, *Metaphors Be With You* is aimed at a target audience of quotation lovers. But for those who take their quotations seriously—writers, journalists, researchers, reference librarians, anthologists, and a host of others—*Dr. Mardy's Dictionary of Metaphorical Quotations* provides an ocean of information impossible to imagine in a single book.

I mentioned in the Introduction that it is possible to view *Metaphors Be With You* as a gallery of quotations disguised as a book. So far, you've seen only the COURAGE collection. The remaining collections—all 249 of them—await.

Metaphors be with you.

the ten best things ever said on 250 topics

ABILITY

(see also AMBITION and ASPIRATION and GENIUS and
POTENTIAL and SUCCESS and TALENT)

Natural abilities are like natural plants, that need pruning by study.

—FRANCIS BACON (1561–1626)

**Natural ability without education has more often
raised a man to glory and virtue than education without natural ability.**

—MARCUS TULLIUS CICERO

**There are many rare abilities in the world
which Fortune never brings to light.**

—THOMAS FULLER, MD

**Ability and achievement are *bona fides* no one dares question,
no matter how unconventional the man who presents them.**

—J. PAUL GETTY[*]

The winds and waves are always on the side of the ablest navigators.

—EDWARD GIBBON

---

[*]   Bona fide and bona fides (pronounced *FEE-daze*) are Latin expressions meaning "in good
faith" and "good faith," respectively. The former is almost always used as an adjective
for "genuine" (a bona fide offer) and the latter for "credentials" (this is the sense in which
Getty uses the term).

A special ability means
a heavy expenditure of energy in a particular direction,
with a consequent drain from some other side of life.

—CARL JUNG

It is a great ability to be able to conceal one's ability.

—FRANÇOIS, DUC DE LA ROCHEFOUCAULD

Ability is not something to be saved, like money,
in the hope that you can draw interest on it.
The interest comes from the spending.
Unused ability, like unused muscles, will atrophy.

—ELEANOR ROOSEVELT

The abilities of man must fall short on one side or other,
like too scanty a blanket when you are a-bed;
if you pull it upon your shoulders, you leave your feet bare;
if you thrust it down upon your feet, your shoulders are uncovered.

—WILLIAM TEMPLE

Intelligence is quickness to apprehend as distinct from ability,
which is capacity to act wisely on the thing apprehended.

—ALFRED NORTH WHITEHEAD

ABSENCE

(see also FRIENDSHIP and LOVE and RELATIONSHIPS)

The heart may think it knows better;
the senses know that absence blots people out.

—ELIZABETH BOWEN

Can flowers but droop in absence of the sun,
Which waked their sweets?

—JOHN DRYDEN

When you part from your friend, you grieve not;
For that which you love most in him may be clearer in his absence,
as the mountain to the climber is clearer from the plain.

—KAHLIL GIBRAN

Friendship, like love, is destroyed by long absence,
though it may be increased by short intermissions.

—SAMUEL JOHNSON

Sometimes, when one person is missing,
the whole world seems depopulated.

—ALPHONSE DE LAMARTINE

Absence lessens the minor passions and increases the great ones,
as the wind douses a candle and kindles a fire.

—FRANÇOIS, DUC DE LA ROCHEFOUCAULD

The longest absence is less perilous to love
than the terrible trials of incessant proximity.

—OUIDA (MARIA LOUISE RAMÉ)

How like a Winter hath my absence been
From thee.

—WILLIAM SHAKESPEARE

Fond as we are of our loved ones,
there comes at times during their absence an unexplained peace.

—ANNE SHAW

Where you used to be, there is a hole in the world,
which I find myself constantly walking around in the day-time,
and falling into at night.

—EDNA ST. VINCENT MILLAY

ACTION

(see also THOUGHT and WORDS)

Sentiment without action is the ruin of the soul.

—EDWARD ABBEY

Action is indeed the sole medium of expression for ethics.

—JANE ADDAMS

Action is the antidote to despair.

—JOAN BAEZ

Action springs not from thought, but from a readiness for responsibility.

—DIETRICH BONHOEFFER

An action is the perfection and publication of thought.

—RALPH WALDO EMERSON

I have always thought the actions of men
the best interpreters of their thoughts.

—JOHN LOCKE

Every man feels instinctively
that all the beautiful sentiments in the world
weigh less than a single lovely action.

—JAMES RUSSELL LOWELL

Dreams grow holy put in action.

—ADELAIDE PROCTOR

Action is eloquence.

—WILLIAM SHAKESPEARE

From thinking proceeds speaking;
thence to acting is often but a single step.
But how irrevocable and tremendous!

—GEORGE WASHINGTON

ADOLESCENCE

(see also AGE & AGING and CHILDHOOD and
CHILDREN and FAMILY and MATURITY and
YOUTH and YOUTH & AGE)

Adolescence is society's permission slip
for combining physical maturity with psychological irresponsibility.

—TERRI APTER

Young birds on their first flight.

—GEORGES BERNANOS, ON ADOLESCENTS

You don't have to suffer to be a poet.
Adolescence is enough suffering for anyone.

—JOHN CIARDI

All the best human impulses can be traced back to adolescence.

—HELENE DEUTSCH

Human life is a continuous thread
which each of us spins to his own pattern, rich and complex in meaning.
There are no natural knots in it.
Yet knots form, nearly always in adolescence.

—EDGAR Z. FRIEDENBERG

Adolescence isn't a training ground for adulthood now;
it is a holding pattern for aging youth.

—ELLEN GOODMAN

We carry adolescence around in our bodies all our lives.

—GARRISON KEILLOR

Adolescence is a kind of emotional seasickness.
Both are funny, but only in retrospect.

—ARTHUR KOESTLER

Adolescence is a twentieth-century invention
most parents approach with dread
and look back on with the relief of survivors.

—FAYE MOSKOWITZ

Adolescence is a tough time for parent and child alike.
It is a time between: between childhood and maturity,
between parental protection and personal responsibility,
between life stage-managed by grown-ups and life privately held.

—ANNA QUINDLEN

ADVENTURE

(see also CURIOSITY and DIFFICULTIES and DISCOVERY
and OBSTACLES and PROBLEMS and TROUBLE)

Never forget that life can only be nobly inspired and rightly lived
if you take it bravely, gallantly, as a splendid adventure.

—ANNIE BESANT

A little *tumult*, now and then, is an agreeable quickener of sensation;
such as a revolution, a battle, or an *adventure* of any lively description.

—GEORGE NOEL GORDON, LORD BYRON

An adventure is only an inconvenience rightly considered.
An inconvenience is only an adventure wrongly considered.

—G. K. CHESTERTON

A task, any task, undertaken in an adventurous spirit
acquires the merit of romance.

—JOSEPH CONRAD

Life is either a daring adventure or nothing.

—HELEN KELLER

How narrow is the line
which separates an adventure from an ordeal.

—HAROLD NICOLSON

They sicken of the calm, who know the storm.

—DOROTHY PARKER

What a large volume of adventures may be grasped
within this little span of life by him who interests his heart in every thing;
and who, having eyes to see what time and chance
are perpetually holding out to him as he journeyeth on his way.

—LAURENCE STERNE

Adventure is hardship aesthetically considered.

—BARRY TARGAN

Life ought to be a struggle of desire towards adventures
whose nobility will fertilize the soul.

—REBECCA WEST

ADVERSITY

(see also DIFFICULTIES and OBSTACLES and PROBLEMS
and SUFFERING and TROUBLE)

Gold is tried in fire,
and acceptable men in the furnace of adversity.

—THE APOCRYPHA, ECCLESIASTICUS 2:5

Adversity has the same effect on a man
that severe training does on the pugilist—
it reduces him to his fighting weight.

—JOSH BILLINGS (HENRY WHEELER SHAW)

If we had no winter, the spring would not be so pleasant:
if we did not sometimes taste of adversity,
prosperity would not be so welcome.

—ANNE BRADSTREET

He that has never known adversity
is but half acquainted with others, or with himself.

—CHARLES CALEB COLTON

There is no education like adversity.

—BENJAMIN DISRAELI

It is not given to everyone to shine in adversity.

—JANE AIKEN HODGE

Adversity has the effect of eliciting talents which,
in prosperous circumstances, would have lain dormant.

—HORACE

Perhaps adversity is a great teacher,
but he charges a high price for his lessons,
and often the profit we take from them
is not worth the price they have cost us.

—JEAN-JACQUES ROUSSEAU

Adversity in immunological doses has its uses;
more than that crushes.

—JOHN UPDIKE

What molting time is to birds,
so adversity or misfortune is . . . for us humans.

—VINCENT VAN GOGH

ADVICE

(see also EXPERIENCE and LEARNING and WISDOM and
WRITING ADVICE)

It is an easy thing for one whose foot
Is on the outside of calamity to give advice.

—AESCHYLUS

Unsolicited advice is the junk mail of life.

—AUTHOR UNKNOWN[*]

[*] This saying is often attributed to Bern Williams, a man whose identity has never been
established.

The brain may take advice, but not the heart.

—TRUMAN CAPOTE

To ask advice is in nine cases out of ten to tout for flattery.

—JOHN CHURTON COLLINS

**Good advice is like a tight glove; it fits the circumstances,
and it does not fit other circumstances.**

—CHARLES READE

**A man takes contradiction and advice much more easily than people think,
only he will not bear it when violently given,
even though it be well-founded.
Hearts are flowers; they remain open to the softly-falling dew,
but shut up in the violent downpour of rain.**

—JEAN PAUL RICHTER

**The true secret of giving advice is, after you have honestly given it,
to be perfectly indifferent whether it is taken or not,
and never persist in trying to set people right.**

—HANNAH WHITALL SMITH

No enemy is worse than bad advice.

—SOPHOCLES

It's queer how ready people always are
with advice in any real or imaginary emergency,
and no matter how many times experience has shown them to be wrong,
they continue to set forth their opinions
as if they had received them from the Almighty!

—ANNE SULLIVAN

Insistent advice may develop into interference,
and interference, someone has said, is the hind hoof of the devil.

—CAROLYN WELLS

AGE & AGING

(see also AGE & AGING—MIDDLE AGE and AGE &
AGING—OLD AGE and MATURITY and YOUTH and
YOUTH & AGE)

To know how to grow old is the masterwork of wisdom,
and one of the most difficult chapters in the great art of living.

—HENRI FRÉDÉRIC AMIEL

Age will not be defied.

—FRANCIS BACON (1561–1626)

As you get older, you find that often the wheat,
disentangling itself from the chaff, comes out to meet you.

—GWENDOLYN BROOKS

We need to break through the age mystique by continuing to grow,
solving problems, making social changes.
We need to see our age as an uncharted adventure.

—BETTY FRIEDAN

We all run on two clocks. One is the outside clock,
which ticks away our decades and brings us ceaselessly to the dry season.
The other is the inside clock,
where you are your own timekeeper and determine your own chronology,
your own internal weather, and your own rate of living.

—MAX LERNER

Age imprints more wrinkles in the mind than it does on the face.

—MICHEL DE MONTAIGNE

The more sand has escaped from the hourglass of our life,
the clearer we should see through it.

—JEAN PAUL RICHTER

It is a mistake to regard age as a downhill grade toward dissolution.
The reverse is true.
As one grows older one climbs with surprising strides.

—GEORGE SAND

Old and young, we are all on our last cruise.

—ROBERT LOUIS STEVENSON

In spite of illness, in spite even of the arch-enemy sorrow,
one *can* remain alive long past the usual date of disintegration
if one is unafraid of change, insatiable in intellectual curiosity,
interested in big things, and happy in small ways.

—EDITH WHARTON

AGE & AGING—MIDDLE AGE

(see also AGE & AGING and AGE & AGING—OLD AGE and
MATURITY and YOUTH and YOUTH & AGE)

Years ago we discovered the exact point, the dead center of middle age.
It occurs when you are too young to take up golf
and too old to rush up to the net.

—FRANKLIN P. ADAMS

The power of hoping through everything,
the knowledge that the soul survives its adventures,
that great inspiration comes to the middle-aged.
God has kept that good wine until now.

—G. K. CHESTERTON

Forty is ten years older than thirty-nine.

—FRANK IRVING COBB

The really frightening thing about middle age
is the knowledge that you'll grow out of it.

—DORIS DAY

Whoever, in middle age, attempts to realize
the wishes and hopes of his early youth, invariably deceives himself.

—JOHANN WOLFGANG VON GOETHE

I think middle age is the best time, if we can escape
the fatty degeneration of the conscience which often sets in at about fifty.

—WILLIAM RALPH INGE

The afternoon of human life must also have a significance of its own
and cannot be merely a pitiful appendage to life's morning.

—CARL JUNG

He was then in his fifty-fourth year, when even in the case of poets,
reason and passion begin to discuss a peace treaty
and usually conclude it not very long afterwards.

—G. C. LICHTENBERG

Is it not possible that middle age can be looked upon as a period
of second flowering, second growth, even a kind of second adolescence?

—ANNE MORROW LINDBERGH

The best way to defeat the numbing ambivalence of middle age
is to surprise yourself—by pulling off some cartwheel
of thought or action never even imagined at a younger age.

—GAIL SHEEHY

AGE & AGING—OLD AGE

(see also AGE & AGING and AGE & AGING—MIDDLE AGE
and MATURITY and YOUTH and YOUTH & AGE)

I inhabit a weak, frail, decayed tenement,
battered by the winds and broken in upon by the storms;
and, from all I can learn, the landlord does not intend to repair.

—JOHN ADAMS, AT AGE NINETY

One keeps forgetting old age up to the very brink of the grave.

—COLETTE (SIDONIE-GABRIELLE COLETTE)

Old age was growing inside me.
It kept catching my eye from the depths of the mirror.
I was paralyzed sometimes as I saw it make its way for me
so steadily when nothing inside me was ready for it.

—SIMONE DE BEAUVOIR

In old age our bodies are worn-out instruments,
on which the soul tries in vain to play the melodies of youth.
But because the instrument has lost its strings, or is out of tune,
it does not follow that the musician has lost his skill.

—HENRY WADSWORTH LONGFELLOW

Old age is like a plane flying through a storm.
Once you're aboard, there's nothing you can do.

—GOLDA MEIR

Old age is rather like another country.
You will enjoy it more if you have prepared yourself before you go.

—B. F. SKINNER

Do not go gentle into that good night.
Old age should burn and rave at close of day;
Rage, rage, against the dying of the light.

—DYLAN THOMAS

And what would it be to grow old?
For, after a certain distance, every step we take in life
we find the ice growing thinner below our feet,
and all around us and behind us we see our contemporaries going through.

—ROBERT LOUIS STEVENSON

I will offer here, as a sound maxim, this:
That we can't reach old age by another man's road.

—MARK TWAIN

Old age is a special problem for me because I've never been able
to shed the mental image I have of myself—a lad of about nineteen.

—E. B. WHITE

AIMS & AIMING

(see also AMBITION and ASPIRATION and DREAMS
[Aspirational] and GOALS and PURPOSE)

An ignorance of means may minister
To greatness, but an ignorance of aims
Makes it impossible to be great at all.

—ELIZABETH BARRETT BROWNING

We aim above the mark to hit the mark.

—RALPH WALDO EMERSON

Despair is the price one pays for setting oneself an impossible aim.

—GRAHAM GREENE

Be winged arrows, aiming at fulfillment and goal,
even though you will tire without having reached the mark.

—PAUL KLEE

Aim at Heaven and you will get earth 'thrown in':
aim at earth and you will get neither.

—C. S. LEWIS

If you would hit the mark, you must aim a little above it;
Every arrow that flies feels the attraction of earth.

—HENRY WADSWORTH LONGFELLOW

Not failure, but low aim, is crime.

—JAMES RUSSELL LOWELL

An aim in life is the only fortune worth the finding;
and it is not to be found in foreign lands, but in the heart itself.

—ROBERT LOUIS STEVENSON

In the long run men hit only what they aim at.
Therefore, though they should fail immediately,
they had better aim at something high.

—HENRY DAVID THOREAU

A noble aim,
Faithfully kept, is as a noble deed,
In whose pure sight all virtue doth succeed.

—WILLIAM WORDSWORTH

AMBITION

(see also AIMS & AIMING and ASPIRATION and DREAMS
[Aspirational] and GOALS and PURPOSE)

**Ambition is the subtlest beast of the intellectual and moral field.
It is wonderfully adroit in concealing itself from its owner.**

—JOHN ADAMS

Ambition is a dream with a V-8 engine.

—AUTHOR UNKNOWN[*]

Well it is known that ambition can creep as well as soar.

—EDMUND BURKE

**The greatest evil which fortune can inflict on men
is to endow them with small talents and great ambition.**

—LUC DE CLAPIERS (MARQUIS DE VAUVENARGUES)

**A slave has but one master;
an ambitious man has as many masters as there are people
who may be useful in bettering his position.**

—JEAN DE LA BRUYÈRE

---

[*] This observation is widely attributed to Elvis Presley, but there's no evidence that he said
it. Some Elvis attributions have him adding, "Ain't nowhere else in the world where you
can go from driving a truck to a Cadillac overnight."

Ambition is not a vice of little people.

—MICHEL DE MONTAIGNE

If ambition doesn't hurt you, you haven't got it.

—KATHLEEN THOMPSON NORRIS

Though ambition in itself is a vice, yet it is often the parent of virtues.

—QUINTILIAN

Ambition, old as mankind, the immemorial weakness of the strong.

—VITA SACKVILLE-WEST

**There is a loftier ambition than merely to stand high in the world.
It is to stoop down and lift mankind a little higher.**

—HENRY VAN DYKE

ANGER

(see also HATRED and JEALOUSY and PASSION and
QUARRELS and RESENTMENT)

**Bitterness is like cancer. It eats upon the host.
But anger is like fire. It burns all clean.**

—MAYA ANGELOU

Anger is an acid that can do more harm to the vessel
in which it is stored than to anything on which it is poured.

—AUTHOR UNKNOWN[*]

Anger can give energy to the mind
but only if it is harnessed and held in control.

—PEARL S. BUCK

Anger is momentary madness,
so control your passion or it will control you.

—HORACE

Anger blows out the lamp of the mind.
In the examination of a great and important question,
everyone should be serene, slow-pulsed and calm.

—ROBERT G. INGERSOLL

Anger is a signal, and one worth listening to.

—HARRIET LERNER

Anger is the fluid that love bleeds when you cut it.

—C. S. LEWIS

Anger is loaded with information and energy.

—AUDRE LORDE

[*] This is commonly attributed to Mark Twain, but it has never been found in any of his
writings or talks.

Anger is the common refuge of insignificance.
People who feel their character to be slight,
hope to give it weight by inflation.
But the blown bladder at its fullest distention is still empty.

—HANNAH MORE

When anger spreads through the breast,
guard thy tongue from barking idly.

—SAPPHO

ANIMALS

(see also and CATS and CATS & DOGS and DOGS)

I like handling newborn animals.
Fallen into life from an unmappable world,
they are the ultimate immigrants,
full of wonder and confusion.

—DIANE ACKERMAN

Sex is a sideshow in the world of the animal,
for the dominant color of that world is fear.

—ROBERT ARDREY

Until one has loved an animal,
a part of one's soul remains unawakened.

—AUTHOR UNKNOWN[*]

An animal's eyes have the power to speak a great language.

—MARTIN BUBER

Whenever you observe an animal closely,
you have the feeling that a person sitting inside is making fun of you.

—ELIAS CANETTI

Animals are such agreeable friends—
they ask no questions, they pass no criticisms.

—GEORGE ELIOT

Animals often strike us as passionate machines.

—ERIC HOFFER

From the oyster to the eagle, from the swine to the tiger,
all animals are to be found in men and each of them
exists in some man, sometimes several at a time.
Animals are nothing but the portrayal of our virtues and vices
made manifest to our eyes, the visible reflections of our souls.
God displays them to us to give us food for thought.

—VICTOR HUGO

[*] This beautiful observation is widely attributed to Anatole France, but has not been found
in his works.

Any glimpse into the life of an animal quickens our own
and makes it so much the larger and better in every way.

—JOHN MUIR

We call them dumb animals, and so they are,
for they cannot tell us how they feel,
but they do not suffer less because they have no words.

—ANNA SEWELL

ANSWERS

(see also CURIOSITY and DOUBT and QUESTIONS and
QUESTIONS & ANSWERS)

The trouble with life isn't that there is no answer,
it's that there are so many answers.

—RUTH BENEDICT

A soft answer turneth away wrath.

—THE BIBLE, PROVERBS 15:1

The answer, my friend, is blowin' in the wind.

—BOB DYLAN

A correct answer is like an affectionate kiss.

—JOHANN WOLFGANG VON GOETHE

Life is made up of constant calls to action,
and we seldom have time for more than hastily contrived answers.

—LEARNED HAND

Most people today don't want honest answers
insofar as honest means unpleasant or disturbing.
They want a soft answer that turneth away anxiety.
They want answers that are, in effect, escapes.

—LOUIS KRONENBERGER

Ah, what a dusty answer gets the soul
When hot for certainties in this our life!

—GEORGE MEREDITH

Teachers who offer you the ultimate answers
do not possess the ultimate answers, for if they did,
they would know that the ultimate answers cannot be given,
they can only be received.

—TOM ROBBINS

In the book of life, the answers are not in the back.

—CHARLES M. SCHULZ, CHARLIE BROWN SPEAKING

An answer is invariably the parent
of a great family of new questions.

—JOHN STEINBECK

APHORISMS

(see also LANGUAGE and QUOTATIONS and WRITING)

Aphorisms are essentially an aristocratic genre of writing.

—W. H. AUDEN

How many of us have been incited to reason,
have first learned to think, to draw conclusions, to extract a moral
from the follies of life by some dazzling aphorism.

—EDWARD GEORGE BULWER-LYTTON

Aphorisms give you more for your time and money
than any other literary form.
Only the poem comes near to it, but then most good poems
either start off from an aphorism or arrive at one.

—LOUIS DUDEK

An aphorism is the last link in a long chain of thought.

—MARIE VON EBNER-ESCHENBACH

Aphorisms are literature's hand luggage. Light and compact,
they fit easily into the overhead compartment of your brain.

—JAMES GEARY

The aphorism is a personal observation inflated into a universal truth,
a private posing as a general.

—STEFAN KANFER

An aphorism can never be the whole truth;
it is either a half-truth or a truth-and-a-half.

—KARL KRAUS (1874–1936)

Certain brief sentences are peerless in their ability
to give one the feeling that nothing remains to be said.

—JEAN ROSTAND

Aphorisms are salted and not sugared almonds at Reason's feast.

—LOGAN PEARSALL SMITH

An aphorism is a one-line novel.

—LEONID SUKHORUKOV

APOLOGY

(see also ERROR and FORGIVENESS and MISTAKES and
RELATIONSHIPS)

Apologizing doesn't always mean you're wrong
and the other person is right.
It just means you value your relationship more than your ego.

—AUTHOR UNKNOWN

Apologize, *v.i.* To lay the foundation for a future offense.

—AMBROSE BIERCE

Apology is birthed in the womb of regret.

—GARY CHAPMAN AND JENNIFER THOMAS

A stiff apology is a second insult. . . .
The injured party does not want to be compensated
because he has been wronged;
he wants to be healed because he has been hurt.

—G. K. CHESTERTON

Right actions for the future
are the best apologies for wrong ones in the past—
the best evidence of regret for them that we can offer.

—TRYON EDWARDS

An apology is the superglue of life!
It can repair just about anything.

—LYNN JOHNSTON

Apology is humanity's perfect response to imperfection. . . .
Apology sends the clearest signal that we have
the strength of character to reconcile ourselves with the truth.

—JOHN KADOR

Apologies rebuild the bridge
that gets severed when we hurt someone else.

—CHARLOTTE KASL

Apology is a lovely perfume;
it can transform the clumsiest moment into a gracious gift.

—MARGARET LEE RUNBECK

Is it not true that the ability to apologize
is one of the elements of true greatness?
It is the small-souled man who will not stoop to apologize.

—J. OSWALD SANDERS

ART

(see also [Works of] ART and ARTISTS and BEAUTY and
CREATIVITY and IMAGINATION)

Life beats down and crushes the soul,
and art reminds you that you have one.

—STELLA ADLER

In art as in lovemaking,
heartfelt ineptitude has its appeal and so does heartless skill,
but what you want is *passionate virtuosity.*

—JOHN BARTH

**The reward of art is not fame or success but intoxication:
that is why so many bad artists are unable to give it up.**

—CYRIL CONNOLLY

To make us feel small in the right way is a function of art.

—E. M. FORSTER

Art, that great undogmatized church.

—ELLEN KEY

**I think of Art, at its most significant, as a DEW line,
a Distant Early Warning system, that can always be relied on
to tell the old culture what is beginning to happen to it.**

—MARSHALL MCLUHAN

**We all know that Art is not truth.
Art is a lie that makes us realize truth.**

—PABLO PICASSO

Art enables us to find ourselves and lose ourselves at the same time.

—THOMAS MERTON

**The primary benefit of practicing any art,
whether well or badly,
is that it enables one's soul to grow.**

—KURT VONNEGUT JR.

Art is the most intense mode of individualism that the world has known.

—OSCAR WILDE

[Works of] ART

(see also ART and ARTISTS and BEAUTY and
CREATIVITY and IMAGINATION)

Every great work of art has two faces,
one toward its own time and one toward the future, toward eternity.

—DANIEL BARENBOIM

A work of art should be like a well-planned crime.

—CONSTANTIN BRANCUSI

Every work of art is one half of a secret handshake,
a challenge that seeks the password,
a heliograph flashed from a tower window,
an act of hopeless optimism in the service of bottomless longing.

—MICHAEL CHABON

A work of art is the trace of a magnificent struggle.

—ROBERT HENRI

Any work of art, regardless of its form or formlessness, is great
when it makes you feel that its creator has dipped into your very heart.

—FANNIE HURST

A work of art that contains theories
is like an object on which the price tag has been left.

—MARCEL PROUST

You use a glass mirror to see your face;
you use works of art to see your soul.

—GEORGE BERNARD SHAW

To say that a work of art is good,
but incomprehensible to the majority of men,
is the same as saying of food that it is very good
but that most people can't eat it.

—LEO TOLSTOY

The creation of a work of art, like an act of love,
is our one small "yes" at the center of a vast "no."

—GORE VIDAL

A work of art has an author and yet, when it is perfect,
it has something which is essentially anonymous about it.

—SIMONE WEIL

ARTISTS

(see also ART and [Works of] ART and BEAUTY and
CREATIVITY and IMAGINATION)

If the artist does not fling himself, without reflecting, into his work . . .
as the soldier flings himself into the enemy's trenches, and if,
once in this crater, he does not work like a miner . . .
he is simply looking on at the suicide of his own talent.

—HONORÉ DE BALZAC

Every artist dips his brush in his own soul,
and paints his own nature into his pictures.

—HENRY WARD BEECHER

The serious artist . . . is like an object caught by a wave and swept to shore.
He's obsessed by his material;
it's like a venom working in his blood and the art is the antidote.

—TRUMAN CAPOTE

The artist of to-day . . . walks at first with his companions,
till one day he falls through a hole in the brambles,
and from that moment is following the dark rapids of an underground river
which may sometimes flow so near the surface
that the laughing picnic parties are heard above.

—CYRIL CONNOLLY

Every production of an artist
should be the expression of an adventure of his soul.

—W. SOMERSET MAUGHAM

Every artist is an unhappy lover.
And unhappy lovers want to tell their story.

—IRIS MURDOCH

Artists are the antennae of the race.

—EZRA POUND

If there is any reason to single out artists
as being more necessary to our lives than any others,
it is because they provide us with light that cannot be extinguished.
They go into dark rooms and poke at their souls
until the contours of our own are familiar to us.

—PHYLLIS THEROUX

The wretched Artist himself is alternatively
the lowest worm that ever crawled when no fire is in him:
or the loftiest God that ever sang when the fire is going.

—CAITLIN THOMAS

ASPIRATION

(see also AIMS & AIMING and AMBITION and DREAMS
[Aspirational] and GOALS and MOTIVATION)

Far away there in the sunshine are my highest aspirations.
I cannot reach them: but I can look up, and see their beauty;
believe in them, and follow where they lead.

—LOUISA MAY ALCOTT

The barriers are not erected
which can say to aspiring talents and industry,
"Thus far and no farther."

—LUDWIG VAN BEETHOVEN

Ah, but a man's reach should exceed his grasp,
Or what's a heaven for?

—ROBERT BROWNING

Make no little plans; they have no magic to stir men's blood.

—DANIEL BURNHAM

We never know how high we are
Till we are called to rise;
And then, if we are true to plan
Our statures touch the skies.

—EMILY DICKINSON

One can never consent to creep when one feels an impulse to soar.

—HELEN KELLER

He who bears in his heart a cathedral to be built is already victorious.

—ANTOINE DE SAINT-EXUPÉRY

If a man constantly aspires, is he not elevated?

—HENRY DAVID THOREAU

We are all in the gutter, but some of us are looking at the stars.

—OSCAR WILDE

Too low they build, who build beneath the stars.

—EDWARD YOUNG (1683–1765)

AUTHENTICITY

(see also INDIVIDUALISM and INTEGRITY and HYPOCRISY)

Let the world know you as you are, not as you think you should be, because sooner or later, if you are posing, you will forget the pose, and then where are you?

—FANNY BRICE

Action is the language of the body
and should harmonize with the spirit within.

—MARCUS TULLIUS CICERO

You can't change the music of your soul.

—KATHARINE HEPBURN

What's a man's first duty? The answer's brief: to be himself.

—HENRIK IBSEN

The best way to define a man's character would be
to seek out the particular mental or moral attitude in which,
when it came upon him,
he felt himself most deeply and intensely active and alive.
At such moments there is a voice inside which speaks and says:
"*This* is the real me!"

—WILLIAM JAMES

One should stick by one's own soul, and by nothing else.
In one's soul, one knows the truth from the untruth, and life from death.
And if one betrays one's own soul-knowledge, one is the worst of traitors.

— D. H. LAWRENCE

One cannot violate the promptings of one's nature
without having that nature recoil upon itself.

—JACK LONDON

If a man can reach the latter days of his life with his soul intact,
he has mastered life.

—GORDON PARKS

This above all: to thine own self be true,
And it must follow, as the night the day,
Thou canst not then be false to any man.

—WILLIAM SHAKESPEARE

AUTHORS

(see also BOOKS and FICTION and LITERATURE and
NOVELISTS and NOVELS and READING and WRITERS
and WRITING)

Authors are sometimes like tomcats:
they distrust all the other toms, but they are kind to kittens.

—MALCOLM COWLEY

The author is like the host at a party. It is his party,
but he must not enjoy himself so much that he neglects his guests.
His enjoyment is not so much his own as it is theirs.

—CHARLES P. CURTIS

Choose an author as you choose a friend.

—WENTWORTH DILLON

An author in his book must be like God in the universe,
present everywhere and visible nowhere.

—GUSTAVE FLAUBERT

Authorship of any sort is a fantastic indulgence of the ego.

—JOHN KENNETH GALBRAITH

I never saw an author in my life, saving perhaps one,
that did not purr as audibly as a full-grown domestic cat
on having his fur smoothed the right way by a skillful hand.

—OLIVER WENDELL HOLMES SR.

The author always loads his dice,
but he must never let the reader see that he has done so.

—W. SOMERSET MAUGHAM

The author lives with one foot in an everyday world
and the other feeling about anxiously
for a foothold in another more precarious one.

—MARY ROBERTS RINEHART

Every author, however modest, keeps a most outrageous vanity
chained like a madman in the padded cell of his breast.

—LOGAN PEARSALL SMITH

The author's character is read from title-page to end.
Of this he never corrects the proofs.

—HENRY DAVID THOREAU

AUTOMOBILES

Cars today are almost the exact equivalent
of the great Gothic cathedrals:
I mean the supreme creation of an era,
conceived with passion by unknown artists,
and consumed in image if not in usage by a whole population
which appropriates them as a purely magical object.

—ROLAND BARTHES

A car can massage organs which no masseur can reach.
It is the one remedy for the disorders of the great sympathetic nervous system.

—JEAN COCTEAU

The automobile traveler is a king on a vinyl bucket-seat throne,
changing direction with the turn of a wheel,
changing the climate with a flick of the button,
changing the music with the switch of a dial.

—ANDREW H. MALCOLM

The automobile reaches to the heart of the American self-image
in the way the horse once did in the West.

—JESSICA TUCHMAN MATHEWS

The car has become a secular sanctuary for the individual,
his shrine to the self, his mobile Walden Pond.

—EDWARD MCDONAGH

The car has become the carapace, the protective and
aggressive shell, of urban and suburban man.

—MARSHALL MCLUHAN

No other man-made device since the shields and lances
of the ancient knights fulfills a man's ego like an automobile.

—WILLIAM ROOTES

The automobile is a peculiarly fertile species that reproduces freely
and appears to have no natural enemies
sufficiently powerful to hold its growth in check.

—GLENN SEABORG

In the 1950s, America was at the wheel of the world
and Americans were at the wheel of two-toned
(and sometimes even more-toned) cars,
tail-finned, high-powered, soft-spring rolling sofas.

—GEORGE F. WILL

As hand-to-hand combat has gradually disappeared . . .
Americans have turned to the automobile
to satisfy their love of direct aggression.

—TOM WOLFE

BABIES

(see also AGE & AGING and CHILDREN and FAMILY and MARRIAGE and PARENTS & PARENTHOOD)

A babe is nothing but a bundle of possibilities.

—HENRY WARD BEECHER

The human baby . . . is a mosaic of animal and angel.

—JACOB BRONOWSKI

The babe in arms is a channel through which
the energies we call fate, love, and reason visibly stream.

—RALPH WALDO EMERSON

Babies are such a nice way to start people.

—DON HEROLD

The baby, assailed by eyes, ears, nose, skin, and entrails at once,
feels it all as one great blooming, buzzing confusion.

—WILLIAM JAMES

A loud noise at one end
and no sense of responsibility at the other.

—RONALD KNOX, DESCRIBING A BABY[*]

---

[*] In his 1965 California gubernatorial campaign, Ronald Reagan famously tweaked Knox's remark when he said, "The Government is like a baby's alimentary canal, with a healthy appetite at one end and no responsibility at the other."

Every new baby is a blind desperate vote for survival:
people who find themselves unable
to register an effective political protest against extermination
do so by a biological act.

—LEWIS MUMFORD

They lie flat on their noses at first
in what appears to be a drunken slumber,
then flat on their backs kicking and screaming,
demanding impossibilities in a foreign language.

—KATHERINE ANNE PORTER, ON BABIES

A baby is God's opinion that the world should go on.

—CARL SANDBURG

A soiled baby, with a neglected nose,
cannot be conscientiously regarded as a thing of beauty;
and inasmuch as babyhood spans but three short years,
no baby is competent to be a joy "forever."

—MARK TWAIN[*]

---

[*]   In this observation, Twain cleverly references the immortal words of John Keats, who
     wrote in *Endymion* (1818): "A thing of beauty is a joy for ever:/ Its loveliness increases."

BEAUTY

(see also ART and [Works of] ART and ARTISTS and MALE-
FEMALE DYNAMICS and NATURE)

There is nothing that makes its way
more directly to the soul than beauty.

—JOSEPH ADDISON

Personal beauty is a greater recommendation
than any letter of reference.

—ARISTOTLE

Bait, *n*. A preparation that renders the hook more palatable.
The best kind is beauty.

—AMBROSE BIERCE

There are various orders of beauty,
causing men to make fools of themselves in various styles,
from the desperate to the sheepish.

—GEORGE ELIOT

Beauty is everywhere a welcome guest.

—JOHANN WOLFGANG VON GOETHE

Beauty can pierce one like a pain.

—THOMAS MANN

The ideal has many names, and beauty is but one of them.

—W. SOMERSET MAUGHAM

In every man's heart there is a secret nerve
that answers to the vibrations of beauty.

—CHRISTOPHER MORLEY

Beauty itself doth of itself persuade
The eyes of men without an orator.

—WILLIAM SHAKESPEARE

Beauty is only a promise of happiness.

—STENDHAL (MARIE-HENRI BEYLE)

BELIEF

(see also DOUBT and KNOWLEDGE and PRAYER and
QUESTIONS & ANSWERS and THOUGHT)

There is no belief, however foolish, that will not
gather its faithful adherents who will defend it to the death.

—ISAAC ASIMOV

Human psychology has a near-universal tendency
to let belief be colored by desire.

—RICHARD DAWKINS

A man must not swallow more beliefs than he can digest.

—HAVELOCK ELLIS

We are so constituted that we believe the most incredible things;
and, once they are engraved upon the memory,
woe to him who would endeavor to erase them.

—JOHANN WOLFGANG VON GOETHE

To have a reason to get up in the morning,
it is necessary to possess a guiding principle.
A belief of some kind.
A bumper sticker, if you will.

—JUDITH GUEST

A belief is a lever that, once pulled,
moves almost everything else in a person's life.

—SAM HARRIS

Believe that life *is* worth living,
and your belief will help create the fact.

—WILLIAM JAMES

One person with a belief
is a social power equal to ninety-nine who have only interests.

—JOHN STUART MILL

My own education operated by a succession of eye-openers
each involving the repudiation of some previously held belief.

—GEORGE BERNARD SHAW

Old beliefs die hard even when demonstrably false.

—EDWARD O. WILSON

BLUES

(see also ART and ARTISTS and JAZZ and MUSIC and
STRUGGLE and SUFFERING)

They've laughed to shield their crying
then shuffled through the dreams
and stepped 'n fetched a country
to write the blues with screams.

—MAYA ANGELOU

There are all different shades of blues.

—BETTY CARTER (LILLIE MAE JONES)

Rock is like a battery that must always go back to blues to get recharged.

—ERIC CLAPTON

As a form, the blues is an autobiographical chronicle
of personal catastrophe expressed lyrically.

—RALPH ELLISON

The blues came from nothingness, from want, from desire.
And when a man sang or played the blues,
a small part of the want was satisfied.

—W. C. HANDY

When we sing the blues,
we're singing out our hearts, we're singing out our feelings.
Maybe we're hurt and just can't answer back,
then we sing or maybe even hum the blues.

—ZORA NEALE HURSTON

The blues was like that problem child that you may have had in the family.
You was a little bit ashamed to let anybody see him, but you loved him.
You just didn't know how other people would take it.

—B. B. KING

The spirituals and the blues were not created out of sweet deceit.
Spirituals and blues contain sublimated
bitterness and humility, pathos and bewilderment.

—CLAUDE MCKAY

The Blues had a Baby and the World Called it Rock and Roll.

—BROWNIE MCGHEE, TITLE OF 1960 SONG

We today have the blues, too, but it is a blues of our day.
It's more of the mind and heart and not of the beating of the back.

—JOE WILLIAMS

BOOKS

(see also AUTHORS and BOOKSTORES and FICTION and
LIBRARIES and NOVELISTS and NOVELS and READING
and WRITERS and WRITING)

In the case of good books,
the point is not to see how many of them you can get through,
but rather how many can get through to you.

—MORTIMER J. ADLER

Some books are to be tasted, others to be swallowed,
and some few to be chewed and digested.

—FRANCIS BACON (1561–1626)

To read good books is like holding a conversation
with the most eminent minds of past centuries and, moreover,
a studied conversation in which these authors
reveal to us only the best of their thoughts.

—RENÉ DESCARTES

There are books . . . which take rank in your life
with parents and lovers and passionate experiences,
so medicinal, so stringent, so revolutionary, so authoritative.

—RALPH WALDO EMERSON

The book is the most efficient technological instrument
for learning that has ever been devised by the human mind.

—NORTHROP FRYE

A book should serve as an ice-axe to break the frozen sea within us.

—FRANZ KAFKA

Many readers judge the power of a book
by the shock it gives their feelings—
as some savage tribes determine the power of muskets by their recoil;
that being considered best which fairly prostrates the purchaser.

—HENRY WADSWORTH LONGFELLOW

All books are either dreams or swords,
You can cut, or you can drug, with words.

—AMY LOWELL

How many a man has dated a new era in his life from the reading of a book.

—HENRY DAVID THOREAU

By bedside and easy chair, books promise
a cozy, swift, and silent release from this world into another,
with no current involved but the free
and scarcely detectable crackle of brain cells.

—JOHN UPDIKE

BOOKSTORES

(see also AUTHORS and BOOKS and LIBRARIES and
NOVELISTS and NOVELS and READING and WRITERS
and WRITING)

Alas! Where is human nature so weak as in a book-store!

—HENRY WARD BEECHER

Booksellers, who are a race apart and one and all delightful company,
as befits those in whom the ideal and the practical are so nicely blended.

—CYRIL CONNOLLY

When I visit a new bookstore,
I demand cleanliness, computer monitors, and rigorous alphabetization.
When I visit a secondhand bookstore, I prefer indifferent housekeeping,
sleeping cats, and sufficient organizational chaos to fuel my fantasies.

—ANNE FADIMAN

There is nothing like the smell of a bookstore.
If you ask me, it's actually a combination of smells: part library,
part new-book smell, and part expectation for what you might find.

—KATHRYN FITZMAURICE

Even an ice cream parlor—a definite advantage—does not
alleviate the sorrow I feel for a town lacking a bookstore.

—NATALIE GOLDBERG

Bookshops are the first and foremost of fine sights
in all the fair cities of the world,
and the surest retreats of delectable temptation.

—HOLBROOK JACKSON

We visit bookshops not so often to buy any one special book,
but rather to rediscover,
in the happier and more expressive words of others,
our own encumbered soul.

—CHRISTOPHER MORLEY

Those of us who read because we love it more than anything . . .
feel about bookstores the way some people feel about jewelers.

—ANNA QUINDLEN

I love bookstores. A bookstore is one of the only
pieces of physical evidence we have that people are still thinking.

—JERRY SEINFELD

A bookstore is one of the few places where all the cantankerous,
conflicting, alluring voices of the world co-exist in peace and order,
and the avid reader is as free as a person can possibly be,
because she is free to choose among them.

—JANE SMILEY

BORES & BOREDOM

If you have once thoroughly bored somebody
it is next to impossible to unbore him.

—ELIZABETH VON ARNIM

Society is now one polished horde,
Formed of two mighty tribes, the *Bores* and *Bored*.

—GEORGE NOEL GORDON, LORD BYRON

Boredom is the fear of self.

—COMTESSE DIANE DE BEAUSACQ

The bore is usually considered a harmless creature,
or of that class of irrational bipeds who hurt only themselves.

—MARIA EDGEWORTH

If you haven't struck oil in five minutes, stop boring!

—GEORGE JESSEL

Boredom is the self being stuffed with itself.

—WALKER PERCY

I am never bored anywhere;
being bored is an insult to oneself.

—JULES RENARD

I am one of those unhappy persons
who inspire bores to the highest flights of their art.

—EDITH SITWELL

A healthy male adult bore consumes each year
one and a half times his own weight in other people's patience.

—JOHN UPDIKE

The secret of being a bore is to tell everything.

—VOLTAIRE

BRAIN

(see also MIND and THINKING & THINKERS and
IDEAS and THOUGHT)

The mind, of course, is just what the brain does for a living.

—SHARON BEGLEY

Where the heart lies, let the brain lie also.

—ROBERT BROWNING

I consider that a man's brain originally is like a little empty attic,
and you have to stock it with such furniture as you choose.

—ARTHUR CONAN DOYLE

The chief function of the body is to carry the brain around.

—THOMAS A. EDISON

Knowledge fills a large brain;
it merely inflates a small one.

—SYDNEY J. HARRIS

The human brain is both a broadcasting and a receiving station.

—NAPOLEON HILL

Brains, on the whole, are like hearts,
and they go where they are appreciated.

—ROBERT S. MCNAMARA

It is good to rub and polish our brains against that of others.

—MICHEL DE MONTAIGNE

If little else, the brain is an educational toy.

—TOM ROBBINS

The brain is like a muscle.
When we think well, we feel good.

—CARL SAGAN

I not only use all the brains I have, but all I can borrow.

—WOODROW WILSON

BUSINESS

(see also MONEY and SUCCESS and SUCCESS & FAILURE
and WEALTH and WORK)

Business once lost, does not easily return to the old hands.

—ABIGAIL ADAMS

**In the business world, the rearview mirror
is always clearer than the windshield.**

—WARREN BUFFETT

There is only one valid definition of business: to create a customer.

—PETER F. DRUCKER

Drive thy Business, or it will drive thee.

—BENJAMIN FRANKLIN

**In business you get what you want
by giving other people what they want.**

—ALICE FOOTE MACDOUGALL

Business is a combination of war and sport.

—ANDRÉ MAUROIS

More businesses die of indigestion than starvation.

—DAVID PACKARD, QUOTING AN UNNAMED ENGINEER

Perpetual devotion to what a man calls his business
is only to be sustained
by perpetual neglect of many other things.

—ROBERT LOUIS STEVENSON

A businessman is a hybrid of a dancer and a calculator.

—PAUL VALÉRY

Being good in business is the most fascinating kind of art.

—ANDY WARHOL

CANCER

(see also DEATH & DYING and ILLNESS and PAIN and
SUFFERING)

Growth for the sake of growth is the ideology of the cancer cell.

—EDWARD ABBEY

Nobody knows what the cause is,
Though some pretend they do;
It's like some hidden assassin
Waiting to strike at you.

—W. H. AUDEN, ON CANCER

When you hear the word *cancer,*
it's as if someone took the game of Life and tossed it in the air.
All the pieces go flying. The pieces land on a new board.
Everything has shifted.

—REGINA BRETT

Cancer is such a ruthless adversary
because it behaves as if it has its own fiendishly cunning agenda.

—PAUL DAVIES

Carcinoma works cunningly from the inside out.
Detection and treatment often work
more slowly and gropingly, from the outside in.

—CHRISTOPHER HITCHENS

Cancer cells behave like the members of a barbarian horde run amok—
leaderless and undirected, but with a single-minded purpose:
to plunder everything within reach.

—SHERWIN B. NULAND

Cancer cells are those which have forgotten how to die.

—HAROLD PINTER, QUOTING AN UNNAMED NURSE

All of a sudden I've become a member
in an elite club that I'd rather not belong to.

—GILDA RADNER

Cancer is a demonic pregnancy.

—SUSAN SONTAG

An individual doesn't get cancer, a family does.

—TERRY TEMPEST WILLIAMS

CATS

(see also ANIMALS and DOGS and CATS & DOGS)

I love in the cat that independent and almost ungrateful temper
which prevents him from attaching himself to anyone

—FRANÇOIS-RENÉ DE CHATEAUBRIAND

The cat purrs itself to sleep,
being the only creature that sings its own lullaby.

—MALCOLM DE CHAZAL

Before a Cat will condescend
To treat you as a trusted friend,
Some little token of esteem
Is needed, like a dish of cream.

—T. S. ELIOT

The cat is the only non-gregarious domestic animal.

—FRANCIS GALTON

Cats are connoisseurs of comfort.

—JAMES HERRIOT

Cats seem to go on the principle that
it never does any harm to ask for what you want.

—JOSEPH WOOD KRUTCH

There is nothing so lowering to one's self-esteem
as the affectionate contempt of a beloved cat.

—AGNES REPPLIER

Cats . . . appear to regard human beings who may be domiciled with them
rather as part of the furniture than as comrades.

—LOUIS ROBINSON

A cat does furnish a room.
Like a graceful vase, a cat, even when motionless, seems to flow.

—GEORGE F. WILL

The real objection to the great majority of cats
is their insufferable air of superiority.
Cats, as a class, have never completely got over the snootiness
caused by the fact that in Ancient Egypt they were worshiped as gods.

—P. G. WODEHOUSE

CATS & DOGS

(see also ANIMALS and CATS and DOGS)

Dogs are high on life.
Cats need catnip.

—MARY BLY

Dogs will come when called.
Cats will take a message and get back to you.

—MISSY DIZICK

If animals could speak as fabulists have feigned,
the dog would be a blunt, blundering, outspoken, honest fellow,
but the cat would have the rare talent of never saying a word too much.

—PHILIP GILBERT HAMERTON

We own a dog—he is with us as a slave
and inferior because we wish him to be.
But we *entertain* a cat—he adorns our hearth as a guest, fellow-lodger,
and equal because *he* wishes to be there.

—H. P. LOVECRAFT

Dogs want only love
but cats demand worship.

—L. M. MONTGOMERY

Dogs . . . can be made to feel guilty about anything,
including the sins of their owners.
Cats refuse to take the blame for anything—including their own sins.

—ELIZABETH PETERS (BARBARA MERTZ)

A man who owns a dog is, in every sense of the word, its master;
the term expresses accurately their mutual relations.
But it is ridiculous when applied to the limited possession of a cat.

—AGNES REPPLIER

I love both the way a dog looks up to me
and a cat condescends to me.

—GLADYS TABER

Walking is a human habit into which dogs readily fall
but it is a distasteful form of exercise to a cat
unless he has a purpose in view.

—CARL VAN VECHTEN

If a dog jumps in your lap, it is because he is fond of you.
If a cat does the same thing, it is because your lap is warmer.

—ALFRED NORTH WHITEHEAD

CHANGE

(see also GROWTH and TIME and YEARS)

The need for change bulldozed a road
down the center of my mind.

—MAYA ANGELOU

Before you'll change, something important must be at risk.

—RICHARD BACH

Most of us are about as eager to be changed as we were to be born,
and go through our changes in a similar state of shock.

—JAMES BALDWIN

No one can persuade another to change.
Each of us guards a gate of change
that can only be unlocked from the inside.
We cannot open the gate of another,
either by argument or emotional appeal.

—MARILYN FERGUSON

All changes, even the most longed for, have their melancholy;
for what we leave behind us is a part of ourselves;
we must die to one life before we can enter into another!

—ANATOLE FRANCE

The more things change, the more they remain the same.

—ALPHONSE KARR

There is no sin punished more implacably by nature
than the sin of resistance to change.

—ANNE MORROW LINDBERGH

None of us knows what the next change is going to be,
what unexpected opportunity is just around the corner,
waiting to change all the tenor of our lives.

—KATHLEEN THOMPSON NORRIS

Changes are not only possible and predictable,
but to deny them is to be an accomplice
to one's own unnecessary vegetation.

—GAIL SHEEHY

Change is the process by which the future invades our lives.

—ALVIN TOFFLER

CHARACTER

(see also CONSCIENCE and INTEGRITY and MATURITY
and VICE and VIRTUE)

Character builds slowly,
but it can be torn down with incredible swiftness.

—FAITH BALDWIN

Character—the willingness to accept responsibility for one's own life—
is the source from which self-respect springs.

—JOAN DIDION

Character is not cut in marble—
it is not something solid and unalterable.
It is something living and changing,
and may become diseased as our bodies do.

—GEORGE ELIOT

No change of circumstances can repair a defect of character.

—RALPH WALDO EMERSON

Talent develops in quiet places,
character in the full current of human life.

—JOHANN WOLFGANG VON GOETHE

Resistance, whether to one's appetites or to the ways of the world,
is a chief factor in the shaping of character.

—ERIC HOFFER

The hell to be endured hereafter, of which theology tells,
is no worse than the hell we make for ourselves in this world
by habitually fashioning our characters in the wrong way.

—WILLIAM JAMES

No man can climb out beyond the limitations of his own character.

—JOHN MORLEY

Character is much easier kept than recovered.

—THOMAS PAINE

Another flaw in the human character is that everybody wants to build
and nobody wants to do maintenance.

—KURT VONNEGUT JR.

CHILDHOOD

(see also ADOLESCENCE and CHILDREN and FAMILY
and MOTHERS & MOTHERHOOD and PARENTS &
PARENTHOOD and YOUTH)

When childhood dies, its corpses are called adults.

—BRIAN ALDISS

So, like a forgotten fire,
a childhood can always flare up again within us.

—GASTON BACHELARD

Everything else you grow out of,
but you never recover from childhood.

—BERYL BAINBRIDGE

But childhood, prolonged, cannot remain a fairyland.
It becomes a hell.

—LOUISE BOGAN

The actual American childhood
is less Norman Rockwell and Walt Disney
than Nathaniel Hawthorne and Edgar Allan Poe.

—SUSAN CHEEVER

There is always one moment in childhood
when the door opens and lets the future in.

—GRAHAM GREENE

Childhood is a short season.

—HELEN HAYES

Childhood is the world of miracle and wonder;
as if creation rose, bathed in light out of the darkness,
utterly new and fresh and astonishing.
The end of childhood is when things cease to astonish us.

—EUGÈNE IONESCO

The childhood shows the man,
As morning shows the day.

—JOHN MILTON

Childhood is Last Chance Gulch for happiness.
After that, you know too much.

—TOM STOPPARD

CHILDREN

(see also ADOLESCENCE and CHILDHOOD and FAMILY
and MOTHERS & MOTHERHOOD and PARENTS &
PARENTHOOD and YOUTH)

In every child who is born, under no matter what circumstances,
and of no matter what parents,
the potentiality of the human race is born again.

—JAMES AGEE

A wise woman once said to me that
there are only two lasting bequests we can hope to give our children.
One of these she said is roots, the other, wings.

—W. HODDING CARTER II[*]

Children aren't coloring books.
You don't get to fill them with your favorite colors.

—KHALED HOSSEINI

If from infancy you treat children as gods
they are liable in adulthood to act as devils.

—P. D. JAMES

Warmth is the vital element for the growing plant
and for the soul of the child.

—CARL JUNG

At every step the child should be allowed
to meet the real experiences of life;
the thorns should never be plucked from his roses.

—ELLEN KEY

A child's nature is too serious a thing to admit of its
being regarded as a mere appendage to another human being.

—CHARLES LAMB

---

[*]   Almost all Internet sites attribute the observation directly to Carter, ignoring his qualifying comment.

The hearts of small children are delicate organs.
A cruel beginning in this world can twist them into curious shapes.

—CARSON MCCULLERS

Children are the living messages we send to a time we will not see.

—NEIL POSTMAN

The child is father of the man.

—WILLIAM WORDSWORTH

CIVILIZATION

(see also HISTORY and KNOWLEDGE and LEARNING)

You think that a wall as solid as the earth
separates civilization from barbarism.
I tell you the division is a thread, a sheet of glass.

—JOHN BUCHAN

The three great elements of modern civilization:
Gunpowder, Printing, and the Protestant Religion.

—THOMAS CARLYLE

Civilization: if it is not in man's heart—well, then, it is nowhere.

—GEORGES DUHAMEL

Civilization is a stream with banks.
The stream is sometimes filled with blood from people killing, stealing,
shouting, and doing things historians usually record,
while on the banks, unnoticed, people build homes, make love,
raise children, sing songs, write poetry and even whittle statues.
The story of civilization is the story of what happened on the banks.

—WILL DURANT

All civilization has from time to time
become a thin crust over a volcano of revolution.

—HAVELOCK ELLIS

The civilized man has built a coach,
but has lost the use of his feet.

—RALPH WALDO EMERSON

Civilization is a perishable commodity.

—HELEN MACINNES

We wear the cape of civilization
But our souls live in the stone age.

—NIZAR QABBANI

A civilization which develops only on its material side,
and not in corresponding measure on its mental and spiritual side,
is like a vessel with a defective steering gear,
which gets out of control at a constantly accelerating pace,
and drifts toward catastrophe.

—ALBERT SCHWEITZER

Civilization, as we know it, is a movement and not a condition,
a voyage and not a harbor.

—ARNOLD J. TOYNBEE

COMMITTEES

(see also BUSINESS and SUCCESS and SUCCESS &
FAILURE and WORK)

A camel is a horse designed by a committee.

—AUTHOR UNKNOWN

A committee is a group that keeps minutes and loses hours.

—MILTON BERLE

The only good thing ever done by a committee
was the King James Version.

—RITA MAE BROWN

A *cul-de-sac* down which ideas are lured, and then quietly strangled.
—BARNETT COCKS, HIS DEFINITION OF A COMMITTEE

The psychology of committees
is a special case of the psychology of mobs.
—CELIA GREEN

What is a committee? A group of the unwilling,
picked from the unfit, to do the unnecessary.
—RICHARD HARKNESS

If you want to kill any idea in the world,
get a committee working on it.
—CHARLES F. KETTERING

Committees are consumers and sometimes sterilizers of ideas,
rarely creators of them.
—HENRY KISSINGER

A committee is an animal with four back legs.
—JOHN LE CARRÉ

A committee is organic rather than mechanical in its nature:
it is not a structure but a plant.
It takes root and grows, it flowers, wilts, and dies,
scattering the seed from which other committees will bloom in their turn.
—C. NORTHCOTE PARKINSON

COMMUNICATION

(see also CONVERSATION and LANGUAGE and
LISTENING and SPEECH and WORDS)

**The single biggest problem in communication
is the illusion that it has taken place.**

—AUTHOR UNKNOWN[*]

Self-expression must pass into communication for its fulfillment.

—PEARL S. BUCK

**In the last analysis, what we *are* communicates
far more eloquently than anything we *say* or *do*.**

—STEPHEN R. COVEY

**To be a recipient of a communication
is to have an enlarged and changed experience.**

—JOHN DEWEY

**The most important thing in communication
is to hear what isn't being said.**

—PETER F. DRUCKER

Many attempts to communicate are nullified by saying too much.

—ROBERT K. GREENLEAF

[*]   While widely attributed to George Bernard Shaw, this quotation has never been found in
his works.

Take the two popular words today, "information" and "communication."
They are often used interchangeably, but they signify quite different things.
Information is *giving out*; communication is *getting through*.

—SYDNEY J. HARRIS

The most important things are the hardest to say,
because words diminish them.

—STEPHEN KING

There is no pleasure to me without communication;
there is not so much as a sprightly thought comes into my mind
but I grieve that I have no one to tell it to.

—MICHEL DE MONTAIGNE

If you want to communicate with another thinking human being,
get in touch with your thoughts.
Put them in order; give them a purpose;
use them to persuade, to instruct, to discover, to seduce.

—WILLIAM SAFIRE

COMPLIMENTS

(see also CRITICISM and FLATTERY and PRAISE
and VANITY)

**There is no effect more disproportionate to its cause
than the happiness bestowed by a small compliment.**

—ROBERT BRAULT

All compliments exceed the truth.

—MARGARET CAVENDISH

Guard against that vanity which courts a compliment, or is fed by it.

—THOMAS CHALMERS

Compliments cost nothing, yet many pay dear for them.

—THOMAS FULLER, MD

**Nothing is so silly as the expression
of a man who is being complimented.**

—ANDRÉ GIDE

**A compliment is a gift, not to be thrown away carelessly
unless you want to hurt the giver.**

—ELEANOR HAMILTON

A compliment is something like a kiss through a veil.

—VICTOR HUGO

Some folks pay a compliment like they expected a receipt.

—FRANK MCKINNEY "KIN" HUBBARD

This was really a compliment to be pleased with—
a nice little handsome pat of butter
made up by a neat-handed ... dairy-maid
instead of the grease fit only for cartwheels
which one is dosed with by the pound.

—WALTER SCOTT

I can live for two months on a good compliment.

—MARK TWAIN

COMPUTERS

(see also INTERNET & WORLD WIDE WEB and
LEARNING and TECHNOLOGY)

A computer terminal is not some clunky old television
with a typewriter in front of it.
It is an interface where the mind and body
can connect with the universe and move bits of it about.

—DOUGLAS ADAMS

I have bought this wonderful machine—a computer.
Now I am rather an authority on gods, so I identified the machine—
it seems to me to be an Old Testament god with a lot of rules and no mercy.

—JOSEPH CAMPBELL

If the automobile had followed the same development cycle as the computer,
a Rolls-Royce would today cost $100, get a million miles per gallon,
and explode once a year, killing everyone inside.

—ROBERT X. CRINGELY

What a computer is to me
is the most remarkable tool that we have ever come up with.
It's the equivalent of a bicycle for our minds.

—STEVE JOBS

We think basically you watch television to turn your brain off,
and you work on your computer when you want to turn your brain on.

—STEVE JOBS

The PC is the LSD of the '90s.

—TIMOTHY LEARY

The computer is by all odds the most extraordinary
of all the technological clothing ever devised by man,
since it is the extension of our central nervous system.
Beside it, the wheel is a mere hula-hoop.

—MARSHALL MCLUHAN

Your computer is a backup of your soul, a multilayered, menu-driven
representation of who you are, who you care about, and how you sin.

—MICHAEL MARSHALL

With the internet, a computer is a door rather than a box.

—CLAY SHIRKY

Terrified of being alone, yet afraid of intimacy, we experience
widespread feelings of emptiness, of disconnection, of the unreality of self.
And here the computer, a companion without emotional demands,
offers a compromise. You can be a loner, but never alone.

—SHERRY TURKLE

CONSCIENCE

(see also ERROR and MISTAKES and SIN and VICE and
VICE & VIRTUE and VIRTUE)

A good conscience is to the soul what health is to the body.

—JOSEPH ADDISON

Labor to keep alive in your breast
that little spark of celestial fire, called conscience.

—AUTHOR UNKNOWN[*]

[*] George Washington is widely cited as the author of this quotation, but he simply copied
it from a school notebook when he was a teenager and adopted it as a "Rule of Civility"
in adulthood. The saying was originally authored around 1595 by a French Jesuit priest
whose name has been lost to history.

We know little about the conscience except that it is soluble in alcohol.
—THOMAS BLACKBURN, QUOTING AN UNNAMED PSYCHOLOGIST

Conscience is thoroughly well-bred
and soon leaves off talking to those who do not wish to hear it
—SAMUEL BUTLER (1835–1902)

The fact that human conscience remains partially infantile
throughout life is the core of human tragedy.
—ERIK H. ERIKSON

I cannot and will not cut my conscience to fit this year's fashions.
—LILLIAN HELLMAN

Before I can live with other folks I've got to live with myself.
The one thing that doesn't abide by majority rule is a person's conscience.
—HARPER LEE

Each man's soul is a menagerie where Conscience,
the animal-tamer, lives with a collection of wild beasts.
—AUSTIN O'MALLEY

The voice of conscience is so delicate that it is easy to stifle;
but it is also so clear that it is impossible to mistake.
—GERMAINE DE STAËL

Conscience is a man's compass,
and though the needle sometimes deviates,
though one often perceives irregularities in directing one's course by it,
still one must try to follow its direction.

—VINCENT VAN GOGH

CONVERSATION

(see also COMMUNICATION and IDEAS and LISTENING
and RELATIONSHIPS and SPEECH and THOUGHT)

Someone has said that conversation is sex for the soul.

—ISABEL ALLENDE

The true spirit of conversation consists in
building on another man's observation, not overturning it.

—EDWARD GEORGE BULWER-LYTTON

There is no arena in which vanity displays
itself under such a variety of forms as in conversation.

—GERMAINE DE STAËL

The art of conversation,
or the qualifications for a good companion, is a certain self-control,
which now holds the subject, now lets it go.

—RALPH WALDO EMERSON

The real art of conversation
is not only to say the right thing in the right place,
but, far more difficult still,
to leave unsaid the wrong thing at the tempting moment.

—DOROTHY NEVILL

Ideal conversation must be an exchange of thought, and not,
as many of those who worry most about their shortcomings believe,
an eloquent exhibition of wit or oratory.

—EMILY POST

It is not what we learn in conversation that enriches us.
It is the elation that comes of swift contact
with the tingling currents of thought.

—AGNES REPPLIER

There is no such thing as conversation. It is an illusion.
There are intersecting monologues, that is all.

—REBECCA WEST

Ah, good conversation—there's nothing like it, is there?
The air of ideas is the only air worth breathing.

—EDITH WHARTON

The only proper intoxication is conversation.

—OSCAR WILDE

COURAGE

(see also COWARDICE and FEAR and HEROES &
HEROISM and RISK & RISK-TAKING)

Courage and perseverance have a magical talisman,
before which difficulties disappear and obstacles vanish into air.

—JOHN QUINCY ADAMS

Courage is Fear
That has said its prayers.

—KARLE WILSON BAKER

Courage is the price that
Life exacts for granting peace.
The soul that knows it not, knows no release
From little things.

—AMELIA EARHART

What a new face courage puts on everything!

—RALPH WALDO EMERSON

Courage has need of reason, but it is not reason's child;
it springs from deeper strata.

—HERMANN HESSE

Courage is reckoned the greatest of all virtues;
because, unless a man has that virtue,
he has no security for preserving any other.

—SAMUEL JOHNSON[*]

It isn't for the moment you are struck that you need courage
but for the long uphill climb back to sanity and faith and security.

—ANNE MORROW LINDBERGH

Courage cannot be counterfeited.
It is one virtue that escapes hypocrisy.

—NAPOLEON BONAPARTE

Life shrinks or expands in proportion to one's courage.

—ANAÏS NIN

What is more mortifying
than to feel that you have missed the plum
for want of courage to shake the tree?

—LOGAN PEARSALL SMITH

[*] Winston Churchill was almost certainly thinking about this quotation when he wrote: "Courage is rightly esteemed the first of human qualities, because, as has been said, it is the quality which guarantees all others."

COWARDICE

(see also COURAGE and FEAR and HEROES & HEROISM
and RISK & RISK-TAKING)

Coward, *n*. One who in a perilous emergency thinks with his legs.

—AMBROSE BIERCE

**Nothing makes us more cowardly and unconscionable
than the desire to be loved by everyone.**

—MARIE VON EBNER-ESCHENBACH

**The most mortifying infirmity in human nature,
to feel in ourselves, or to contemplate in another,
is, perhaps, cowardice.**

—CHARLES LAMB

**It was always himself that the coward abandoned first.
After this all other betrayals came easily.**

—CORMAC MCCARTHY

Cowardice is the mother of cruelty.

—MICHEL DE MONTAIGNE

Where there is no danger, cowards are bold.

—THOMAS PAINE

Cowardice is the unpardonable sin in a man.

—THEODORE ROOSEVELT

Cowards die many times before their deaths
The valiant never taste of death but once.

—WILLIAM SHAKESPEARE

Man gives every reason for his conduct save one,
every excuse for his crimes save one, every plea for his safety save one;
and that one is his cowardice.

—GEORGE BERNARD SHAW

The human race is a race of cowards;
and I am not only marching in that procession
but carrying a banner.

—MARK TWAIN

CREATIVITY

(see also ART and ARTISTS and CURIOSITY and
DISCOVERY and IMAGINATION)

What about the creative state? In it a man is taken out of himself.
He lets down as it were a bucket into his subconscious
and draws up something which is normally beyond his reach.

—E. M. FORSTER

Could Hamlet have been written by a committee,
or the Mona Lisa painted by a club?
Could the New Testament have been composed as a conference report?
Creative ideas do not spring from groups. They spring from individuals.
The divine spark leaps from the finger of God to the finger of Adam.

—A. WHITNEY GRISWOLD

Creative activity could be described as a type of learning process
where teacher and pupil are located in the same individual.

—ARTHUR KOESTLER

Every creative act is a sudden cessation of stupidity.

—EDWIN LAND

The creative act, the defeat of habit by originality, overcomes everything.

—GEORGE LOIS

Creative minds are uneven,
and the best of fabrics have their dull spots.

—H. P. LOVECRAFT

It's the ability to see things a new way, and from that insight
to produce something that didn't exist before—something original.
It sometimes means piercing the mundane to find the marvelous—
or looking beyond the marvelous to find the mundane.

—BILL MOYERS, ON CREATIVITY

Creativity can be described as letting go of certainties.

—GAIL SHEEHY

Creativity is an act of *defiance*. You're challenging the status quo.

—TWYLA THARP

Being creative without talent is a bit like
being a perfectionist and not being able to do anything right.

—JANE WAGNER

CRITICISM

(see also ART and ARTISTS and COMPLIMENTS and
CRITICS and LITERATURE and PRAISE and WRITERS
and WRITING)

Criticism should be a casual conversation.

—W. H. AUDEN

It is from the womb of art that criticism was born.

—CHARLES BAUDELAIRE

The rule in carving holds good as to criticism—
never cut with a knife what you can cut with a spoon.

—CHARLES BUXTON

What embitters the world is not excess of criticism,
but absence of self-criticism.

—G. K. CHESTERTON

Criticism may not be agreeable, but it is necessary.
It fulfills the same function as pain in the human body;
it calls attention to an unhealthy state of things.

—WINSTON CHURCHILL

Criticism, like rain, should be gentle enough
to nourish a man's growth without destroying his roots.

—FRANK A. CLARK

Criticism should not be querulous and wasting,
all knife and root-puller,
but guiding, instructive, inspiring, a south wind, not an east wind.

—RALPH WALDO EMERSON

Criticism is . . . always a kind of compliment.

—JOHN MADDOX

People fed on sugared praises cannot be expected
to feel an appetite for the black broth of honest criticism.

—AGNES REPPLIER

Writing criticism is to writing fiction and poetry
as hugging the shore is to sailing in the open sea.

—JOHN UPDIKE

CRITICS

(see also ART and ARTISTS and COMPLIMENTS and
CRITICISM and LITERATURE and PRAISE
and WRITING)

A critic is a bundle of biases held loosely together by a sense of taste.

—WHITNEY BALLIETT

Critics are like eunuchs in a harem.
They're there every night, they see it done every night,
they see how it should be done every night,
but they can't do it themselves.

—BRENDAN BEHAN

Critics are like horse-flies which hinder the horses
in their plowing of the soil.

—ANTON CHEKHOV

To be a critic, you have to have maybe three percent education,
five percent intelligence, two percent style,
and ninety percent gall and egomania in equal parts.

—JUDITH CRIST

A man is a critic when he cannot be an artist,
in the same way that a man becomes an informer
when he cannot be a soldier.

—GUSTAVE FLAUBERT

Critics and reviewers can be loosely divided into two camps:
Those who never let you forget that
they are judge, jury, and if need be, executioner;
and those who humble themselves before a poem or novel,
waiting for it to reveal its secrets to them.

—MICHAEL DIRDA

Asking a working writer what he thinks about critics
is like asking a lamp-post how it feels about dogs.

—CHRISTOPHER HAMPTON

Insects sting, not in malice, but because they want to live.
It is the same with critics: they desire our blood, not our pain.

—FRIEDRICH NIETZSCHE

A critic is a man who knows the way but can't drive the car.

—KENNETH TYNAN

Pigs at a pastry cart.

—JOHN UPDIKE, ON CRITICS

CURIOSITY

(see also ANSWERS and DISCOVERY and IMAGINATION
and LEARNING and QUESTIONS)

**The greatest weapons in the conquest of knowledge
are an understanding mind and
the inexorable curiosity that drives it on.**

—ISAAC ASIMOV

**The first and the simplest emotion which we discover
in the human mind is Curiosity.**

—EDMUND BURKE

**If you bring curiosity to your work
it will cease to be merely a job and become a door
through which you enter the best that life has to give you.**

—ROBERTSON DAVIES

Never lose a holy curiosity.

—ALBERT EINSTEIN

Curiosity is lying in wait for every secret.

—RALPH WALDO EMERSON

A man who knows the price of everything and the value of nothing.

—OSCAR WILDE, DESCRIBING A CYNIC

DEATH & DYING

(see also AGE & AGING—OLD AGE and CANCER and
GRIEF & GRIEVING and ILLNESS and LIFE)

The timing of death, like the ending of a story,
gives a changed meaning to what preceded it.

—MARY CATHERINE BATESON

Tears are sometimes an inappropriate response to death.
When a life has been lived
completely honestly, completely successfully, or just completely,
the correct response to death's perfect punctuation mark is a smile.

—JULIE BURCHILL

Death hath so many doors to let out life.

—JOHN FLETCHER AND PHILIP MASSINGER

It will happen to all of us that at some point
you'll get tapped on the shoulder and told,
not just that the party is over, but slightly worse:
the party's going on but you have to leave.
And it's going on without you.

—CHRISTOPHER HITCHENS

Watching a peaceful death of a human being reminds us of a falling star;
one of a million lights in a vast sky that flares up for a brief moment
only to disappear into the endless night forever.

—ELISABETH KÜBLER-ROSS

There is only one way to be prepared for death: to be sated.
In the soul, in the heart, in the spirit, in the flesh. To the brim.

—HENRY DE MONTHERLANT

Death persecutes before it executes.

—CYNTHIA OZICK

We are all under sentence of death,
but with a sort of indefinite reprieve.

—WALTER PATER

Death,
The undiscovered country from whose bourn
No traveller returns.

—WILLIAM SHAKESPEARE

In any man who dies there dies with him
his first snow and kiss and fight.
It goes with him. . . .
Not people die but worlds die in them.

—YEVGENY YEVTUSHENKO

DECISIONS & DECISION-MAKING

(see also ACTION and BUSINESS and DISCIPLINE and
PROBLEMS and RISK & RISK-TAKING)

The man who insists upon seeing with perfect clearness
before he decides, never decides.

—HENRI FRÉDÉRIC AMIEL

A peacefulness follows any decision, even the wrong one.

—RITA MAE BROWN

If decisions were a choice between alternatives, decisions would come easy.
Decision is the selection and formulation of alternatives.

—KENNETH BURKE

Every decision is liberating, even if it leads to disaster.
Otherwise, why do so many people
walk upright and with open eyes into their misfortune?

—ELIAS CANETTI

Every decision is like a murder,
and our march forward is over the stillborn bodies
of all our possible selves that we'll never be.

—RENÉ DUBOS

The key to good decision making is not knowledge.
It is understanding.
We are swimming in the former.
We are desperately lacking in the latter.

—MALCOLM GLADWELL

The man who in wavering times is inclined to be wavering
only increases the evil, and spreads it wider and wider;
but the man of firm decision fashions the universe.

—JOHANN WOLFGANG VON GOETHE

It is better to stir up a question without deciding it,
than to decide it without stirring it up.

—JOSEPH JOUBERT

Decision is a sharp knife that cuts clear and straight
and lays bare the fat and the lean;
indecision, a dull one that hacks and tears
and leaves ragged edges behind it.

—GEORGE HORACE LORIMER

Life puts no greater burdens upon a man
than the necessity of making decisions.

—FRANK YERBY

DEFEAT

(see also FAILURE and SUCCESS and SUCCESS &
FAILURE and VICTORY and VICTORY & DEFEAT)

History to the defeated
May say Alas but cannot help or pardon.

—W. H. AUDEN

Man is not made for defeat.
A man can be destroyed but not defeated.

—ERNEST HEMINGWAY

When defeat comes,
accept it as a signal that your plans are not sound,
rebuild those plans, and set sail once more toward your coveted goal.

—NAPOLEON HILL

Defeat is simply a signal to press onward.

—HELEN KELLER

A wise man fights to win,
but he is twice a fool who has no plan for possible defeat.

—LOUIS L'AMOUR

There could be no honor in a sure success
but much might be wrested from a sure defeat.

—T. E. LAWRENCE

The deepest personal defeat suffered by human beings
is constituted by the difference between
what one was capable of becoming
and what one has in fact become.

—ASHLEY MONTAGU

No man is defeated without until he has first been defeated within.

—ELEANOR ROOSEVELT

The injustice of defeat lies in the fact that its most innocent victims
are made to look like heartless accomplices.

—ANTOINE DE SAINT-EXUPÉRY

What is important is not that you have a defeat but how you react to it.
There is always the possibility to transform a defeat
into something else, something new, something strong.

—LINA WERTMULLER

DIFFICULTIES

(see also ADVERSITY and OBSTACLES and PROBLEMS
and SUFFERING and TROUBLE)

**The habits of a vigorous mind
are formed in contending with difficulties.**

—ABIGAIL ADAMS

**Conquering any difficulty always gives one a secret joy,
for it means pushing back a boundary-line and adding to one's liberty.**

—HENRI FRÉDÉRIC AMIEL

**Difficulty, my brethren, is the nurse of greatness—
a harsh nurse, who roughly rocks her foster-children
into strength and athletic proportion.**

—WILLIAM CULLEN BRYANT

**Every difficulty slurred over
will be a ghost to disturb your repose later on.**

—FRÉDÉRIC CHOPIN

Man needs difficulties; they are necessary for health.

—CARL JUNG

**What is required of us is that we *love the difficult* and learn to deal with it.
In the difficult are the friendly forces, the hands that work on us.**

—RAINER MARIA RILKE

As we advance in life it becomes more and more difficult,
but in fighting the difficulties,
the inmost strength of the heart is developed.

—VINCENT VAN GOGH

To overcome difficulties is to experience the full delight of existence,
no matter where the obstacles are encountered.

—ARTHUR SCHOPENHAUER

Providence has hidden a charm in difficult undertakings,
which is appreciated only by those who dare to grapple with them.

—ANNE SOPHIE SWETCHINE

When you are face to face with a difficulty,
you are up against a discovery.

—WILLIAM THOMSON (LORD KELVIN)

DISCIPLINE

(see also CHARACTER and FAILURE and GROWTH and
HABIT and SUCCESS and TALENT)

True freedom is impossible
without a mind made free by discipline.

—MORTIMER J. ADLER

Some people regard discipline as a chore.
For me, it is a kind of order that sets me free to fly.

—JULIE ANDREWS

The discipline of desire is the backbone of character.

—WILL DURANT AND ARIEL DURANT

No horse gets anywhere until he is harnessed.
No stream or gas drives anything until it is confined.
No Niagara is ever turned into light and power until it is tunneled.
No life ever grows great until it is focused, dedicated, disciplined.

—HARRY EMERSON FOSDICK

Self-discipline is the free man's yoke.
Either he is his own master or he will be his own slave.

—JOHN W. GARDNER

Seek freedom and become captive of your desires.
Seek discipline and find your liberty.

—FRANK HERBERT

Self-respect is the fruit of discipline,
the sense of dignity grows with the ability to say No to oneself.

—ABRAHAM JOSHUA HESCHEL

If men live decently it is because discipline
Saves their very lives for them.

—SOPHOCLES

If we do not discipline ourselves, the world will do it for us.
Control from without flourishes when discipline from within grows weak.

—MARY H. ROBINSON

I cannot conceive of a good life which isn't,
in some sense, a self-disciplined life.

—PHILIP TOYNBEE

DISCOVERY

(see also CREATIVITY and CURIOSITY and
IMAGINATION and SCIENCE & SCIENTISTS and TRUTH)

A discovery is said to be an accident meeting a prepared mind.

—AUTHOR UNKNOWN[*]

They are ill discoverers that think there is no land,
when they see nothing but sea.

—FRANCIS BACON (1561–1626)[†]

---

[*] This observation is widely attributed to Albert Szent-Györgi, but the observation has not
been found in his works.

[†] Three centuries later, André Gide was likely inspired by Bacon's observation when he
wrote in *The Counterfeiters* (1925), "One doesn't discover new lands without consenting
to lose sight of the shore for a very long time."

The greatest obstacle to discovery is not ignorance—
it is the illusion of knowledge.

—DANIEL J. BOORSTIN

No great discovery was ever made in science
except by one who lifted his nose above the grindstone of details
and ventured on a more comprehensive vision.

—ALBERT EINSTEIN

Art is partly communication but only partly. The rest is discovery.

—WILLIAM GOLDING

Most new discoveries are suddenly-seen things that were always there.

—SUSANNE K. LANGER

Discovery follows discovery, each both raising and answering questions,
each ending a long search,
and each providing the new instruments for a new search.

—J. ROBERT OPPENHEIMER

Discovery comes only to a mind immersed in its pursuit.

—MICHAEL POLANYI

The only real voyage of discovery, the only Fountain of Youth,
consists not in seeking new landscapes but in having new eyes.

—MARCEL PROUST

What is it that confers the noblest delight?
What is that which swells a man's breast with pride
above that which any other experience can bring to him?
Discovery!

—MARK TWAIN

DIVORCE

(see also FAMILY [Positive] and FAMILY [Not-So-Positive]
and MARRIAGE [Wise] and MARRIAGE [Wry & Witty])

A divorce is like an amputation; you survive, but there's less of you.

—MARGARET ATWOOD

Divorce is the psychological equivalent of a triple coronary bypass.
After such a monumental assault on the heart,
it can take a whole decade to amend
all the habits and attitudes that led up to it.

—MARY KAY BLAKELY

Divorce is the one human tragedy that reduces everything to cash.

—RITA MAE BROWN

There is something fantastic about getting divorced.
Everyone should do it to experience the extraordinary sense of freedom
after being in marriage jail.

—DELIA EPHRON

Divorce is a game played by lawyers.

—CARY GRANT

There is a rhythm to the ending of a marriage
just like the rhythm of a courtship—only backward.
You try to start again but get into blaming over and over.
Finally you are both worn out, exhausted, hopeless.
Then lawyers are called in to pick clean the corpses.

—ERICA JONG

There are four stages to a marriage.
First there's the affair, then the marriage,
then children and finally the fourth stage,
without which you cannot know a woman, the divorce.

—NORMAN MAILER

Divorce is very expensive,
both economically and psychologically as well,
but it probably isn't any more so than
living with someone who isn't really on your side.

—MERLE SHAIN

I find to my astonishment that an unhappy marriage
goes on being unhappy when it is over.

—REBECCA WEST

In the dissolution of sentimental partnerships it is seldom that
both associates are able to withdraw their funds at the same time.

—EDITH WHARTON

DOGS

(see also ANIMALS and CATS and CATS & DOGS)

Dogs need to sniff the ground;
it's how they keep abreast of current events.
The ground is a giant dog newspaper,
containing all kinds of late-breaking news items, which,
if they are especially urgent, are often continued in the next yard.

—DAVE BARRY

The dog was created specially for children.
He is the god of frolic.

—HENRY WARD BEECHER

The dog is a Yes-animal,
very popular with people who can't afford to keep a Yes-man.

—ROBERTSON DAVIES

Dogs laugh, but they laugh with their tails.

—MAX EASTMAN

We know ourselves to be such lamentably imperfect characters,
that we long for an affection altogether ignorant of our faults.
Heaven has accorded this to us in the uncritical canine attachment.

—PHILIP GILBERT HAMERTON

To his dog, every man is Napoleon;
hence the constant popularity of dogs.

—ALDOUS HUXLEY

All dogs can be guide dogs of a sort,
leading us to places we didn't even know we needed or wanted to go.

—CAROLINE KNAPP

Dogs live with man as courtiers round a monarch,
steeped in the flattery of his notice and enriched with sinecures.
To push their favor in this world of pickings and caresses is,
perhaps, the business of their lives.

—ROBERT LOUIS STEVENSON

My little old dog:
A heart-beat at my feet.

—EDITH WHARTON

DOUBT

(see also BELIEF and KNOWLEDGE and QUESTIONS and
QUESTIONS & ANSWERS and THOUGHT)

Doubt is not below knowledge, but above it.

—ALAIN (ÉMILE-AUGUSTE CHARTIER)

**Doubt is the vestibule which *all* must pass,
before they can enter into the temple of wisdom.**

—CHARLES CALEB COLTON

A quart of doubt to an ounce of truth is the safest brew.

—JOHN OLIVER HOBBES (PEN NAME OF PEARL CRAIGIE)

**Doubt comes in at the window,
when Inquiry is denied at the door.**

—BENJAMIN JOWETT

**Doubt must be no more than vigilance,
otherwise it can become dangerous.**

—G. C. LICHTENBERG

I respect faith, but doubt is what gets you an education.

—WILSON MIZNER

I think there is no suffering greater than what is caused
by the doubts of those who want to believe.

—FLANNERY O'CONNOR

Modest doubt is call'd the beacon of the wise.

—WILLIAM SHAKESPEARE

There lives more faith in honest doubt,
Believe me, than in half the creeds.

—ALFRED, LORD TENNYSON

Doubt springs eternal in the human breast.

—THORNTON WILDER[*]

DREAMS [Aspirational]

(see also AIMS & AIMING and ASPIRATION and DREAMS
[Nocturnal] and GOALS and VISION and WISHES &
WISHING)

Dream lofty dreams, and as you dream, so shall you become.

—JAMES ALLEN

[*]   Wilder is playing off "Hope springs eternal in the human breast," from Alexander Pope's
An Essay on Man (1733).

I've dreamt in my life dreams that have stayed with me ever after,
and changed my ideas: they've gone through and through me,
like wine through water, and altered the color of my mind.

—EMILY BRONTË

Dreams nourish the soul just as food nourishes the body.

—PAULO COELHO

What happens to a dream deferred?
Does it dry up
like a raisin in the sun?
Or fester like a sore—
And then run?
Does it stink like rotten meat?
Or crust and sugar over—
like a syrupy sweet?
Maybe it just sags
Like a heavy load.
Or does it explode?

—LANGSTON HUGHES[*]

---

[*] This 1951 poem, formally titled "Harlem," served as the inspiration for Lorraine Hansberry's *A Raisin in the Sun* (1959), the first Broadway play written by a black woman, and the first with a black director, Lloyd Richards.

Sometimes we have the dream
but we are not ourselves ready for the dream.
We have to grow to meet it.

—LOUIS L'AMOUR

Throw your dream into space like a kite,
and you do not know what it will bring back,
a new life, a new friend, a new love, or a new country.

—ANAÏS NIN

If one advances confidently in the direction of his dreams,
and endeavors to live the life which he has imagined,
he will meet with a success unexpected in common hours.

—HENRY DAVID THOREAU

Dreams come true; without that possibility,
nature would not incite us to have them.

—JOHN UPDIKE

Saddle your dreams afore you ride 'em.

—MARY WEBB

You have to have a dream so you can get up in the morning.

—BILLY WILDER

DREAMS [Nocturnal]

(see also DREAMS [Aspirational] and SLEEP and WISHES & WISHING)

Dreams have only the pigmentation of fact.

—DJUNA BARNES

**A man who doesn't dream is like a man who doesn't sweat.
He stores up a lot of poison.**

—TRUMAN CAPOTE

**Dreaming permits each and every one of us
to be quietly and safely insane every night of our lives.**

—WILLIAM DEMENT

Dreams wherein we often see ourselves in masquerade.

—RALPH WALDO EMERSON

**The interpretation of dreams is the royal road
to a knowledge of the unconscious activities of the mind.**

—SIGMUND FREUD

Dreams say what they mean, but they don't say it in daytime language.

—GAIL GODWIN

The dream is the small hidden door
in the deepest and most intimate sanctum of the soul,
which opens to that primeval cosmic night that was soul
long before there was conscious ego.

—CARL JUNG

Dreams are the true interpreters of our inclinations;
but there is art required to sort and understand them.

—MICHEL DE MONTAIGNE

In bed my real love has always been
the sleep that rescued me by allowing me to dream.

—LUIGI PIRANDELLO

In the drowsy dark caves of the mind
dreams build their nest with fragments
dropped from day's caravan.

—RABINDRANATH TAGORE

EDUCATION

(see also CURIOSITY and DISCOVERY and KNOWLEDGE
and LEARNING and TEACHERS & TEACHING)

What sculpture is to a block of marble,
education is to an human soul.

—JOSEPH ADDISON

The roots of education are bitter, but the fruit is sweet.

—ARISTOTLE

To live for a time close to great minds
is the best kind of education.

—JOHN BUCHAN

Education is simply the soul of a society
as it passes from one generation to another.

—G. K. CHESTERTON

Education is a progressive discovery of our own ignorance.

—WILL DURANT

To be able to be caught up into the world of thought—
that is to be educated.

—EDITH HAMILTON

My idea of education is to unsettle the minds of the young
and to inflame their intellects.

—ROBERT MAYNARD HUTCHINS

'Tis education forms the common mind,
Just as the twig is bent, the tree's inclined.

—ALEXANDER POPE

It is as impossible to withhold education from the receptive mind,
as it is impossible to force it upon the unreasoning.

—AGNES REPPLIER

What does education often do?
It makes a straight-cut ditch of a free, meandering brook.

—HENRY DAVID THOREAU

ELOQUENCE

(see also COMMUNICATION and ENGLISH—THE
LANGUAGE and LANGUAGE and SPEECH and WORDS)

Eloquence is the poetry of prose.

—WILLIAM CULLEN BRYANT

Eloquence is the power to translate a truth
into language perfectly intelligible to the person to whom you speak.

—RALPH WALDO EMERSON

Eloquence may set fire to reason.

—OLIVER WENDELL HOLMES JR.

Eloquence, when at its highest pitch,
leaves little room for reason or reflection;
but addressing itself entirely to the fancy or the affections,
captivates the willing hearers, and subdues their understanding.

—DAVID HUME

There is no eloquence which does not agitate the soul.

—WALTER SAVAGE LANDOR

Eloquence lies as much in the tone of the voice,
in the eyes, and in the speaker's manner,
as in his choice of words.

—FRANÇOIS, DUC DE LA ROCHEFOUCAULD

Eloquence is feeling pouring itself to other minds,
courting their sympathy.

—JOHN STUART MILL

Shame on all eloquence which leaves us with a taste for itself
and not for its substance.

—MICHEL DE MONTAIGNE

Eloquence is a painting of thought.

—BLAISE PASCAL

You are eloquent enough if truth speaks through you.

—PUBLILIUS SYRUS

ENGLISH—THE LANGUAGE

(see also COMMUNICATION and ELOQUENCE and
LANGUAGE and SPEECH and WORDS)

**Modern English is the Wal-Mart of languages:
convenient, huge, hard to avoid, superficially friendly,
and devouring all rivals in its eagerness to expand.**

—MARK ABLEY

**English is the great Wurlitzer of language,
the most perfect all-purpose instrument ever invented.**

—MICHAEL ARLEN

**One cannot but be impressed by
the amazing hospitality of the English language.**

—ROBERT BURCHFIELD

**It is a language which is being molded by writers to do delicate things
and yet be in the grasp of superficially educated people.**

—RAYMOND CHANDLER, ON AMERICAN ENGLISH

**I like to be beholden to the great metropolitan English speech,
the sea which receives tributaries from every region under heaven.**

—RALPH WALDO EMERSON

He mobilized the English language and sent it into battle.

—EDWARD R. MURROW, ON WINSTON CHURCHILL IN WWII

The problem with defending the purity of the English language
is that English is about as pure as a cribhouse whore.
We don't just borrow words;
on occasion, English has pursued other languages down alleyways
to beat them unconscious and rifle their pockets for new vocabulary

—JAMES D. NICOLL

English, no longer an English language, now grows from many roots;
and those whom it once colonized are carving out
large territories within the language for themselves.
The Empire is striking back.

—SALMAN RUSHDIE

English is a stretch language; one size fits all.

—WILLIAM SAFIRE

There is no such thing as "the Queen's English."
The property has gone into the hands of a joint stock company
and we own the bulk of the shares!

—MARK TWAIN, ON AMERICAN ENGLISH

ENTHUSIASM

(see also CURIOSITY and PASSION and ZEAL)

Nothing is so contagious as enthusiasm.

—EDWARD GEORGE BULWER-LYTTON

All noble enthusiasms pass through a feverish stage,
and grow wiser and more serene.

—WILLIAM ELLERY CHANNING

Nothing great was ever achieved without enthusiasm.
For what is enthusiasm but the oblivion
and swallowing-up of self in an object dearer than self?

—SAMUEL TAYLOR COLERIDGE

Every great and commanding movement
in the annals of the world is the triumph of some enthusiasm.

—RALPH WALDO EMERSON

Enthusiasm is a volcano
on whose top never grows the grass of hesitation.

—KAHLIL GIBRAN

Enthusiasm is the great hill-climber.

—ELBERT HUBBARD

Indeed, there is an eloquence in true enthusiasm
that is not to be doubted.

—WASHINGTON IRVING

The sense of this word among the Greeks
affords the noblest definition of it: enthusiasm signifies *God in us.*

—GERMAINE DE STAËL

Enthusiasm is to a person what gasoline is
to the engine of an automobile: the vital moving force.

—W. CLEMENT STONE

We grow old by deserting our ideals.
Years may wrinkle the skin, but to give up enthusiasm wrinkles the soul.

—SAMUEL ULLMAN

ENVY

(see also JEALOUSY and VICE and VICE & VIRTUE)

Few men have the strength of character
to rejoice in a friend's success without a touch of envy.

—AESCHYLUS

As iron is eaten away by rust,
so the envious are consumed by their own passion.

—ANTISTHENES

The envious die not once,
but as often as the envied win applause.

—BALTASAR GRACIÁN

Envy is a littleness of soul,
which cannot see beyond a certain point,
and if it does not occupy the whole space,
feels itself excluded.

—WILLIAM HAZLITT

Even in envy may be discerned something of an instinct of justice,
something of a wish to see universal fair-play, and things on a level.

—LEIGH HUNT

An envious heart makes a treacherous ear.

—ZORA NEALE HURSTON

We often pride ourselves on even the most criminal passions,
but envy is a timid and shame-faced passion we never dare acknowledge.

—FRANÇOIS, DUC DE LA ROCHEFOUCAULD

Envy is a symptom of lack of appreciation
of our own uniqueness and self worth.

—ELIZABETH O'CONNOR

Base envy withers at another's joy,
And hates that excellence it cannot reach.

—JAMES THOMSON

A show of envy is an insult to oneself.

—YEVGENY YEVTUSHENKO

ERROR

(see also FAILURE and FOLLY and MISTAKES and TRUTH & ERROR)

The weak have one weapon:
the errors of those who are strong.

—GEORGE BIDAULT

There is no error so monstrous
that it fails to find its defenders among the ablest men.

—JOHN DALBERG (LORD ACTON)

To kill an error is as good a service as,
and sometimes even better than,
the establishing of a new truth or fact.

—CHARLES DARWIN

Error is acceptable as long as we are young;
but one must not drag it along into old age.

—JOHANN WOLFGANG VON GOETHE

Generally speaking, the errors of religion are dangerous;
those in philosophy only ridiculous.

—DAVID HUME

Give me a fruitful error any time,
full of seeds, bursting with its own corrections.

—VILFREDO PARETO

The most powerful cause of error
is the war existing between the senses and reason.

—BLAISE PASCAL

With Pleasure own your Errors past,
And make each day a Critic on the last.

—ALEXANDER POPE

By our errors we see deeper into life.

—OLIVE SCHREINER

Error is the ultimate inside job.
Yes, the world can be profoundly confusing;
and yes, other people can mislead or deceive you.
In the end, though, nobody but you
can choose to believe your own beliefs.

—KATHRYN SCHULZ

EVIL

(see also CONSCIENCE and SIN and VICE and VICE &
VIRTUE and VIRTUE)

**Evil is unspectacular and always human
And shares our bed and eats at our own table.**

—W. H. AUDEN

**The belief in a supernatural source of evil is not necessary;
men alone are quite capable of every wickedness.**

—JOSEPH CONRAD

**No evil dooms us hopelessly except the evil we love,
and desire to continue in, and make no effort to escape from.**

—GEORGE ELIOT

Man produces evil as a bee produces honey.

—WILLIAM GOLDING

**Whoever fights with monsters should see to it
that he does not become one himself.
And when you stare for a long time into an abyss,
the abyss stares back into you.**

—FRIEDRICH NIETZSCHE

Men never do evil so completely and cheerfully
as when they do it from religious conviction.

—BLAISE PASCAL

In all men is evil sleeping;
the good man is he who will not awaken it,
in himself or in other men.

—MARY RENAULT

The evil that men do lives after them;
The good is oft interred with their bones.

—WILLIAM SHAKESPEARE

There are a thousand hacking at the branches of evil
to one who is striking at the root.

—HENRY DAVID THOREAU

Evil when we are in its power is not felt as evil
but as a necessity, or even a duty.

—SIMONE WEIL

EXAMPLE

(see also EDUCATION and LEARNING and PARENTS &
PARENTHOOD and TEACHERS & TEACHING)

Example is the best precept.

—AESOP

He preaches well who lives well.

—MIGUEL DE CERVANTES

**A superior who works on his own development
sets an almost irresistible example.**

—PETER F. DRUCKER

**People never improve unless they look to
some standard or example higher and better than themselves.**

—TRYON EDWARDS

**It is not so much the example of others we imitate
as the reflection of ourselves in their eyes
and the echo of ourselves in their words.**

—ERIC HOFFER

Children have more need of models than critics.

—JOSEPH JOUBERT

They who set an example make a highway.
Others follow the example, because it is easier
to travel on a highway than over untrodden grounds.

—HORACE MANN

Example moves the world more than doctrine.
The great exemplars are the poets of action,
and it makes little difference
whether they be forces for good or forces for evil.

—HENRY MILLER

Example is not the *main* thing in influencing others.
It is the *only* thing.

—ALBERT SCHWEITZER

There is a transcendent power in example.
We reform others unconsciously when we walk uprightly.

—ANNE SOPHIE SWETCHINE

EXCELLENCE

(see also AIMS & AIMING and ABILITY and ASPIRATION
and GREATNESS and MEDIOCRITY and TALENT)

The sad truth is that excellence makes people nervous.

—SHANA ALEXANDER

The secret of joy in work is contained in one word—excellence.

—PEARL S. BUCK

The study of what is excellent is food for the mind and body.

—LEONARDO DA VINCI

It is a wretched taste to be gratified with mediocrity
when the excellent lies before us.

—ISAAC D'ISRAELI

We are what we repeatedly do.
Excellence, then, is not an act but a habit.

—WILL DURANT[*]

Excellence encourages one about life generally;
it shows the spiritual wealth of the world.

—GEORGE ELIOT

From time to time there appear on the face of the earth
men of rare and consummate excellence,
who dazzle us by their virtue,
and whose outstanding qualities shed a stupendous light.

—JEAN DE LA BRUYÈRE

[*]   Almost all Internet quotation sites mistakenly attribute this observation to Aristotle.

We are going to relentlessly chase perfection,
knowing full well we will not catch it,
because nothing is perfect.
But we are going to relentlessly chase it,
because in the process we will catch excellence.

—VINCE LOMBARDI

To rest in the arms of perfection
is the desire of any man intent upon creating excellence.

—THOMAS MANN

It takes a long time to bring excellence to maturity.

—PUBLILIUS SYRUS

EXPECTATION

(see also HOPE and WISHES & WISHING)

A life that is burdened with expectations is a heavy life.
Its fruit is sorrow and disappointment.

—DOUGLAS ADAMS

Life is so constructed, that the event does not,
cannot, will not, meet the expectation.

—CHARLOTTE BRONTË

There is one illusion that has much to do with most of our happiness,
and still more to do with most of our unhappiness.
It may be told in a word. We expect too much.

—JOSEPH FARRELL

Expectation improperly indulged in must end in disappointment.

—SAMUEL JOHNSON

Expectation . . . quickens desire, while possession deadens it.

—HANNAH MORE

Expectation is hope colored by fancy.

—LADY MORGAN (SYDNEY OWENSON MORGAN)

To expect too much is to have a sentimental view of life
and this is a softness that ends in bitterness.

—FLANNERY O'CONNOR

"Blessed is the man who expects nothing,
for he shall never be disappointed"
was the ninth beatitude which a man of wit . . . added to the eighth.

—ALEXANDER POPE

Oft expectation fails and most oft there
Where most it promises.

—WILLIAM SHAKESPEARE

All expectation hath something of torment.

—BENJAMIN WHICHCOTE

EXPERIENCE

(see also EDUCATION and HISTORY and LEARNING and
LIFE and MATURITY and PAST)

Experience is a good teacher, but she sends in terrific bills.

—MINNA ANTRIM

Everything you experience is what constitutes *you* as a human being,
but the experience passes away and the person's left.
The person is the residue.

—ILKA CHASE

To most men, experience is like the stern lights of a ship,
which illumine only the track it has passed.

—SAMUEL TAYLOR COLERIDGE

Experience has two things to teach:
the first, that we must correct a great deal;
the second, that we must not correct too much.

—EUGÈNE DELACROIX

Experience is a hard teacher
because she gives the test first, the lesson afterward.

—VERNON LAW

One thorn of experience is worth a whole wilderness of warning.

—JAMES RUSSELL LOWELL

A strong and well-constituted man digests his experiences
(deeds and misdeeds) just as he digests his meats,
even when he has some tough morsels to swallow.

—FRIEDRICH NIETZSCHE

Experience comprises illusions lost, rather than wisdom gained.

—JOSEPH ROUX

We should be careful to get out of an experience
only the wisdom that is in it—and stop there;
lest we be like the cat that sits down on a hot stove-lid.
She will never sit down on a hot-stove lid again—and that is well;
but also she will never sit down on a cold one any more.

—MARK TWAIN

Experience is the name every one gives to their mistakes.

—OSCAR WILDE

FACTS

(see also ERROR and KNOWLEDGE and SCIENCE &
SCIENTISTS and TRUTH and TRUTH & ERROR)

Facts are stubborn things.

—ABEL BOYER[*]

In the spider-web of facts, many a truth is strangled.

—PAUL ELDRIDGE

**If a man will kick a fact out of the window,
when he comes back he finds it again in the chimney corner.**

—RALPH WALDO EMERSON

A single fact will often spoil an interesting argument.

—WILLIAM FEATHER

**When the mind withdraws into itself
and dispenses with facts it makes only chaos.**

—EDITH HAMILTON

Facts do not cease to exist because they are ignored.

—ALDOUS HUXLEY

---

[*] This saying, which has long bedeviled quotation sleuths, is commonly attributed to John
Adams. While Adams did, in fact, say "Facts are stubborn things" to the jury in the 1770
Boston Massacre trial, it was Abel Boyer, an English lexicographer and historian, who
first presented it in a 1717 newsletter.

The facts we see depend on where we are placed,
and the habits of our eyes.

—WALTER LIPPMANN

In science, all facts, no matter how trivial or banal,
enjoy democratic equality.

—MARY MCCARTHY

The facts are *always* friendly.
Every bit of evidence one can acquire, in any area,
leads one that much closer to what is true.

—CARL ROGERS

Let us not underrate the value of a fact;
it will one day flower in a truth.

—HENRY DAVID THOREAU

FAILURE

(see also DEFEAT and SUCCESS and SUCCESS & FAILURE
and VICTORY and VICTORY & DEFEAT)

They fail, and they alone, who have not striven.

—THOMAS BAILEY ALDRICH

A man's life is interesting primarily when he has failed—I well know.
For it's a sign that he tried to surpass himself.

—GEORGES CLEMENCEAU

The only failure a man ought to fear
is failure of cleaving to the purpose he sees to be best.

—GEORGE ELIOT

Learning starts with failure,
the first failure is the beginning of education.

—JOHN HERSEY

Half the failures in life
arise from pulling in one's horse as he is leaping.

—JULIUS C. HARE AND AUGUSTUS W. HARE

There is not a fiercer hell than the failure in a great object.

—JOHN KEATS

Virtually nothing comes out right the first time.
Failures, repeated failures,
are finger posts on the road to achievement.

—CHARLES F. KETTERING

Failure can get to be a rather comfortable old friend.

—MIGNON MCLAUGHLIN

Supposing you have tried and failed again and again,
you may have a fresh start any moment you choose,
for this thing that we call "failure" is not the falling down,
but the staying down.

—MARY PICKFORD

I cannot give you the formula for success, but I can
give you the formula for failure, which is: Try to please everybody.

—HERBERT BAYARD SWOPE

FAME

(see also AIMS & AIMING and AMBITION and
ASPIRATION and DREAMS [Aspirational] and GOALS
and HEROES & HEROISM and SUCCESS)

Fame is a pearl many dive for and only a few bring up.

—LOUISA MAY ALCOTT

It's such a corrosive chemical: fame.

—CANDICE BERGEN

Worldly fame is but a breath of wind that blows now this way,
and now that, and changes name as it changes direction.

—DANTE ALIGHIERI

Fame is a fickle food
Upon a shifting plate.

—EMILY DICKINSON

Fame is a powerful aphrodisiac.

—GRAHAM GREENE

Fame and tranquility can never be bedfellows.

—MICHEL DE MONTAIGNE

Those whom the gods wish to destroy, they first make famous.

—JOYCE CAROL OATES[*]

I don't think I realized that the cost of fame
is that it's open season on *every moment* of your life.

—JULIA ROBERTS

So this was fame at last!
Nothing but a vast debt to be paid to the world
in energy, in blood, in time.

—MAY SARTON

Blessed is he whose fame does not outshine his truth.

—RABINDRANATH TAGORE

---

[*] Oates is playing off the proverb "Whom the gods would destroy they first make mad," which was derived from a fifth-century BC fragment from Euripides.

FAMILY [Positive]

(see also BABIES and CHILDREN and FAMILY
[Not-So-Positive] and MARRIAGE and MOTHERS &
MOTHERHOOD and PARENTS & PARENTHOOD)

The family is the association established by nature
for the supply of man's everyday wants.

—ARISTOTLE

A glance of heaven to see,
To none on earth is given;
And yet a happy family
Is but an earlier heaven.

—JOHN BOWRING

The family fireside is the best of schools.

—ARNOLD H. GLASOW

Good families are fortresses
with many windows and doors to the outer world.

—JANE HOWARD

Family. A snug kind of word.

—FANNIE HURST

Without a family, man, alone in the world, trembles with the cold.

—ANDRÉ MAUROIS

The family is the country of the heart.

—GIUSEPPE MAZZINI

The family is one of nature's masterpieces.

—GEORGE SANTAYANA

Perhaps the greatest social service that can be rendered
by anybody to the country and to mankind
is to bring up a family.

—GEORGE BERNARD SHAW

The family—that dear octopus
from whose tentacles we never quite escape,
nor, in our inmost hearts, ever wish to.

—DODIE SMITH

FAMILY [Not-So-Positive]

(see also BABIES and CHILDREN and FAMILY [Positive]
and MARRIAGE and MOTHERS & MOTHERHOOD and
PARENTS & PARENTHOOD)

The family.
I believe more unhappiness comes from this source than from any other—
I mean the attempt to prolong family connection unduly,
and to make people hang together artificially
who would never naturally do so.

—SAMUEL BUTLER (1835–1902)

If Mr. Vincent Price were to be co-starred with Miss Bette Davis
in a story by Mr. Edgar Allan Poe directed by Mr. Roger Corman,
it could not fully express the pent-up violence and depravity
of a single day in the life of the average family.

—QUENTIN CRISP

Family quarrels are bitter things. They don't go by any rules.
They're not like aches or wounds;
they're more like splits in the skin that won't heal.

—F. SCOTT FITZGERALD

If a kingdom be . . . a great family, a family likewise is a little kingdom,
torn with factions and exposed to revolutions.

—SAMUEL JOHNSON

A family is but too often a commonwealth of malignants.

—ALEXANDER POPE

The Family is a petty despotism.

—GEORGE BERNARD SHAW

If a man's character is to be abused, say what you will,
there's nobody like a relation to do the business.

—WILLIAM MAKEPEACE THACKERAY

All happy families resemble one another,
but each unhappy family is unhappy in its own way.

—LEO TOLSTOY

Families are great murderers of the creative impulse.
—BRENDA UELAND

Unhappy families are conspiracies of silence.
The one who breaks the silence is never forgiven.
—JEANETTE WINTERSON

FANATICISM

(see also BELIEF and IDEAS and POLITICS & RELIGION
and WAR and ZEAL)

From fanaticism to barbarism is only one step.
—DENIS DIDEROT

The fanatical believer is not conscious
of his envy, malice, pettiness, and dishonesty.
There is a wall of words between his consciousness and his real self.
—ERIC HOFFER

Defined in psychological terms, a fanatic
is a man who consciously over-compensates for a secret doubt.
—ALDOUS HUXLEY

Fanatics have their dreams, wherewith they weave
A paradise for a sect.

—JOHN KEATS

The tendency to claim God as an ally
for our partisan values and ends is another childish,
but also universal, corruption of religion.
This is the source of all religious fanaticism.

—REINHOLD NIEBUHR

One defeats the fanatic precisely by *not* being a fanatic oneself,
but on the contrary by using one's intelligence.

—GEORGE ORWELL

Fanatics fear liberty more than they fear persecution.

—ERNEST RENAN

Fanaticism consists in redoubling your effort
when you have forgotten your aim.

—GEORGE SANTAYANA

There is nobody as enslaved as the fanatic,
the person in whom one impulse, one value,
has assumed ascendancy over all others.

—MILTON R. SAPIRSTEIN

The weakness of the fanatic is that those whom he fights
have a secret hold upon him;
and to this weakness he and his group finally succumb.

—PAUL TILLICH

FEAR

(see also ADVENTURE and COURAGE and COWARDICE
and HEROES & HEROISM and RISK & RISK-TAKING)

There are times when fear is good.
It must keep its watchful place
at the heart's controls.

—AESCHYLUS

Fear has a smell, as love does.

—MARGARET ATWOOD

We must travel in the direction of our fear.

—JOHN BERRYMAN

No passion so effectually robs the mind
of all its powers of acting and reasoning as fear.

—EDMUND BURKE

Fear has many eyes.

—MIGUEL DE CERVANTES

Fear is a pair of handcuffs on your soul.

—FAYE DUNAWAY

He has not learned the lesson of life
who does not every day surmount a fear.

—RALPH WALDO EMERSON

When men are ruled by fear,
they strive to prevent the very changes that will abate it.

—ALAN PATON

You gain strength, courage, and confidence
by every experience in which
you really stop to look fear in the face.

—ELEANOR ROOSEVELT

In order to do anything in this world worth doing,
we must not stand shivering on the bank
and thinking of the cold and the danger,
but jump in and scramble through as well as we can.

—SYDNEY SMITH

FICTION

(see also AUTHORS and BOOKS and LITERATURE and
NOVELS and READING and WRITERS and WRITING)

Fiction is fact distilled into truth.

—EDWARD ALBEE

Fiction is the higher autobiography.

—SAUL BELLOW

**Books are acts of composition: you compose them.
You make music: the music is called fiction.**

—E. L. DOCTOROW

**The art of writing fiction
is to sail as dangerously close to the truth as possible
without sinking the ship.**

—KINKY FRIEDMAN

**The house of fiction has in short not one window,
but a million . . . but they are, singly, as nothing
without the posted presence of the watcher.**

—HENRY JAMES

**Fiction is Truth's elder sister. Obviously.
No one in the world knew what truth was till somebody had told a story.**

—RUDYARD KIPLING

Everybody else is working to change, persuade, tempt, and control them.
The best readers come to fiction to be free of all that noise.

—PHILIP ROTH

Fiction is nothing less than the subtlest instrument
for self-examination and self-display that mankind has invented yet.

—JOHN UPDIKE

Fiction reveals truths that reality obscures.

—JESSAMYN WEST

Fiction is like a spider's web, attached ever so lightly perhaps,
but still attached to life at all four corners.
Often the attachment is scarcely perceptible.

—VIRGINIA WOOLF

FLATTERY

(see also COMPLIMENTS and PRAISE and SELF-
DECEPTION and VANITY)

Flattery corrupts both the receiver and the giver.

—EDMUND BURKE

Flatterers look like friends, as wolves like dogs.

—GEORGE CHAPMAN

We swallow greedily any lie that flatters us,
but we sip only little by little at a truth we find bitter.

—DENIS DIDEROT

We love flattery, even though we are not deceived by it,
because it shows that we are of importance enough to be courted.

—RALPH WALDO EMERSON

Flattery must be pretty thick before anybody objects to it.

—WILLIAM FEATHER

Flattery, if judiciously administered, is always acceptable,
however much we may despise the flatterer.

—MARGUERITE GARDINER (LADY BLESSINGTON)

Flattery is counterfeit money which,
but for vanity, would have no circulation.

—FRANÇOIS, DUC DE LA ROCHEFOUCAULD

Flattery is praise without foundation.

—ELIZA LESLIE

The aim of flattery is to soothe and encourage us by assuring
us of the truth of an opinion we have already formed about ourselves.

—EDITH SITWELL

'Tis an old maxim in the schools,
That flattery's the food of fools;
Yet now and then your men of wit
Will condescend to take a bit.

—JONATHAN SWIFT

FLOWERS

(see also BEAUTY and GARDENS & GARDENING and
NATURE)

Flowers are the sweetest things that God ever made,
and forgot to put a soul into.

—HENRY WARD BEECHER

Flowers always make people better, happier, and more hopeful;
they are sunshine, food, and medicine to the soul.

—LUTHER BURBANK

The flower has no weekday self,
dressed as it always is in Sunday clothes.

—MALCOLM DE CHAZAL

Earth laughs in flowers.

—RALPH WALDO EMERSON

The flower is the poetry of reproduction.
It is an example of the eternal seductiveness of life.

—JEAN GIRAUDOUX

The Amen! of Nature is always a flower.

—OLIVER WENDELL HOLMES SR.

A flower is a plant's way of making love.

—BARBARA KINGSOLVER

People from a planet without flowers would think we must be
mad with joy the whole time to have such things about us.

—IRIS MURDOCH

A flowerless room is a soulless room, to my way of thinking;
but even one solitary little vase of a living flower may redeem it.

—VITA SACKVILLE-WEST

One of the most attractive things about the flowers
is their beautiful reserve.

—HENRY DAVID THOREAU

FOLLY

(see also ERROR and FOOLS & FOOLISHNESS and SELF-
DECEPTION and STUPIDITY)

The folly of one man is the fortune of another;
for no man prospers so suddenly as by others' errors.

—FRANCIS BACON (1561–1626)

Profit from folly rather than participate in it.

—WARREN BUFFETT

If we wise people make eminent fools of ourselves
on any particular occasion,
we must endure the legitimate conclusion
that we carry a few grains of folly to our ounce of wisdom.

—GEORGE ELIOT

There is, perhaps, no surer mark of folly,
than an attempt to correct the natural infirmities of those we love.

—HENRY FIELDING

The most exquisite folly is made of wisdom spun too fine.

—BENJAMIN FRANKLIN

To flee vice is the beginning of virtue,
and to have got rid of folly is the beginning of wisdom.

—HORACE

Folly pursues us throughout our lives,
and the man whom we call wise is he whose follies
are proportionate to his age and to his fortune.

—FRANÇOIS, DUC DE LA ROCHEFOUCAULD

What curious little corners of folly
are to be found in even the sanest brain!

—QUEEN MARIE OF ROMANIA (MARIE ALEXANDRA VICTORIA)

The most costly of all follies
is to believe passionately in the palpably not true.

—H. L. MENCKEN

The ultimate result of shielding men from the effects of folly
is to fill the world with fools.

—HERBERT SPENCER

FOOLS & FOOLISHNESS

(see also ERROR and FOLLY and SELF-DECEPTION and
STUPIDITY)

Fine clothes may disguise,
but foolish words will disclose a fool.

—AESOP

A fool bolts pleasure, then complains of moral indigestion.

—MINNA ANTRIM

To be intimate with a foolish friend is like going to bed to a razor.

—BENJAMIN FRANKLIN*

Every man is a damn fool for at least five minutes every day.
Wisdom consists in not exceeding that limit.

—ELBERT HUBBARD

Silence is all the genius a fool has.

—ZORA NEALE HURSTON

A learned fool is a greater fool than an ignorant fool.

—MOLIÈRE

People are never so near playing the fool
as when they think themselves wise.

—MARY WORTLEY MONTAGU

Fools rush in where Angels fear to tread.

—ALEXANDER POPE

Fools are a family over all the world.

—JAMES SHIRLEY

---

* This is the correct original phrasing, but the observation is now almost always presented as if it ended "with a razor."

There's no system foolproof enough to defeat a sufficiently great fool.

—EDWARD TELLER

FORGIVENESS

(see also APOLOGY and ERROR and MISTAKES and
QUARRELS and RELATIONSHIPS)

Without being forgiven,
released from the consequences of what we have done,
our capacity to act would, as it were, be confined
to one single deed from which we could never recover.

—HANNAH ARENDT

Forgiveness is the fragrance the violet sheds on the heel that has crushed it.

—AUTHOR UNKNOWN*

Life is an adventure in forgiveness.
Nothing clutters the soul more than remorse, resentment, recrimination.

—NORMAN COUSINS

Once a woman has forgiven her man,
she must not reheat his sins for breakfast.

—MARLENE DIETRICH

---

* This observation is often mistakenly attributed to Mark Twain. The underlying sentiment goes back centuries, first applied to the forgiving fragrance of cut sandalwood trees, then to flowers in general, and ultimately to violets.

As long as you don't forgive,
who and whatever it is will occupy rent-free space in your mind.

—ISABELLE HOLLAND

When a deep injury is done to us,
we never recover until we forgive.

—ALAN PATON

To err is human; to forgive, divine.

—ALEXANDER POPE

To forgive is to set a prisoner free and discover that the prisoner was you.

—LEWIS B. SMEDES

It is very easy to forgive others their mistakes;
it takes more grit and gumption
to forgive them for having witnessed your own.

—JESSAMYN WEST

Many promising reconciliations have broken down because,
while both parties came prepared to forgive,
neither was prepared to be forgiven.

—CHARLES WILLIAMS

FRIENDS

(see also FAMILY [Positive] and FAMILY [Not-So-Positive]
and FRIENDSHIP and LOVE and RELATIONSHIPS)

A faithful friend is a sturdy shelter:
he that has found one has found a treasure.

—APOCRYPHA, ECCLESIASTICUS 6:14

To the query, "What is a friend?" his reply was,
"A single soul dwelling in two bodies."

—ARISTOTLE, QUOTED BY DIOGENES LAËRTIUS

Friends are the family we choose for ourselves.

—EDNA BUCHANAN

A friend is, as it were, a second self.

—MARCUS TULLIUS CICERO

A friend may well be reckoned the masterpiece of nature.

—RALPH WALDO EMERSON

Friends are God's apology for relations.

—HUGH KINGSMILL

Each friend represents a world in us,
a world possibly not born until they arrive,
and it is only by this meeting that a new world is born.

—ANAÏS NIN

A home-made friend wears longer
than one you buy in the market.

—AUSTIN O'MALLEY

Friends do not live in harmony merely,
as some say, but in melody.

—HENRY DAVID THOREAU

A friend: one who walks in when the rest of the world walks out.

—WALTER WINCHELL

FRIENDSHIP

(see also FAMILY [Positive] and FAMILY [Not-So-Positive]
and FRIENDS and LOVE and RELATIONSHIPS)

Wishing to be friends is quick work,
but friendship is a slow-ripening fruit.

—ARISTOTLE

It is one of the severest tests of friendship to tell your friend of his faults . . .
so to love a man that you cannot bear to see the stain of a sin upon him,
and to speak painful truth through loving words—that *is* friendship.

—HENRY WARD BEECHER

Friendship is Love without his wings!

—GEORGE NOEL GORDON, LORD BYRON

Friendship is a sheltering tree.

—SAMUEL TAYLOR COLERIDGE

To let friendship die away by negligence and silence is certainly not wise.
It is voluntarily to throw away
one of the greatest comforts of this weary pilgrimage.

—SAMUEL JOHNSON

For friendship is an art,
and very few persons are born with a natural gift for it.

—KATHLEEN THOMPSON NORRIS

Friendship loves a free air,
and will not be penned up in straight and narrow enclosures.

—WILLIAM PENN

Though friendship is not quick to burn,
It is explosive stuff.

—MAY SARTON

True friendship can afford true knowledge.
It does not depend on darkness and ignorance.

—HENRY DAVID THOREAU

The path of social advancement is, and must be,
strewn with broken friendships.

—H. G. WELLS

FUTURE

(see also PAST and TIME and YEARS)

Never let the future disturb you.
You will meet it, if you have to, with the same
weapons of reason which today arm you against the present.

—MARCUS AURELIUS

You can never plan the future by the past.

—EDMUND BURKE

The future is a convenient place for dreams.

—ANATOLE FRANCE

The future: A consolation for those who have no other.

—MARGUERITE GARDINER (LADY BLESSINGTON)

Sometimes it's like I can see the future
stretched out in front of me——just as plain as day.
The future hanging over there at the edge of my days.
Just waiting for me.

—LORRAINE HANSBERRY

The future remains uncertain and so it should,
for it is the canvas upon which we paint our desires.

—FRANK HERBERT

No one can walk backwards into the future.

—JOSEPH HERGESHEIMER

I like the dreams of the future better than the history of the past.

—THOMAS JEFFERSON

The best way to predict the future is to invent it.

—ALAN KAY

The future has a way of arriving unannounced.
Its arrival is jolting when people have not prepared for it.

—GEORGE F. WILL

GARDENS & GARDENING

(see also BEAUTY and FLOWERS and NATURE)

A modest garden . . . contains,
for those who know how to look and to wait,
more instruction than a library.

—HENRI FRÉDÉRIC AMIEL

Gardening is not a rational act.

—MARGARET ATWOOD

God Almighty first planted a garden.
And, indeed, it is the purest of human pleasures.

—FRANCIS BACON (1561–1626)

A garden is a kinetic work of art, not an object but a process,
open-ended, biodegradable, nurturant, like all women's artistry.
A garden is the best alternative therapy.

—GERMAINE GREER

The kiss of the sun for pardon,
The song of the birds for mirth,
One is nearer God's Heart in a garden
Than anywhere else on earth.

—DOROTHY FRANCES GURNEY

Gardening has compensations out of all proportion to its goals.
It is creation in the pure sense.

—PHYLLIS MCGINLEY

All gardening is landscape painting.

—ALEXANDER POPE

A garden is always a series of losses
set against a few triumphs, like life itself.

—MAY SARTON

I realized that I was really nothing more than a custodian
to a mystery that was beyond my comprehension.
I think that's what hooks one on gardening forever.
It is the closest one can come to being present at the creation.

—PHYLLIS THEROUX

Gardening is civil and social,
but it wants the vigor and freedom of the forest and the outlaw.

—HENRY DAVID THOREAU

GENEROSITY

(see also KINDNESS and LOVE and VIRTUE)

That's what I consider true generosity.
You give your all and yet you always feel as if it costs you nothing.

—SIMONE DE BEAUVOIR

Generosity gives assistance rather than advice.

—LUC DE CLAPIERS (MARQUIS DE VAUVENARGUES)

Generosity is the most natural outward expression
of an inner attitude of compassion and loving-kindness.

—TENZIN GYATSO, THE FOURTEENTH DALAI LAMA

Generosity lies less in giving much
than in giving at the right moment.

—JEAN DE LA BRUYÈRE

What is called generosity is usually only the vanity of giving;
we enjoy the vanity more than the thing given.

—FRANÇOIS, DUC DE LA ROCHEFOUCAULD

Generosity with strings is not generosity: it is a deal.

—MARYA MANNES

We'd all like a reputation for generosity
and we'd all like to buy it cheap.

—MIGNON MCLAUGHLIN

He who gives only what he would as readily throw away
gives without generosity;
for the essence of generosity is in self-sacrifice.

—HENRY TAYLOR

Generosity is luck going in the opposite direction, away from you.
If you're generous to someone, if you do something to help him out,
you are in effect making him lucky. This is important.
It's like inviting yourself into a community of good fortune.

—TWYLA THARP

Generosity is often the stalking horse of control.

—ANNE TRUITT

GENIUS

(see also ABILITY and CREATIVITY and GREATNESS and
TALENT and TALENT & GENIUS)

The meaning of genius is that it doesn't have to work
to attain what people without it must labor for—and not attain.

—MARGARET C. ANDERSON

I have known no man of genius who had not to pay,
in some affliction or defect either physical or spiritual,
for what the gods had given him.
—MAX BEERBOHM

What is genius—but the power of expressing a new individuality?
—ELIZABETH BARRETT BROWNING

One of the marks of true genius is a quality of abundance.
A rich, rollicking abundance,
enough to give indigestion to ordinary people.
Great artists turn it out in rolls, in swatches.
They cover whole ceilings with paintings,
they chip out a mountainside in stone,
they write not one novel but a shelf full.
—CATHERINE DRINKER BOWEN

In every work of genius we recognize our own rejected thoughts:
they come back to us with a certain alienated majesty.
—RALPH WALDO EMERSON

A genius is a promontory jutting out into the infinite.
—VICTOR HUGO

The principle mark of genius is not perfection,
but originality, the opening of new frontiers;
once this is done, the conquered territory becomes common property.
—ARTHUR KOESTLER

Towering genius disdains a beaten path.
It seeks regions hitherto unexplored.

—ABRAHAM LINCOLN

Blessed the geniuses who know that egomania is not a duty.

—MARIANNE MOORE

When a true genius appears in the world,
you may know him by this sign;
that the dunces are all in confederacy against him.

—JONATHAN SWIFT

GOALS

(see also AIMS & AIMING and ASPIRATION and DREAMS
[Aspirational] and PURPOSE and VISION)

A goal is a dream with a deadline.

—AUTHOR UNKNOWN[*]

It is not possible to run a course aright
when the goal itself has not been rightly placed.

—FRANCIS BACON (1561–1626)

Without some goal and some effort to reach it, no man can live.

—FYODOR DOSTOEVSKY

---

[*] This observation is widely attributed to the self-help author Napoleon Hill, but it has not
been found in his works.

One should not pursue goals that are easily achieved.
One must develop an instinct for what one can just barely achieve
through one's greatest efforts.

—ALBERT EINSTEIN

What man actually needs is not a tensionless state
but rather the striving and struggling for a worthwhile goal.

—VICTOR FRANKL

By losing your goal—you have lost your way, too!

—FRIEDRICH NIETZSCHE

To tend, unfailingly, unflinchingly,
towards a goal, is the secret of success.

—ANNA PAVLOVA

To live only for some future goal is shallow.
It's the sides of the mountain that sustain life, not the top.
Here's where things grow.

—ROBERT M. PIRSIG

We must walk consciously only part way toward our goal,
and then leap in the dark to our success.

—HENRY DAVID THOREAU

What you get by achieving your goals is not as important
as what you become by achieving your goals.

—ZIG ZIGLAR

GOSSIP

(see also ENVY and VICE)

Gossip is the art-form of the man and woman in the street,
and the proper subject for gossip,
as for all art, is the behavior of mankind.

—W. H. AUDEN

Gossip is a sort of smoke that comes
from the dirty tobacco-pipes of those who diffuse it;
it proves nothing but the bad taste of the smoker.

—GEORGE ELIOT

Gossip is vice enjoyed vicariously—
the sweet, subtle satisfaction without the risk.

—ELBERT HUBBARD

Gossip . . . was like any other commodity in the marketplace.
You received it only if you had something of value to give.

—P. D. JAMES

It's the gossip columnist's business
to write about what is none of his business.

—LOUIS KRONENBERGER

Of course we women gossip on occasion.
But our appetite for it is not as avid as a man's.
It is in the boys' gyms, the college fraternity houses, the club locker rooms,
the paneled offices of business that gossip reaches its luxuriant flower.

—PHYLLIS MCGINLEY

The widespread interest in gossip is inspired,
not by a love of knowledge but by malice:
no one gossips about other people's secret virtues.

—BERTRAND RUSSELL

People are universally interested in gossip.
Gossip is just news running ahead of itself in a red satin dress.

—LIZ SMITH

Gossip, even when it avoids the sexual,
bears about it a faint flavor of the erotic.

—PATRICIA MEYER SPACKS

GRATITUDE

(see also INGRATITUDE)

Gratitude is the sign of noble souls.

—AESOP

Gratitude is not only the greatest of virtues,
but the parent of all the others.

—MARCUS TULLIUS CICERO

Gratitude is one of the least articulate of the emotions,
especially when it is deep.

—FELIX FRANKFURTER

Gratitude is a fruit of great cultivation;
you do not find it among gross people.

—SAMUEL JOHNSON

Gratitude is the most exquisite form of courtesy.

—JACQUES MARITAIN

Gratitude is the memory of the heart.

—JEAN MASSIEU

From the moment we expect gratitude, we forfeit it.

—IVAN PANIN

He who receives a benefit with gratitude
repays the first installment on his debt.

—LUCIUS ANNAEUS SENECA (SENECA THE YOUNGER)

Feeling gratitude and not expressing it
is like wrapping a present and not giving it.

—WILLIAM ARTHUR WARD

No one is as capable of gratitude as one
who has emerged from the kingdom of night.

—ELIE WIESEL

GREATNESS

(see also EXAMPLE and EXCELLENCE and GENIUS and
HEROES & HEROISM and LEADERS & LEADERSHIP)

All rising to great place is by a winding stair.

—FRANCIS BACON (1561–1626)

Greatness is a road that leads toward something unknown.

—CHARLES DE GAULLE

To be great is to be misunderstood.

—RALPH WALDO EMERSON

Mountains appear more lofty the nearer they are approached;
but great men, to retain their altitude,
must only be viewed from a distance.

—MARGUERITE GARDINER (LADY BLESSINGTON)

True greatness is free, kind, familiar, and popular;
it lets itself be touched and handled,
it loses nothing by being seen at close quarters;
the better one knows it, the more one admires it.

—JEAN DE LA BRUYÈRE

Lives of great men all remind us
We can make our lives sublime,
And, departing, leave behind us
Footprints on the sands of time.

—HENRY WADSWORTH LONGFELLOW

Failure is the true test of greatness.

—HERMAN MELVILLE

It is the privilege of greatness
to confer intense happiness with insignificant gifts.

—FRIEDRICH NIETZSCHE

Fortunately there is excess in greatness:
it can lose more than mediocrity possesses, and still be great.

—VIRGINIA MOORE

Be not afraid of greatness.
Some are born great, some achieve greatness,
and some have greatness thrust upon 'em.

—WILLIAM SHAKESPEARE

GRIEF & GRIEVING

(see also DEATH & DYING and SORROW)

When we grieve, tears and guilt get mixed together.

—ART BUCHWALD

The only education in grief that any of us ever gets is a crash course.

—GAIL CALDWELL

Grief is the price Love pays for being in the same world with Death.

—MARGARET DELAND

I measure every Grief I meet
With narrow, probing, eyes—
I wonder if It weighs like Mine—
Or has an Easier size.

—EMILY DICKINSON

While grief is fresh, every attempt to divert it only irritates.
You must wait till grief be *digested*,
and then amusement will dissipate the remains of it.

—SAMUEL JOHNSON

O, well it has been said, that there is no grief
like the grief which does not speak!
—HENRY WADSWORTH LONGFELLOW[*]

Grief is the price we pay for Love.
—MARY RIDPATH MANN

There are some griefs so loud
They could bring down the sky,
And there are griefs so still
None knows how deep they lie.
—MAY SARTON

Nothing becomes so offensive so quickly as grief.
When fresh it finds someone to console it,
but when it becomes chronic, it is ridiculed, and rightly.
—LUCIUS ANNAEUS SENECA (SENECA THE YOUNGER)

Every one can master a grief but he that has it.
—WILLIAM SHAKESPEARE

[*] Longfellow refers here to a line from the character Malcolm in Shakespeare's *Macbeth* (1606): "Give sorrow words. The grief that does not speak / Whispers the o're-fraught heart and bids it break."

GROWTH

(see also CHANGE and LIFE and PROGRESS)

Growth itself contains the germ of happiness.

—PEARL S. BUCK

A man's growth is seen in the successive choirs of his friends.

—RALPH WALDO EMERSON

**In some ways, spiritual growth resembles a game of leapfrog.
As soon as we've got past one puzzling question,
we discover we're faced with another.**

—JEAN GRASSO FITZPATRICK

**Just as we outgrow a pair of trousers, we outgrow
acquaintances, libraries, principles, etc., at times before they're worn out
and at times—and this is the worst of all—before we have new ones.**

—G. C. LICHTENBERG

**One can choose to go back toward safety or forward toward growth.
Growth must be chosen again and again;
fear must be overcome again and again.**

—ABRAHAM MASLOW

**All growth is a leap in the dark,
a spontaneous, unpremeditated act without benefit of experience.**

—HENRY MILLER

Growth is the only evidence of life.

—JOHN HENRY NEWMAN[*]

The base from which all growth is predicated then,
is in the future, not from the past.
Growing is always into, not away from.

—MARGARET LEE RUNBECK

If we don't change, we don't grow.
If we don't grow, we are not really living.
Growth demands a temporary surrender of security.

—GAIL SHEEHY

What is the most rigorous law of our being? Growth.
No smallest atom of our moral, mental,
or physical structure can stand still a year.
It grows—it must grow; nothing can prevent it.

—MARK TWAIN

---

[*] This saying is generally attributed directly to Cardinal Newman, but he was summarizing a piece of doctrine from the English preacher and biblical scholar Thomas Scott (1747–1821). It became something of a motto for Newman.

HABIT

(see also CHARACTER and DISCIPLINE and SUCCESS
and TALENT)

Habit, a particularly insidious thug
who chokes passion and smothers love.
Habit puts us on autopilot.

—DIANE ACKERMAN

Habit is a compromise effected between an individual and his environment.

—SAMUEL BECKETT

Habit, *n.* A shackle for the free.

—AMBROSE BIERCE

Old habits are strong and jealous.

—DOROTHEA BRANDE

It seems, in fact, as though the second half
of a man's life is usually made up of nothing but
the habits he has accumulated during the first half.

—FYODOR DOSTOEVSKY

One nail drives out another; habit is overcome by habit.

—DESIDERIUS ERASMUS

Habit is a cable.
We weave a thread of it every day, and at last we cannot break it.

—HORACE MANN

Ill habits gather by unseen degrees—
As brooks make rivers, rivers run to seas.

—OVID

Habit is habit, and not to be flung out of the window
by any man, but coaxed downstairs a step at a time.

—MARK TWAIN

It is the habit of having habits, of turning a trail into a rut,
that must be incessantly fought against if one is to remain alive.

—EDITH WHARTON

HAPPINESS [Wise]

(see also HAPPINESS [Wry & Witty] and JOY and
LAUGHTER)

Happiness sneaks in through a door you didn't know you left open.

—JOHN BARRYMORE

Happiness comes most to persons who seek her least,
and think least about her.
It is not an object to be sought; it is a state to be induced.
It must follow and not lead. It must overtake you, and not you overtake it.

—JOHN BURROUGHS

That is happiness;
to be dissolved into something complete and great.
When it comes to one, it comes as naturally as sleep.

—WILLA CATHER

Happiness makes up in height for what it lacks in length.

—ROBERT FROST

Happiness hangs by a hair.

—MARY O'HARA

Happiness is not a station you arrive at, but a manner of traveling.

—MARGARET LEE RUNBECK

If you want to understand the meaning of happiness,
you must see it as a reward and not as a goal.

—ANTOINE DE SAINT-EXUPÉRY

But O, how bitter a thing it is
to look into happiness through another man's eyes!

—WILLIAM SHAKESPEARE

I am still determined to be cheerful and to be happy
in whatever situation I may be, for I have
also learned from experience that the greater part of our happiness
or misery depends upon our dispositions, and not upon our circumstances;
we carry the seeds of the one, or the other about with us,
in our minds wherever we go.

—MARTHA WASHINGTON

HAPPINESS [Wry & Witty]

(see also HAPPINESS [Wise] and JOY and LAUGHTER)

Happiness, *n.* An agreeable sensation
arising from contemplating the misery of another.

—AMBROSE BIERCE

Happiness? A good cigar, a good meal, a good cigar and a good woman—
or a bad woman; it depends on how much happiness you can handle.

—GEORGE BURNS

We must select the illusion which appeals to our temperament
and embrace it with passion, if we want to be happy.

—CYRIL CONNOLLY

Happiness . . . is not something that can be demanded from life,
and if you are not happy you had better stop worrying about it
and see what treasures you can pluck from your own brand of unhappiness.

—ROBERTSON DAVIES

The search for happiness is one of the chief sources of unhappiness.

—ERIC HOFFER

If one were to build the house of happiness,
the largest space would be the waiting room.

—JULES RENARD

To be without some of the things you want
is an indispensable part of happiness.

—BERTRAND RUSSELL

We all look for happiness,
but without knowing where to find it:
like drunkards who look for their house,
knowing dimly that they have one.

—VOLTAIRE

There are lots of ways of being miserable, but there's only one way
of being comfortable, and that is to stop running round after happiness.
If you make up your mind not to be happy
there's no reason why you shouldn't have a fairly good time.

—EDITH WHARTON

Happiness is no laughing matter.

—RICHARD WHATELY

HATRED

(see also ANGER and FANATACISM and FEAR and LOVE
and LOVE & HATE)

**Hatred rarely does any harm to its object. It is the hater who suffers.
His soul is warped and his life poisoned
by dwelling on past injuries or projecting schemes of revenge.**

—MAX AITKEN (LORD BEAVERBROOK)

**I imagine that one of the reasons people cling to their hates
so stubbornly is because they sense, once hate is gone,
that they will be forced to deal with pain.**

—JAMES BALDWIN

**He who says he is in the light
and hates his brother is in the darkness still.**

—THE BIBLE, 1 JOHN 2:9

The price of hating other human beings is loving oneself less.

—ELDRIDGE CLEAVER

Hating people is like burning down your own house to get rid of a rat.

—HARRY EMERSON FOSDICK

Passionate hatred can give meaning and purpose to an empty life.

—ERIC HOFFER

Like an unchecked cancer,
hate corrodes the personality and eats away its vital unity.
Hate destroys a man's sense of values and his objectivity.
It causes him to describe the beautiful as ugly and the ugly as beautiful,
and to confuse the true with the false and the false with the true.

—MARTIN LUTHER KING JR.

Hatred is like an acid.
It can do more damage to the container in which it is stored
than to the object on which it is poured.

—ANN LANDERS

Hatred is a deathwish for the hated, not a lifewish for anything else.

—AUDRE LORDE

One drop of hatred in your soul will spread
and discolor everything like a drop of black ink in white milk.

—ALICE MUNRO

HEROES & HEROISM

(see also COURAGE and COWARDICE and FEAR and
GREATNESS and RISK & RISK-TAKING)

Everyone is necessarily the hero of his own life story.

—JOHN BARTH

No man is a hero to his valet.

—ANNE-MARIE BIGOT (MADAME DU CORNUEL)

**The legacy of heroes—
the memory of a great name and the inheritance of a great example.**

—BENJAMIN DISRAELI

**The greatest obstacle to being heroic
is the doubt whether one may not be going to prove one's self a fool;
the truest heroism is to resist the doubt; and the profoundest wisdom,
to know when it ought to be resisted, and when to be obeyed.**

—NATHANIEL HAWTHORNE

**Life, misfortune, isolation, abandonment, poverty,
are battlefields which have their heroes;
obscure heroes, sometimes greater than the illustrious heroes.**

—VICTOR HUGO

Without heroes, we're all plain people
and don't know how far we can go.

—BERNARD MALAMUD

Calculation never made a hero.

—JOHN HENRY NEWMAN

Do not let the hero in your soul perish,
in lonely frustration for the life you deserved,
but have never been able to reach.

—AYN RAND

Whoe'er excels in what we prize,
Appears a hero in our eyes.

—JONATHAN SWIFT

To be a hero, one must give an order to oneself.

—SIMONE WEIL

HISTORY

(see also CIVILIZATION and PAST)

We can think of history as a kind of layer cake
in which a number of different layers run side by side through time,
each with a dynamic of its own, and yet each from time to time
profoundly penetrating and interacting with others.

—KENNETH E. BOULDING

All true histories contain instruction;
though, in some, the treasure may be hard to find,
and when found, so trivial in quantity that the dry, shriveled kernel
scarcely compensates for the trouble of cracking the nut.

—ANNE BRONTË

If men could learn from history, what lessons it might teach us!

—SAMUEL TAYLOR COLERIDGE

History is a vast early warning system.

—NORMAN COUSINS

If you didn't know history, you didn't know anything.
You were a leaf that didn't know it was part of a tree.

—MICHAEL CRICHTON

History is a gallery of pictures in which
there are few originals and many copies.
—ALEXIS DE TOCQUEVILLE

What experience and history teach is this—
that people and governments never have learned anything from history,
or acted upon any lessons they might have drawn from it.
—GEORG WILHELM FRIEDRICH HEGEL

History is a guide to navigation in perilous times.
History is who we are and why we are the way we are.
—DAVID MCCULLOUGH

The very ink with which all history is written is merely fluid prejudice.
—MARK TWAIN

History is a conversation
and sometimes a shouting match between present and past,
though often the voices we most want to hear are barely audible.
—LAUREL THATCHER ULRICH

HOPE

(see also EXPECTATION and FEAR and WISHES & WISHING)

When hope is taken away from a people
moral degeneration follows swiftly after.

—PEARL S. BUCK

While there is life, there is hope.

—MARCUS TULLIUS CICERO

A great Hope fell
You heard no noise
The Ruin was within.

—EMILY DICKINSON

Those who are animated by hope
can perform what would seem impossibilities
to those who are under the depressing influence of fear.

—MARIA EDGEWORTH

A ship should not ride on a single anchor,
nor life on a single hope.

—EPICTETUS

The very least you can do in your life
is to figure out what you hope for.
And the most you can do is live inside that hope.
Not admire it from a distance but live right in it, under its roof.

—BARBARA KINGSOLVER

Hope is itself a species of happiness, and, perhaps,
the chief happiness which this world affords.

—SAMUEL JOHNSON

Take hope from the heart of man
and you make him a beast of prey.

—OUIDA (MARIA LOUISE RAMÉ)

Never give out while there is hope;
but hope not beyond reason;
for that shows more desire than judgment.

—WILLIAM PENN

Hope springs eternal in the human breast.

—ALEXANDER POPE

HUMILITY

(see also GREATNESS and MATURITY and VANITY and
VIRTUE)

You aspire to great things? Begin with little ones.
You desire to erect a very high building?
Think first of the foundation of humility.

—SAINT AUGUSTINE

Nothing is more deceitful than the appearance of humility.
It is often only carelessness of opinion, and sometimes an indirect boast.

—JANE AUSTEN

Whoever exalts himself will be humbled,
and whoever humbles himself will be exalted.

—THE BIBLE, MATTHEW 23:12

Humility is the most difficult of all virtues to achieve;
nothing dies harder than the desire to think well of oneself.

—T. S. ELIOT

Humility is often only a feigned submissiveness
by which men hope to bring other people to submit to them;
it is a more calculated sort of pride.

—FRANÇOIS, DUC DE LA ROCHEFOUCAULD

The moment that humility becomes self-conscious, it becomes hubris.
One cannot be humble and aware of oneself at the same time.

—MADELEINE L'ENGLE

True humility does not know that it is humble.
If it did, it would be proud
from the contemplation of so fine a virtue.

—MARTIN LUTHER

We come nearest to the great when we are great in humility.

—RABINDRANATH TAGORE

Humility like darkness reveals the heavenly lights.

—HENRY DAVID THOREAU

Humility is not thinking less of yourself;
it is thinking of yourself less.

—RICK WARREN

HUMOR

(see also LAUGHTER and [Sense of] HUMOR and WIT and
WIT & HUMOR)

Among all kinds of writing, there is none in which
authors are more apt to miscarry than in works of humor,
as there is none in which they are more ambitious to excel.

—JOSEPH ADDISON

Humor is a social lubricant
that helps us get over some of the bad spots.

—STEVE ALLEN

Humor is but another weapon against the universe.

—MEL BROOKS

Humor is an affirmation of dignity,
a declaration of man's superiority to all that befalls him.

—ROMAIN GARY

Humor has a tremendous place in this sordid world.
It's more than just a matter of laughing.
If you can see things out of whack,
then you can see how things can be in whack.

—THEODOR SEUSS GEISEL (DR. SEUSS)

Humor is a rubber sword—
it allows you to make a point without drawing blood.

—MARY HIRSCH

Humor is an antidote to isolation.

—ELIZABETH JANEWAY

Humor is hope's companion in arms.
It is not brash, it is not cheap, it is not heartless.
Among other things, I think humor is a shield, a weapon, a survival kit.

—OGDEN NASH

Humor can be dissected, as a frog can,
but the thing dies in the process
and the innards are discouraging to any but the pure scientific mind.

—E. B. WHITE

Humor is not a mood but a way of looking at the world.

—LUDWIG WITTGENSTEIN

[Sense of] HUMOR

(see also HUMOR and LAUGHTER and WIT and WIT & HUMOR)

Of all the band of personal traitors
the sense of humor is the most dangerous.

—MARGERY ALLINGHAM

A person without a sense of humor is like a wagon without springs:
jolted by every pebble in the road.

—AUTHOR UNKNOWN[*]

A sense of humor is a measurement of the extent to which we realize
that we are trapped in a world almost totally devoid of reason.
Laughter is how we express the anxiety we feel at this knowledge.

—DAVE BARRY

Certainly if there is any worldly talent worth cultivating,
it's a sense of humor.

—MICHAEL DIRDA

A sense of humor is a sense of proportion.

—KAHLIL GIBRAN

---

[*] This saying was inspired by an 1869 observation from Henry Ward Beecher: "A man
without mirth is like a wagon without springs, in which one is caused disagreeably to jolt
by every pebble over which it runs."

Common sense and a sense of humor are the same things,
moving at different speeds.
A sense of humor is just common sense, dancing.

—CLIVE JAMES

Humor, a good sense of it, is to Americans what manhood is to Spaniards
and we will go to great lengths to prove it.

—GARRISON KEILLOR

Among animals, *one* has a sense of humor.

—MARIANNE MOORE

A sense of humor, properly developed,
is superior to any religion so far devised.

—TOM ROBBINS

The real marriage of true minds is for any two people
to possess a sense of humor or irony pitched in exactly the same key,
so that their joint glances at any subject
cross like interarching searchlights.

—EDITH WHARTON

HYPOCRISY

(see also AUTHENTICITY and INTEGRITY and VICE and
VICE & VIRTUE)

The hypocrite's crime is that he bears false witness against himself.

—HANNAH ARENDT

Woe to you, scribes and Pharisees, hypocrites!
For you are like whitewashed tombs, which outwardly appear beautiful,
but within they are full of dead men's bones and all uncleanness.

—THE BIBLE, MATTHEW 23:27

A criminal is twice a criminal when he adds hypocrisy to his crime.

—MARIE CORELLI

Every man alone is sincere.
At the entrance of a second person, hypocrisy begins.

—RALPH WALDO EMERSON

No man, for any considerable period,
can wear one face to himself and another to the multitude,
without finally getting bewildered as to which may be the true.

—NATHANIEL HAWTHORNE

If it were not for the intellectual snobs who pay—in solid cash—
the tribute which philistinism owes to culture,
the arts would perish with their starving practitioners.
Let us thank heaven for hypocrisy.

—ALDOUS HUXLEY

Hypocrisy is the tribute which vice pays to virtue.

—FRANÇOIS, DUC DE LA ROCHEFOUCAULD

For neither man nor angel can discern
Hypocrisy, the only evil that walks
Invisible, except to God alone.

—JOHN MILTON

In our interactions with people,
a benevolent hypocrisy is frequently required—
acting as though we do not see through the motives of their actions.

—FRIEDRICH NIETZSCHE

Hypocrisy in anything whatever
may deceive the cleverest and most penetrating man,
but the least wide-awake of children recognizes it,
and is revolted by it, however ingeniously it may be disguised.

—LEO TOLSTOY

IDEAS

(see also BRAIN and MIND and THINKING & THINKERS
and THOUGHT and WISDOM)

Not to engage in this pursuit of ideas
is to live like ants instead of like men.

—MORTIMER J. ADLER

One can live in the shadow of an idea without grasping it.

—ELIZABETH BOWEN

There are well-dressed foolish ideas just as there are well-dressed fools.

—NICOLAS CHAMFORT

An idea launched like a javelin in proverbial form strikes with sharper point
on the hearer's mind and leaves implanted barbs for meditation.

—DESIDERIUS ERASMUS

Ideas move rapidly when their time comes.

—CAROLYN HEILBRUN

Every now and then a man's mind is stretched by a new idea or sensation,
and never shrinks back to its former dimensions.

—OLIVER WENDELL HOLMES SR.

One can resist the invasion of armies;
one cannot resist the invasion of ideas.

—VICTOR HUGO[*]

He who receives an idea from me
receives instruction himself without lessening mine;
as he who lights his taper at mine receives light without darkening me.

—THOMAS JEFFERSON

An idea is a light turned on in a man's soul.

—AYN RAND

Ideas won't keep. Something must be done about them.

—ALFRED NORTH WHITEHEAD

IGNORANCE

(see also FOLLY and FOOLS & FOOLISHNESS and
ILLUSION and KNOWLEDGE and LEARNING and
STUPIDITY)

To be ignorant of one's ignorance is the malady of the ignorant.

—A. BRONSON ALCOTT

---

[*] This is widely—and mistakenly—presented as: "There is nothing so powerful as an idea whose time has come." However, nothing in Hugo's original phrasing (*On résiste à l'invasion des armées; on ne résiste pas à l'invasion des idées*) warrants the erroneous version.

Against logic there is no armor like ignorance.

—AUTHOR UNKNOWN[*]

A great deal of intelligence can be invested in ignorance
when the need for illusion is great.

—SAUL BELLOW

Knowledge slowly builds up what Ignorance in an hour pulls down.

—GEORGE ELIOT

Nothing is more terrible than ignorance in action.

—JOHANN WOLFGANG VON GOETHE

Contrary to popular superstition, ignorance is not bliss.
Ignorance is impotence; it is fear; it is cruelty;
it is all the things that make for unhappiness.

—WINIFRED HOLTBY

Ignorance, when it is voluntary, is criminal.

—SAMUEL JOHNSON

[*] Almost all Internet sites attribute this observation to Dr. Laurence J. Peter, author of *The Peter Principle* (1968), but the saying made its first appearance in an October 10, 1901 issue of *Life* magazine, eighteen years before Peter's birth.

Ignorance is not a simple lack of knowledge
but an active aversion to knowledge, the refusal to know,
issuing from cowardice, pride, or laziness of mind.

—RYSZARD KAPUSCINSKI

Ignorance is always afraid of change.
It fears the unknown and sticks to its rut,
however miserable it may be there.

—JAWAHARLAL NEHRU

There is no darkness but ignorance.

—WILLIAM SHAKESPEARE

ILLNESS

(see also CANCER and DEATH & DYING and PAIN and
SUFFERING)

A man's illness is his private territory and,
no matter how much he loves you and how close you are,
you stay an outsider. You are healthy.

—LAUREN BACALL[*]

---

[*] Bacall was writing about husband Humphrey Bogart's battle with esophageal cancer,
which took his life in 1957 (at age 57), less than a year after it was diagnosed.

A critical illness is like a great permission, an authorization. . . .
All your life you think you have to hold back your craziness,
but when you're sick you can let it go in all its garish colors.

—ANATOLE BROYARD

Those who have never been ill
are incapable of real sympathy for a great many misfortunes.

—ANDRÉ GIDE

A long illness seems to be placed between life and death,
in order to make death a comfort
both to those who die and to those who remain.

—JEAN DE LA BRUYÈRE

Illness is in part what the world has done to a victim,
but in a larger part it is what the victim
has done with his world, and with himself.

—DR. KARL MENNINGER

Illness is friendship's proving ground, the uncharted territory
where one's actions may be the least sure-footed but also the most indelible.

—LETTY COTTIN POGREBIN

Illness is the doctor to whom we pay most heed;
to kindness, to knowledge, we make promise only; pain we obey.

—MARCEL PROUST

Illness is the opposite of freedom. It makes everything impossible.
You lose so many things when you're ill.

—FRANÇOISE SAGAN

Illness is the night-side of life, a more onerous citizenship.
Everyone who is born holds dual citizenship,
in the kingdom of the well and in the kingdom of the sick.

—SUSAN SONTAG

Considering how common illness is,
how tremendous the spiritual change that it brings . . .
it becomes strange indeed that illness has not taken its place
with love and battle and jealousy among the prime themes in literature.

—VIRGINIA WOOLF

ILLUSION

(see also FOLLY and FOOLS & FOOLISHNESS and
IGNORANCE and SELF-DECEPTION and STUPIDITY and
TRUTH and TRUTH & ERROR)

The most all-around, practical, long-wearing illusions
are the ones that you weave yourself.

—PEG BRACKEN

But time strips our illusions of their hue,
And one by one in turn, some grand mistake
Casts off its bright skin yearly, like a snake.

—GEORGE NOEL GORDON, LORD BYRON

Reason dissipates the illusions of life,
but does not console us for their departure.

—MARGUERITE GARDINER (LADY BLESSINGTON)

How strange when an illusion dies
It's as though you've lost a child.

—JUDY GARLAND

Life consists in molting our illusions.
We form creeds today only to throw them away tomorrow.
The eagle molts a feather because he is growing a better one.

—ELBERT HUBBARD

Rob the average man of his life-illusion,
and you rob him of his happiness at the same stroke.

—HENRIK IBSEN

No death is so sad and final as the death of an illusion.

—ARTHUR KOESTLER

Lost Illusion is the undisclosed title of every novel.

—ANDRÉ MAUROIS

Better a dish of illusion, one might say,
and a hearty appetite for life,
than a feast of reality and indigestion therewith.

—HARRY A. OVERSTREET

Though illusion often cheers and comforts,
it ultimately and invariably weakens and constricts the spirit.

—IRVIN D. YALOM

IMAGINATION

(see also ART and ARTISTS and CREATIVITY and
DREAMS [Aspirational] and VISION)

Imagination is the highest kite that can fly.

—LAUREN BACALL

Imagination took the reins,
and reason, slow-paced, though sure-footed, was unequal
to a race with so eccentric and flighty a companion.

—FANNY BURNEY

**The Possible's slow fuse is lit
By the Imagination.**

—EMILY DICKINSON

Imagination is a very high sort of seeing.

—RALPH WALDO EMERSON

My imagination is a monastery and I am its monk.

—JOHN KEATS

To imagine the unimaginable is the highest use of the imagination.

—CYNTHIA OZICK

Imagination continually outruns the creature it inhabits.

—KATHERINE ANNE PORTER

Perhaps imagination is only intelligence having fun.

—GEORGE SCIALABBA

**If the imagination is to yield any real product,
it must have received a great deal of material from the external world.**

—ARTHUR SCHOPENHAUER

This world is but canvas to our imaginations.

—HENRY DAVID THOREAU

INDIVIDUALISM

(see also AUTHENTICITY and COURAGE and
COWARDICE and FEAR and INTEGRITY)

To be nobody-but-yourself—
in a world which is doing its best, night and day,
to make you everybody else—means to fight the hardest battle
which any human being can fight, and never stop fighting.

—E. E. CUMMINGS

Individuality is freedom lived.

—JOHN DOS PASSOS

Two roads diverged in a wood, and I—
I took the road less traveled by,
And that has made all the difference.

—ROBERT FROST

The individual has always had to struggle
to keep from being overwhelmed by the tribe.

—RUDYARD KIPLING

Whatever crushes individuality is despotism,
by whatever name it may be called.

—JOHN STUART MILL

There is not one big cosmic meaning for all,
there is only the meaning we each give to our life,
an individual meaning, an individual plot,
like an individual novel, a book for each person.

—ANAÏS NIN

If a life can have a theme song,
and I believe every worthwhile one has,
mine is a religion, an obsession, or a mania
or all of these expressed in one word: individualism.

—AYN RAND

What is repugnant to every human being is to be reckoned
always as a member of a class and not as an individual person.

—DOROTHY L. SAYERS

If a man does not keep pace with his companions,
perhaps it is because he hears a different drummer.
Let him step to the music which he hears, however measured or far away.

—HENRY DAVID THOREAU

Born *Originals*, how comes it to pass that we die *Copies*?

—EDWARD YOUNG (1683–1765)

INGRATITUDE

(see also GRATITUDE)

**What a miserable thing life is:
you're living in clover, only the clover isn't good enough.**

—BERTOLT BRECHT

We set ourselves to bite the hand that feeds us.

—EDMUND BURKE[*]

**Our gratitude to most benefactors
is the same as our feeling for dentists who have pulled our teeth.
We acknowledge the good they have done
and the evil from which they have delivered us,
but we remember the pain they occasioned and do not love them very much.**

—NICOLAS CHAMFORT

Ingratitude is surely the chief of the intellectual sins of man.

—G. K. CHESTERTON

**Most people return small favors, acknowledge middling ones,
and repay great ones with ingratitude.**

—BENJAMIN FRANKLIN

---

[*]   Written in 1770, this is the origin of *biting the hand that feeds*, the most popular idiom about ingratitude.

Of all crimes that human creatures are capable of committing,
the most horrid and unnatural is ingratitude,
especially when it is committed against parents.

—DAVID HUME

Too great haste in paying off an obligation is a kind of ingratitude.

—FRANÇOIS, DUC DE LA ROCHEFOUCAULD

Every time I fill an office, I make a hundred malcontents and one ingrate.

—LOUIS XIV

How sharper than a serpent's tooth it is
To have a thankless child.

—WILLIAM SHAKESPEARE

If you pick up a starving dog
and make him prosperous, he will not bite you;
that is the principal difference between a dog and a man.

—MARK TWAIN

INTEGRITY

(see also AUTHENTICITY and CHARACTER and
HYPOCRISY and TRUTH and VIRTUE)

Integrity has no need of rules.

—ALBERT CAMUS

Integrity simply means a willingness not to violate one's identity,
in the many ways in which such violation is possible.

—ERICH FROMM

Men of integrity, by their very existence, rekindle the belief
that as a people we can live above the level of moral squalor.

—JOHN W. GARDNER

Integrity, like humility, is a quality which vanishes
the moment we are conscious of it in ourselves.
We see it only in others.

—MADELEINE L'ENGLE

I am sure that in estimating every man's value
either in private or public life,
a pure integrity is the quality we take first into calculation,
and that learning and talents are only the second.

—THOMAS JEFFERSON

If everyone were clothed with integrity,
if every heart were just, frank, kindly,
the other virtues would be well-nigh useless.

—MOLIÈRE

It is necessary to the happiness of man
that he be mentally faithful to himself.

—THOMAS PAINE

There is no such thing as a minor lapse of integrity.

—TOM PETERS

Integrity is so perishable in the summer months of success.

—VANESSA REDGRAVE

Integrity can be neither lost nor concealed
nor faked nor quenched nor artificially come by nor outlived,
nor, I believe, in the long run, denied.

—EUDORA WELTY

INTERNET & WORLD WIDE WEB

(see also COMPUTERS and TECHNOLOGY)

The Net's interactivity gives us powerful new tools for finding information,
expressing ourselves, and conversing with others.
It also turns us into lab rats constantly pressing levers
to get tiny pellets of social or intellectual nourishment.

—NICHOLAS CARR

Doing research on the Web is like using a library
assembled piecemeal by pack rats and vandalized nightly.

—ROGER EBERT

Like the PC, the Internet is a tidal wave.
It will wash over the computer industry and many others,
drowning those who don't learn to swim in its waves.

—BILL GATES

The Internet is becoming the town square
for the global village of tomorrow.

—BILL GATES

My favorite thing about the Internet is that you get to go
into the private world of real creeps without having to smell them.

—PENN JILLETTE

Getting information off the Internet
is like taking a drink from a fire hydrant.

—MITCH KAPOR

It's been my policy to view the Internet
not as an "information highway,"
but as an electronic asylum filled with babbling loonies.

—MIKE ROYKO

The Internet is the first thing that humanity has built
that humanity doesn't understand,
the largest experiment in anarchy that we have ever had.

—ERIC SCHMIDT

The Internet is just a world passing around notes in a classroom.

—JON STEWART

The Internet is the Viagra of big business.

—JACK WELCH

JAZZ

(see also BLUES and MUSIC)

**Jazz is about the only form of art existing today in which there is
this freedom of the individual without the loss of group contact.**

—DAVE BRUBECK

Playing "bop" is like playing Scrabble with all the vowels missing.

—DUKE ELLINGTON[*]

**Thus it came to pass that jazz multiplied all over the face of the earth
and the wiggling of bottoms was tremendous.**

—PETER GAMMOND AND PETER CLAYTON

A jazz musician is a juggler who uses harmonies instead of oranges.

—BENNY GREEN

---

[*] *Bop* was the shortened term for *bebop,* an extension of jazz music that began to enjoy great
popularity in the 1940s (a practitioner was called a *bebopper*).

Jazz is the big brother of the blues.
If a guy's playing blues like we play, he's in high school.
When he starts playing jazz, it's like going on to college,
to a school of higher learning.

—B. B. KING

Jazz is the nobility of the race put into sound

—WYNTON MARSALIS

Jazz is the music of the body.

—ANAÏS NIN

Jazz may be thought of as a current
that bubbled forth from a spring in the slums of New Orleans
to become the mainstream of the twentieth century.

—HENRY PLEASANTS

Jazz music is an intensified feeling of nonchalance.

—FRANÇOISE SAGAN

Jazz came to America three hundred years ago in chains.

—PAUL WHITEMAN

JEALOUSY

(see also ENVY and LOVE [Wise] and LOVE [Wry & Witty]
and LOVE & HATE and MALE-FEMALE DYNAMICS)

Jealousy in romance is like salt in food.
A little can enhance the savor,
but too much can spoil the pleasure
and, under certain circumstances, can be life-threatening.

—MAYA ANGELOU

Jealousy is no more than feeling alone
against smiling enemies.

—ELIZABETH BOWEN

To cure jealousy is to see it for what it is,
a dissatisfaction with self.

—JOAN DIDION

Jealousy is never satisfied with anything short of an omniscience
that would detect the subtlest fold of the heart.

—GEORGE ELIOT

Jealousy: that dragon which slays love
under the pretense of keeping it alive.

—HAVELOCK ELLIS

When however small a measure of jealousy
is mixed with misunderstanding,
there is going to be trouble.

—JOHN IRVING

Jealousy is always born with love
but does not always die with it.

—FRANÇOIS, DUC DE LA ROCHEFOUCAULD

The jealous are troublesome to others,
but a torment to themselves.

—WILLIAM PENN

The knives of jealousy are honed on details.

—RUTH RENDELL

Trifles light as air
Are to the jealous confirmations strong
As proofs of holy writ.

—WILLIAM SHAKESPEARE

JOY

(see also HAPPINESS and LAUGHTER and PLEASURE and
SORROW)

When large numbers of people share their joy in common,
the happiness of each is greater
because each adds fuel to the other's flame.

—SAINT AUGUSTINE

There is no beautifier of complexion, or form, or behavior,
like the wish to scatter joy and not pain around us.

—RALPH WALDO EMERSON

The root of joy, as of duty,
is to put all one's powers towards some great end.

—OLIVER WENDELL HOLMES JR.

Joy's smile is much closer to tears than laughter.

—VICTOR HUGO

Men without joy seem like corpses.

—KÄTHE KOLLWITZ

For happiness one needs security,
but joy can spring like a flower even from the cliffs of despair.

—ANNE MORROW LINDBERGH

When the great joys are stilled, the minor ones must sing.

—MARGARET LEE RUNBECK

You have to sniff out joy, keep your nose to the joy-trail.

—BUFFY SAINTE-MARIE

Those undeserved joys which come uncalled
and make us more pleased than grateful are they that sing.

—HENRY DAVID THOREAU

Grief can take care of itself, but to get the full value of a joy
you must have somebody to divide it with.

—MARK TWAIN

KINDNESS

(see also GENEROSITY and LOVE and VIRTUE)

No act of kindness, no matter how small, is ever wasted.

—AESOP

When kindness has left people, even for a few moments,
we become afraid of them, as if their reason had left them.

—WILLA CATHER

Kindness is love in action.

—HENRY DRUMMOND

Ignorant kindness may have the effect of cruelty.

—GEORGE ELIOT

This is my simple religion.
There is no need for temples; no need for complicated philosophy.
Our own brain, our own heart is our temple;
the philosophy is kindness.

—TENZIN GYATSO, THE FOURTEENTH DALAI LAMA

Wise sayings often fall on barren ground;
but a kind word is never thrown away.

—ARTHUR HELPS

Constant kindness can accomplish much.
As the sun makes ice melt,
kindness causes misunderstanding, mistrust, and hostility to evaporate.

—ALBERT SCHWEITZER

If you stop to be kind, you must swerve often from your path.

—MARY WEBB

So many gods, so many creeds,
So many paths that wind and wind,
While just the art of being kind
Is all the sad world needs.

—ELLA WHEELER WILCOX

That best portion of a good man's life,
His little, nameless, unremembered, acts
Of kindness and of love.

—WILLIAM WORDSWORTH

KISSES & KISSING

(see also LOVE and PASSION and ROMANCE &
ROMANTICS and SEX)

A kiss is like singing into someone's mouth.

—DIANE ACKERMAN

A kiss is a lovely trick designed by nature
to stop speech when words become superfluous.

—INGRID BERGMAN[*]

---

[*] Bergman, who said this in 1977, was almost certainly inspired by Oliver Herford, who wrote in *Cupid's Cyclopedia* (1910): "Kiss: a course of procedure, cunningly devised, for the mutual stoppage of speech at a moment when words are superfluous."

All other caresses are valueless without a kiss;
for is not a kiss the very autograph of love?

—HENRY T. FINCK

The kiss originated when the first male reptile
licked the first female reptile,
implying in a subtle, complimentary way that she was
as succulent as the small reptile he had for dinner the night before.

—F. SCOTT FITZGERALD

For 'twas not into my ear you whispered but into my heart.
'Twas not my lips you kissed, but my soul.

—JUDY GARLAND

The state induced by the kiss is actually self-induced, of course,
for few lips are so gifted with electric and psychedelic possibilities.

—GERMAINE GREER

A kiss can be a comma, a question mark, or an exclamation point.
That's basic spelling that every woman ought to know.

—MISTINGUETT

Lips that taste of tears, they say
Are the best for kissing.

—DOROTHY PARKER

A kiss, when all is said, what is it?
An oath sworn nearer by; a promise made
With greater certainty; a vow which seeks
To make itself more binding; a rosy dot
Placed on the "i" in loving; 'tis a secret
Told to the mouth instead of to the ear.

—EDMOND ROSTAND

A man's kiss is his signature.

—MAE WEST

KNOWLEDGE

(see also EDUCATION and IGNORANCE and KNOWLEDGE
and LEARNING and WISDOM)

Knowledge itself is power.

—FRANCIS BACON (1561–1626)[*]

The more we know, the better we realize that our knowledge
is a little island in the midst of an ocean of ignorance.

—THEODOSIUS DOBZHANSKY

Knowledge of what is does not open the door directly to what should be.

—ALBERT EINSTEIN

[*] In an 1871 book, the French scholar Ernest Renan wrote about Bacon's aphorism:
"'Knowledge is power' is the finest idea ever put into words."

Knowledge is happiness,
because to have knowledge—broad, deep knowledge—
is to know true ends from false, and lofty things from low.

—HELEN KELLER

Knowledge belongs to humanity,
and is the torch which illuminates the world.

—LOUIS PASTEUR

Imparting knowledge is only lighting other men's candles at our lamp,
without depriving ourselves of any flame.

—JANE PORTER

The struggling for knowledge hath a pleasure in it
like that of wrestling with a fine woman.

—GEORGE SAVILE (LORD HALIFAX)

The field of knowledge which even the best of us can master
is like an island surrounded by a limitless ocean of mystery.
And the larger the island of knowledge, the longer the shoreline of wonder.

—RALPH W. SOCKMAN

Knowledge is a comfortable and necessary retreat
and shelter for us in advanced age.
If we do not plant it while young, it will give us no shade when we grow old.

—PHILIP DORMER STANHOPE (LORD CHESTERFIELD)

Knowledge is a potent and subtle distillation of experience,
a rare liquor, and it belongs to the person who has the power
to see, think, feel, taste, smell,
and observe for himself, and who has hunger for it.

—THOMAS WOLFE

LANGUAGE

(see also COMMUNICATION and ELOQUENCE and
ENGLISH—THE LANGUAGE and SPEECH and WORDS
and WRITING)

High thoughts must have high language.

—ARISTOPHANES

One can say of language that it is potentially the only human home,
the only dwelling place that cannot be hostile to man.

—JOHN BERGER

Language is the road map of a culture.
It tells you where its people come from and where they are going.

—RITA MAE BROWN

Language is the apparel
in which your thoughts parade before the public.
Never clothe them in vulgar or shoddy attire.

—GEORGE W. CRANE

In language, the ignorant have prescribed laws to the learned.

—RICHARD DUPPA

Language is the dress of thought.

—SAMUEL JOHNSON

Language is the amber in which
a thousand precious and subtle thoughts
have been safely embedded and preserved.

—RICHARD CHENEVIX TRENCH

A language is a dialect that has an army and a navy.

—MAX WEINREICH

The living language is like a cowpath:
it is the creation of the cows themselves, who, having created it,
follow it or depart from it according to their whims or their needs.
From daily use, the path undergoes change.

—E. B. WHITE

Language is a finding place, not a hiding place.

—JEANETTE WINTERSON

LAUGHTER

(see also HUMOR and [Sense of] HUMOR and JOY and WIT
and WIT & HUMOR)

**Without laughter life on our planet would be intolerable.
So important is laughter to us that humanity highly rewards
members of one of the most unusual professions on earth,
those who make a living by inducing laughter in others.**

—STEVE ALLEN

**So many tangles in life are ultimately hopeless
that we have no appropriate sword other than laughter.**

—GORDON W. ALLPORT

Laughter is the shortest distance between two people.

—AUTHOR UNKNOWN[*]

**Laughter is a form of internal jogging.
It moves your internal organs around. It enhances respiration.
It is an igniter of great expectations.**

—NORMAN COUSINS

**There is nothing in which people more betray their character
than in what they laugh at.**

—JOHANN WOLFGANG VON GOETHE

---

[*]   This quotation is widely attributed to Victor Borge. Borge did offer a similar observation—
one that became a signature line: "A smile is the shortest distance between two people."

Laughter is the sun which drives winter from the human face.

—VICTOR HUGO

Laughter is the great antidote for self-pity,
maybe a specific for the malady.

—MARY MCCARTHY

Against the assault of laughter nothing can stand.

—MARK TWAIN

I was irrevocably betrothed to laughter,
the sound of which has always seemed to me to
be the most civilized music in the world.

—PETER USTINOV

A good laugh overcomes more difficulties
and dissipates more dark clouds than any other one thing.

—LAURA INGALLS WILDER

LEADERS & LEADERSHIP

(see also BUSINESS and EXAMPLE and HEROES &
HEROISM and POLITICIANS and POWER)

The speed of the leader is the speed of the gang.

—MARY KAY ASH

The task of leadership is not to put greatness into humanity,
but to elicit it, for the greatness is already there.

—JOHN BUCHAN

The first responsibility of a leader is to define reality.
The last is to say thank you.
In between the two, the leader must become a servant.

—MAX DE PREE

Leadership is lifting a person's vision to higher sights,
the raising of a person's performance to a higher standard,
the building of a personality beyond its normal limitations.

—PETER F. DRUCKER

You do not lead by hitting people over the head—
that's assault, not leadership.

—DWIGHT D. EISENHOWER

The very essence of leadership is you have to have a vision.
It's got to be a vision you articulate clearly
and forcefully on every occasion.
You can't blow an uncertain trumpet.

—THEODORE HESBURGH

A leader . . . is like a shepherd. He stays behind the flock,
letting the most nimble go out ahead, whereupon the others follow,
not realizing that all along they are being directed from behind.

—NELSON MANDELA, QUOTING A MENTOR

The real leader has no need to lead——he is content to point the way.

—HENRY MILLER

A leader is a dealer in hope.

—NAPOLEON BONAPARTE

Leadership is a potent combination of strategy and character.
But if you must be without one, be without the strategy.

—NORMAN H. SCHWARZKOPF

LEARNING

(see also BOOKS and CURIOSITY and DISCOVERY and
EDUCATION and EXPERIENCE and KNOWLEDGE and
WISDOM)

Learning is not attained by chance,
it must be sought for with ardor and attended to with diligence.

—ABIGAIL ADAMS

The day you stop learning is the day you begin decaying.

—ISAAC ASIMOV

There are some things you learn best in calm, and some in storm.

—WILLA CATHER

Learning acquired in youth arrests the evil of old age.

—LEONARDO DA VINCI

The three pillars of learning;
seeing much, suffering much, and studying much.

—ISAAC D'ISRAELI

The world of learning is so broad,
and the human soul is so limited in power!
We reach forth and strain every nerve,
but we seize only a bit of the curtain that hides the infinite from us.

—MARIA MITCHELL

A little learning is a dangerous thing.

—ALEXANDER POPE[*]

You have learnt something.
That always feels at first as if you had lost something.

—GEORGE BERNARD SHAW

---

[*] This is one of history's most misunderstood sayings. Pope was not suggesting that learn-ing per se was dangerous, only that inadequate learning was (as when people with shallow or superficial knowledge make the mistake of believing they know more than they do— and put themselves and others in danger as a result).

Learning is acquired by reading books:
but the much more necessary learning, the knowledge of the world,
is only to be acquired by reading men,
and studying all the various editions of them.

—PHILIP DORMER STANHOPE (LORD CHESTERFIELD)

There is no royal road to learning;
no short cut to the acquirement of any art.

—ANTHONY TROLLOPE

LIBRARIES & LIBRARIANS

(see also AUTHORS and BOOKS and BOOKSTORES
and LITERATURE and READING and WRITERS and
WRITING)

Here is where people,
One frequently finds,
Lower their voices
And raise their minds.

—RICHARD ARMOUR, ON LIBRARIES

I had always imagined Paradise as a kind of library.

—JORGE LUIS BORGES

A library doesn't need windows. A library is a window.

—STEWART BRAND

A library, to modify the famous metaphor of Socrates,
should be the delivery room for the birth of ideas—
a place where history comes to life.

—NORMAN COUSINS

The library is an arena of possibility, opening both
a window into the soul and a door onto the world.

—RITA DOVE

A man's library is a sort of harem.

—RALPH WALDO EMERSON

A family library is a breeding-place for character.

—GRAHAM GREENE

A library is a place where you can lose your innocence
without losing your virginity.

—GERMAINE GREER

Your library is your portrait.

—HOLBROOK JACKSON

We are the only species on the planet, so far as we know,
to have invented a communal memory
stored neither in our genes nor in our brains.
The warehouse of that memory is called the library.

—CARL SAGAN

LIFE [Wise]

(see also AGE & AGING and DEATH & DYING and LIFE
[Wry & Witty] and WISDOM)

I don't want to get to the end of my life
and find that I lived just the length of it.
I want to have lived the width of it as well.

—DIANE ACKERMAN

The life of every man is a diary
in which he means to write one story, and writes another;
and his humblest hour is when he compares the volume as it is
with what he vowed to make it.

—J. M. BARRIE

Life is like a beautiful flirt, whom we love and to whom, finally,
we grant every condition she imposes as long as she doesn't leave us.

—GIOVANNI GIACOMO CASANOVA

Life is like a library owned by an author.
In it are a few books which he wrote himself,
but most of them were written for him.

—HARRY EMERSON FOSDICK

Life is a verb, not a noun.

—CHARLOTTE PERKINS GILMAN

Life is painting a picture, not doing a sum.

—OLIVER WENDELL HOLMES JR.

Life is like a ten-speed bicycle.
Most of us have gears we never use.

—CHARLES M. SCHULZ

Life is like a play: it's not the length,
but the excellence of the acting that matters.

—LUCIUS ANNAEUS SENECA (SENECA THE YOUNGER)

Life is no "brief candle" to me.
It is a sort of splendid torch which I have got hold of for the moment;
and I want to make it burn as brightly as possible
before handing it on to future generations.

—GEORGE BERNARD SHAW

Life is a rainbow which also includes black.

—YEVGENY YEVTUSHENKO

LIFE [Wry & Witty]

(see also AGE & AGING and DEATH & DYING and LIFE
[Wise] and WIT & HUMOR)

**On the keyboard of life,
always keep one finger on the escape key.**

—SCOTT ADAMS

**Life is a journey, but don't worry,
you'll find a parking spot at the end.**

—ISAAC ASIMOV

**I've learned that life is like a roll of toilet paper.
The closer it gets to the end, the faster it goes.**

—AUTHOR UNKNOWN[*]

**Life is much more manageable when
thought of as a scavenger hunt as opposed to a surprise party.**

—JIMMY BUFFETT

Life is a moderately good play with a badly written third act.

—TRUMAN CAPOTE[†]

---

[*] This observation is widely attributed to Andy Rooney, but there is no evidence he ever said such a thing.

[†] Capote may have been inspired by an observation from Blaise Pascal, who wrote in *Pensées* (1670): "The last act is bloody, however delightful the rest of the play may be."

Life is a near-death experience.

—GEORGE CARLIN

Life is the funny thing that happens to you
on the way to the grave.

—QUENTIN CRISP

For most men,
life is a search for the proper manila envelope
in which to get themselves filed.

—CLIFTON FADIMAN

Life is like a dog-sled team.
If you ain't the lead dog, the scenery never changes.

—LEWIS GRIZZARD

Life is like a sewer.
What you get out of it depends on what you put in.

—TOM LEHRER

LISTENING

(see also COMMUNICATION and CONVERSATION and
FRIENDSHIP and LOVE and RELATIONSHIPS)

**Being heard is so close to being loved
that for the average person they are almost indistinguishable.**

—DAVID W. AUGSBURGER

Listening, not imitation, may be the sincerest form of flattery.

—JOYCE BROTHERS

**Were we as eloquent as angels,
yet should we please . . . much more by listening, than by talking.**

—CHARLES CALEB COLTON

**All of man's life among his kind
is nothing other than a battle to seize the ears of others.**

—MILAN KUNDERA

**Two evils, of almost equal weight, may befall the man of erudition:
never to be listened to, and to be listened to always.**

—WALTER SAVAGE LANDOR

To be able to listen . . . without presupposing, classifying,
improving, controverting, evaluating, approving or disapproving,
without dueling with what is being said,
without rehearsing the rebuttal in advance,
without free-associating to portions of what is being said
so that succeeding portions are not heard at all—
such listening is rare.

—ABRAHAM MASLOW

Listening . . . means taking a vigorous,
human interest in what is being told us.
You can listen like a blank wall or like a splendid auditorium
where every sound comes back fuller and richer.

—ALICE DUER MILLER

The greatest compliment that was ever paid me was when
one asked me what *I thought*, and attended to my answer.

—HENRY DAVID THOREAU

The first duty of love is to listen.

—PAUL TILLICH

Not listening is probably the commonest unkindness of married life.

—JUDITH VIORST

LITERATURE

(see also AUTHORS and BOOKS and FICTION and
NOVELISTS and NOVELS and READING and WRITERS
and WRITING)

What a lost person needs is a map of the territory . . .
so he can see where he is in relation to everything else.
Literature is not only a mirror; it is a map, a geography of the mind.

—MARGARET ATWOOD

Literature takes its revenge on reality by making it the slave of fiction.

—SIMONE DE BEAUVOIR

The use of literature is to afford us a platform
whence we may command a view of our present life.

—RALPH WALDO EMERSON

Literature flourishes best when it is half a trade and half an art.

—WILLIAM RALPH INGE

Great literature cannot grow
from a neglected or impoverished soil

—P. D. JAMES

The reason literacy is important is that
literature is the operating instructions.
The best manual we have.
The most useful guide to the country we're visiting, life.

—URSULA LE GUIN

In literature as in love,
we are astonished at what is chosen by others.

—ANDRÉ MAUROIS

Literature is the most agreeable way of ignoring life.

—FERNANDO PESSOA

Great literature is simply language
charged with meaning to the utmost possible degree.

—EZRA POUND

To turn events into ideas is the function of literature.

—GEORGE SANTAYANA

LONELINESS

(see also FRIENDS and FRIENDSHIP and
RELATIONSHIPS and SOLITUDE)

**Loneliness comes about when I am alone
without being able . . . to keep myself company.**

—HANNAH ARENDT

**A person can be lonely even if he is loved by many people,
because he is still not the "One and Only" to anyone.**

—ANNE FRANK

**Loneliness is never more cruel than when it is felt
in close propinquity with someone who has ceased to communicate.**

—GERMAINE GREER[*]

**What makes loneliness an anguish
Is not that I have no one to share my burden,
But this:
I have only my own burden to bear.**

—DAG HAMMARSKJÖLD

---

[*] This may be the best observation on what might be termed *relationship loneliness*, but it's
not the first. In a 1916 book, Elbert Hubbard wrote, "Loneliness is to endure the presence
of one who does not understand." And in a 1900 entry in his *Notebook*, Anton Chekhov
wrote, "If you are afraid of loneliness, do not marry."

I think it's very important to be alone.
Loneliness is just an idea that, I'm afraid, has something to do with self-pity.

—HELEN HAYES

Loneliness is the way by which destiny endeavors to lead man to himself.

—HERMANN HESSE

No one should ever be afraid alone.
It is the worst form of loneliness and the most corrosive.

—MARION HILLIARD

Loneliness does not come from having no people about one,
but from being unable to communicate
the things that seem important to oneself,
or from holding certain views which others find inadmissible.

—CARL JUNG

To comfort any mortal against loneliness, one other is enough.

—MARJORIE KINNAN RAWLINGS

Loneliness is the poverty of self; solitude is richness of self.

—MAY SARTON

LOVE [Wise]

(see also KISSES & KISSING and LOVE [Wry & Witty]
and LOVE & HATE and MARRIAGE and ROMANCE &
ROMANTICS and SEX)

I never knew how much like heaven this world could be,
when two people love and live for one another!

—LOUISA MAY ALCOTT

Oh, love is real enough; you will find it some day,
but it has one arch-enemy—and that is life.

—JEAN ANOUILH

How do I love thee? Let me count the ways.
I love thee to the depth and breadth and height
My soul can reach, when feeling out of sight.

—ELIZABETH BARRETT BROWNING

There's no such thing as safe love.
Real love means giving someone the power to hurt you.

—JULIAN FELLOWES[*]

[*] The remark comes from a Season Six episode of *Downton Abbey*, as Tom Branson urges Lady Mary to reconsider her class-based hesitation about pursuing a relationship with race-car driver Henry Talbot, a man she is fond of, but exceeds in wealth and status. Years earlier, Branson was a Downton Abbey chauffeur when he won the heart of Lady Sybil, Mary's sister.

Love . . . dies because we don't know how to replenish its source,
it dies of blindness and errors and betrayals.
It dies of illnesses and wounds, it dies of weariness,
of witherings, of tarnishings, but never a natural death.
Every lover should be brought to trial as the murderer of his own love.

—ANAÏS NIN

True love is friendship set on fire.

—PROVERB (AMERICAN)*

Love does not consist of gazing at each other,
but in looking outward together in the same direction.

—ANTOINE DE SAINT-EXUPÉRY

The course of true love never did run smooth.

—WILLIAM SHAKESPEARE

Love must be as much a light as a flame.

—HENRY DAVID THOREAU

All love that has not friendship for its base,
Is like a mansion built upon the sand.

—ELLA WHEELER WILCOX

---

* Quotation scholars agree that this is an American proverb, but most Internet sites mistakenly attribute "Love is friendship set on fire" to the English clergyman Jeremy Taylor (1613–1667). While Taylor's eloquence earned him the sobriquet "the Shakespeare of Divines," there is no evidence he ever wrote anything like this.

LOVE [Wry & Witty]

(see also KISSES & KISSING and LOVE [Wise] and LOVE
& HATE and MARRIAGE and RELATIONSHIPS and
ROMANCE & ROMANTICS and SEX)

Love is an exploding cigar which we willingly smoke.

—LYNDA BARRY

Love is the wild card of existence.

—RITA MAE BROWN

**Love is a fire.
But whether it is going to warm your hearth,
or burn down your house, you can never tell.**

—JOAN CRAWFORD

Love never dies of starvation, but often of indigestion.

—NINON DE LENCLOS

**Of all the icy blasts that blow on love,
a request for money is the most chilling and havoc-wreaking.**

—GUSTAVE FLAUBERT

Love is a perky elf dancing a merry little jig
and then suddenly he turns on you with a miniature machine-gun.

—MATT GROENING[*]

Love's a disease. But curable.

—ROSE MACAULAY

Happiness is the china shop; love is the bull.

—H. L. MENCKEN

Love is like an hourglass,
with the heart filling up as the brain empties.

—JULES RENARD

Love is the ultimate outlaw.
It just won't adhere to any rules.
The most any of us can do is to sign on as its accomplice.

—TOM ROBBINS

---

[*] Well before becoming famous for *The Simpsons*, Groening was a Los Angeles cartoonist best known for *Life Is Hell*, a 1970s underground cartoon strip that reflected his darkly comic view of the universe. In a piece titled "What the Great Philosophers Have Said Vis-à-Vis Love," this was his summary of Kierkegaard's view. His take on the positions of Bertrand Russell and Friedrich Nietzsche—also hilarious—may be seen in *DMDMQ*.

LOVE & HATE

(see also HATRED and LOVE [Wise] and LOVE [Wry &
Witty] and MARRIAGE and ROMANCE & ROMANTICS and
SEX)

So often the truth is told with hate,
and lies are told with love.

—RITA MAE BROWN

Heaven has no rage like love to hatred turned
Nor Hell a fury, like a woman scorned.

—WILLIAM CONGREVE

Hatred is blind, as well as love.

—THOMAS FULLER, MD

Love that is ignorant and hatred have almost the same ends.

—BEN JONSON

If we judge of love by its usual effects,
it resembles hatred more than friendship.

—FRANÇOIS, DUC DE LA ROCHEFOUCAULD

As the best wine doth make the sharpest vinegar,
so the deepest love turneth to the deadliest hate.

—JOHN LYLY

In hatred as in love, we grow like the thing we brood upon.
What we loathe, we graft into our very soul.

—MARY RENAULT

Love and hate have a magical transforming power.
They are the great soul changers.
We grow through their exercise
into the likeness of what we contemplate.

—GEORGE WILLIAM RUSSELL

I hated her now with a hatred more fatal than indifference
because it was the other side of love.

—AUGUST STRINDBERG

Love lights more fires than hate extinguishes.

—ELLA WHEELER WILCOX

MALE-FEMALE DYNAMICS

(see also LOVE and MARRIAGE and MEN & WOMEN and
RELATIONSHIPS and SEX)

In the sex-war thoughtlessness is the weapon of the male,
vindictiveness of the female.

—CYRIL CONNOLLY

If a man is vain, flatter. If timid, flatter. If boastful, flatter.
In all history, too much flattery never lost a gentleman.

—KATHRYN CRAVENS

A man is already halfway in love with any woman who listens to him.

—BRENDAN FRANCIS (EDWARD F. MURPHY)

It's hard to fight an enemy who has outposts in your head.

—SALLY KEMPTON

Nobody will ever win the battle of the sexes.
There is just too much fraternizing with the enemy.

—HENRY KISSINGER

Other wars end eventually in victory, defeat, or exhaustion,
but the war between men and women goes on forever.

—ALISON LURIE

The allurement that women hold out to men
is precisely the allurement that Cape Hatteras holds out to sailors:
they are enormously dangerous and hence enormously fascinating.

—H. L. MENCKEN

When men and women pick one another up for just a bit of fun,
they find they've picked up more than they bargained for,
because men and women have a top story as well as a ground floor,
and you can't have the one without the other.

—GEORGE BERNARD SHAW

When the fine eyes of a woman are veiled with tears
it is the man who no longer sees clearly.

—ACHILLE TOURNIER

Women have served all these centuries as looking-glasses
possessing the magic and delicious power
of reflecting the figure of a man at twice its natural size.

—VIRGINIA WOOLF

MAN—THE ANIMAL

(see also ANIMALS)

Man is the only animal that can remain on friendly terms
with the victims he intends to eat until he eats them.

—SAMUEL BUTLER (1835–1902)

**Man is a talking animal
and he will always let himself be swayed
by the power of the word.**

—SIMONE DE BEAUVOIR

**Man may be defined as the animal that can say "I,"
that can be aware of himself as a separate entity.**

—ERICH FROMM

**There is still this difference between man and all other animals—
he is the only animal whose desires increase as they are fed;
the only animal that is never satisfied.**

—HENRY GEORGE

**Man is the only animal that laughs and weeps;
for he is the only animal that is struck with the difference
between what things are, and what they ought to be.**

—WILLIAM HAZLITT

Man is a clever animal who behaves like an imbecile.

—ALBERT SCHWEITZER

**We are, perhaps uniquely among the earth's creatures,
the worrying animal.**

—LEWIS THOMAS

Man is the only animal that blushes. Or needs to.

—MARK TWAIN

**Man is the unnatural animal, the rebel child of Nature,
and more and more does he turn himself
against the harsh and fitful hand that reared him.**

—H. G. WELLS

**One is tempted to define man as a rational animal
who always loses his temper when he is called upon
to act in accordance with the dictates of reason.**

—OSCAR WILDE

MARRIAGE [Wise]

(see also DIVORCE and FAMILY and LOVE and MALE-
FEMALE DYNAMICS and MARRIAGE [Wry & Witty])

**Marriage must constantly fight against
a monster which devours everything: routine.**

—HONORÉ DE BALZAC

Marriage is our last, best chance to grow up.

—JOSEPH BARTH

Wasn't marriage, like life, unstimulating and unprofitable
and somewhat empty when too well ordered and protected and guarded?
Wasn't it finer, more splendid, more nourishing, when it was, like life itself,
a mixture of the sordid and the magnificent;
of mud and stars; of earth and flowers;
of love and hate and laughter and tears and ugliness and beauty and hurt?

—EDNA FERBER

Marriage is like a war.
There are moments of chivalry and gallantry that attend the
victorious advances and strategic retreats,
the birth or death of children,
the momentary conquest of loneliness,
the sacrifice that ennobles him who makes it.
But mostly there are the long dull sieges,
the waiting, the terror and boredom.
Women understand this better than men;
they are better able to survive attrition.

—HELEN HAYES

In every house of marriage
there's room for an interpreter.

—STANLEY KUNITZ

In married conversation, as in surgery, the knife must be used with care.

—ANDRÉ MAUROIS

In a successful marriage, there is no such thing as one's way.
There is only the way of both,
only the bumpy, dusty, difficult, but always mutual path!

—PHYLLIS MCGINLEY

Marriage is three parts love and seven parts forgiveness of sins.

—LANGDON MITCHELL

Chains do not hold a marriage together.
It is threads, hundreds of tiny threads,
which sew people together through the years.

—SIMONE SIGNORET

Every marriage is a battle between
two families struggling to reproduce themselves.

—CARL A. WHITAKER

MARRIAGE [Wry & Witty]

(see also DIVORCE and FAMILY and LOVE and MALE-
FEMALE DYNAMICS and MARRIAGE [Wise])

The only real argument for marriage
is that it remains the best method for getting acquainted.

—HEYWOOD BROUN

Marriage is a feast where the grace is sometimes better than the dinner.

—CHARLES CALEB COLTON

The dread of loneliness is greater than the fear of bondage,
so we get married.

—CYRIL CONNOLLY

The chains of marriage are so heavy
that it takes two to bear them, sometimes three.

—ALEXANDRE DUMAS, PÈRE

Marrying a man is like buying something
you've been admiring for a long time in a shop window.
You may love it when you get it home,
but it doesn't always go with everything else in the house.

—JEAN KERR

Marriage is not a reform school.

—ANN LANDERS

Marriage is based on the theory that
when a man discovers a particular brand of beer exactly to his taste
he should at once throw up his job and go to work in the brewery.

—GEORGE JEAN NATHAN

Marriage isn't a word—it's a *sentence*!

—KING VIDOR

Marriage is the only adventure open to the cowardly.

—VOLTAIRE[*]

Marriage is a great institution——but I'm not ready for an institution.

—MAE WEST

MATURITY

(see also AGE & AGING—MIDDLE AGE and GROWTH and YOUTH & AGE)

For a conscious being, to exist is to change,
to change is to mature,
to mature is to go on creating oneself endlessly.

—HENRI BERGSON

When I was a child, I spake as a child,
I understood as a child, I thought as a child:
but when I became a man, I put away childish things.

—THE BIBLE, 1 CORINTHIANS 13:11

[*] A number of influential people, including W. H. Auden and Louis Kronenberger, have attributed this saying to Voltaire, but it has never been found in his works—and should therefore be used with this in mind.

Maturity is gratification delayed,
Self-confidence conveyed,
Opportunity parlayed,
Risk delayed,
Self-esteem displayed,
And self-denial repaid.

—MARLENE CAROSELLI

Maturity includes discovering that even an opinion contrary to ours
may contain a vein of truth we could profitably assimilate to our own views.

—SYDNEY J. HARRIS

There is no "trick" in being young: it happens to you.
But the process of maturing is an art to be learned,
an effort to be sustained.

—MARYA MANNES

Compassion for our parents is the true sign of maturity.

—ANAÏS NIN

Maturity is a high price to pay for growing up.

—TOM STOPPARD[*]

---

[*] This observation, from a character in *Where Are They Now?*, a 1970 BBC radio play by
Stoppard, is a tweaking of a remark he made about his own life in a 1969 interview: "Age
is a very high price to pay for maturity."

The awareness of the ambiguity of one's highest achievements
(as well as one's deepest failures) is a definite symptom of maturity.

—PAUL TILLICH

To live with fear and not be afraid is the final test of maturity.

—EDWARD WEEKS

Maturity's reached the day we don't need to be lied to about anything.

—FRANK YERBY

MEDIOCRITY

(see also ABILITY and AIMS & AIMING and ASPIRATION
and EXCELLENCE and GREATNESS and TALENT)

There is always a heavy demand for fresh mediocrity.
In every generation
the least cultivated taste has the largest appetite.

—THOMAS BAILEY ALDRICH

Only mediocrity can be trusted to be always at its best.

—MAX BEERBOHM

Mediocrity knows nothing higher than itself.

—ARTHUR CONAN DOYLE

The mediocre always feel as if they're fighting for their lives
when confronted by the excellent.

—MARIE VON EBNER-ESCHENBACH

To me, the only sin is mediocrity.

—MARTHA GRAHAM

"Elitism" is the slur directed at merit by mediocrity.

—SYDNEY J. HARRIS

In the republic of mediocrity, genius is dangerous.

—ROBERT G. INGERSOLL

Mediocrity is excellence to the mediocre.

—JOSEPH JOUBERT

When small men attempt great enterprises,
they always end by reducing them to the level of their mediocrity.

—NAPOLEON BONAPARTE

Indifference is the revenge the world takes on mediocrities.

—OSCAR WILDE

MEMORY

(see also CHILDHOOD and IMAGINATION and PAST and
SELF-DECEPTION and TIME)

The charm, one might say the genius, of memory
is that it is choosy, chancy, and temperamental;
It rejects the edifying cathedral
and indelibly photographs the small boy outside,
chewing a hunk of melon in the dust.

—ELIZABETH BOWEN

Our memories are card-indexes, consulted, and then
put back in disorder by authorities whom we do not control.

—CYRIL CONNOLLY

The difference between false memories and true ones
is the same as for jewels:
it is always the false ones that look the most real, the most brilliant.

—SALVADOR DALÍ

Memory is a skilled seducer.

—CHRISTINA GARCIA

Each man's memory is his private literature,
and every recollection affects us with something of
the penetrative force that belongs to the work of art.

—ALDOUS HUXLEY

Memory is a complicated thing,
a relative to truth but not its twin.

—BARBARA KINGSOLVER

No memory is ever alone,
it's at the end of a trail of memories,
a dozen trails that each have their own associations.

—LOUIS L'AMOUR

Memory is a crazy woman
that hoards colored rags and throws away food.

—AUSTIN O'MALLEY

For a purely untrustworthy human organ,
the memory is right in there with the penis.

—P. J. O'ROURKE

Memory is the personal journalism of the soul.

—RICHARD SCHICKEL

MEN & WOMEN

(see also LOVE and MALE-FEMALE DYNAMICS and
RELATIONSHIPS and SEX and UNDERSTANDING
OTHERS)

If men and women are to understand each other,
to enter into each other's natures with mutual sympathy,
and to become capable of genuine comradeship,
the foundation must be laid in youth.

—HAVELOCK ELLIS

The feminine in the man is the sugar in the whiskey.
The masculine in the woman is the yeast in the bread.
Without these ingredients the result is flat, without tang or flavor.

—EDNA FERBER

A man has every season,
while a woman only has the right to spring.

—JANE FONDA

A woman's head is always influenced by her heart,
but a man's heart is always influenced by his head.

—MARGUERITE GARDINER (LADY BLESSINGTON)

Men are from Mars, Women are from Venus.

—JOHN GRAY, TITLE OF 1992 BOOK

Women speak in estrogen and men listen in testosterone.

—RICHARD ROEPER

A man falls in love through his eyes,
a woman through her imagination,
and then they both speak of it as an affair of "the heart."

—HELEN ROWLAND

Women might be able to fake orgasms,
but men can fake whole relationships.

—SHARON STONE

Though all human beings need both intimacy and independence,
women tend to focus on the first and men on the second.
It is as if their lifeblood ran in different directions.

—DEBORAH TANNEN

A man's face is his autobiography.
A woman's face is her work of fiction.

—OSCAR WILDE

METAPHOR

(see also LANGUAGE and POETRY and THINKING &
THINKERS and UNDERSTANDING and WRITING)

A noble metaphor, when it is placed to an advantage,
casts a kind of glory around it,
and darts a luster through a whole sentence.

—JOSEPH ADDISON

The greatest thing by far is to be a master of metaphor.

—ARISTOTLE

Metaphors have a way of holding the most truth in the least space.

—ORSON SCOTT CARD

An idea is a feat of association,
and the height of it is a good metaphor.

—ROBERT FROST

A metaphor is both detour and destination,
a digression that gets to the point.

—JAMES GEARY

The metaphor is a shorter simile, or rather a kind of magical coat,
by which the same idea assumes a thousand different appearances.

—OLIVER GOLDSMITH

Effective metaphor does more than shed light
on the two things being compared.
It actually brings to the mind's eye
something that has never before been seen.
It's not just the marriage ceremony linking two things;
it's the child born from the union.

—REBECCA MCCLANAHAN

Metaphor is the energy charge that leaps between images,
revealing their connections.

—ROBIN MORGAN

The metaphor is probably the most fertile power possessed by man.

—JOSÉ ORTEGA Y GASSET

Metaphors are the diplomats of rhetoric;
they lead you urbanely to the brink, but it is you
who states some unique conclusion to your own discovering self.

—MARGARET LEE RUNBECK

MIND

(see also BRAIN and IDEAS and THINKING & THINKERS
and THOUGHT)

Measure your mind's height by the shade it casts.

—ROBERT BROWNING

A mind, like a home, is furnished by its owner,
so if one's life is cold and bare he can blame none but himself.
You have a chance to select from some pretty elegant furnishings.

—LOUIS L'AMOUR

A man's mind is known by the company it keeps.

—JAMES RUSSELL LOWELL, PLAYING OFF THE FAMILIAR PROVERB

The mind is its own place, and in itself
Can make a Heav'n of Hell, a Hell of Heav'n.

—JOHN MILTON

The mind is not a vessel to be filled, but a fire to be kindled.

—PLUTARCH[*]

Untilled soil, however fertile it may be, will bear thistles and thorns;
and so it is with man's mind.

—SAINT TERESA OF AVILA

Mind does dominate body.
We are superior to the house in which we dwell.

—MARGARET ELIZABETH SANGSTER

---

[*] This is an updated version of a Plutarch observation that's been traditionally translated this way: "The correct analogy for the mind is not a vessel that needs filling, but wood that needs igniting."

'Tis the mind that makes the body rich.

—WILLIAM SHAKESPEARE

The forceps of our minds are clumsy forceps,
and crush the truth a little in taking hold of it.

—H. G. WELLS

Where the Mind is biggest, the Heart, the Senses, Magnanimity, Charity,
Tolerance, Kindliness, and the rest of them scarcely have room to breathe.

—VIRGINIA WOOLF

MISTAKES

(see also ERROR and FAILURE and FOLLY and SUCCESS &
FAILURE)

You can spend the entire second half of your life
recovering from the mistakes of the first half.

—SAUL BELLOW

Every great mistake has a halfway moment,
a split second when it can be recalled and perhaps remedied.

—PEARL S. BUCK

Mistakes are a fact of life
It is the response to error that counts.

—NIKKI GIOVANNI

Men heap together the mistakes of their lives
and create a monster which they call Destiny.

—JOHN OLIVER HOBBES (PEARL CRAIGIE)

Mistakes are, after all, the foundations of truth,
and if a man does not know what a thing is,
it is at least an increase in knowledge if he knows what it is not.

—CARL JUNG

Back of every mistaken venture and defeat
is the laughter of wisdom, if you listen.
Every blunder behind us is giving a cheer for us.

—CARL SANDBURG

It is only an error in judgment to make a mistake,
but it argues an infirmity of character to stick to it.

—ADELA ROGERS ST. JOHNS

Mistakes live in the neighborhood of truth and therefore delude us.

—RABINDRANATH TAGORE

Mistakes are the usual bridge between inexperience and wisdom.

—PHYLLIS THEROUX

Mistakes are at the very base of human thought,
embedded there, feeding the structure like root nodules.
If we were not provided with the knack of being wrong,
we could never get anything useful done.

—LEWIS THOMAS

MODERATION

(see also ENTHUSIASM and FANATICISM and FOLLY and
PASSION and VICE & VIRTUE and WISDOM and ZEAL)

Whether zeal or moderation be the point we aim at,
let us keep fire out of the one, and frost out of the other.

—JOSEPH ADDISON

Moderation is the inseparable companion of wisdom,
but with it genius has not even a nodding acquaintance.

—CHARLES CALEB COLTON

This much I think I do know——that a society so riven
that the spirit of moderation is gone, no court can save.

—LEARNED HAND

To enjoy the flavor of life, take big bites. Moderation is for monks.

—ROBERT A. HEINLEIN

I should say that our prevalent belief is in moderation.
We inculcate the virtue of avoiding excesses of all lands—
even including, if you will pardon the paradox, excess of virtue itself.

—JAMES HILTON[*]

---

[*] Most Internet sites mistakenly say *excesses of all kinds.*

Thou shalt not carry moderation into excess.

—ARTHUR KOESTLER

Excess on occasion is exhilarating.
It prevents moderation from
acquiring the deadening effect of habit.

—W. SOMERSET MAUGHAM

Fear and dull disposition, lukewarmness and sloth,
are not seldom wont to cloak themselves
under the affected name of moderation.

—JOHN MILTON

Any plan conceived in moderation must fail
when the circumstances are set in extremes.

—PRINCE KLEMENS VON METTERNICH

Moderation in temper is always a virtue,
but moderation in principle is always a vice.

—THOMAS PAINE[*]

---

[*]   This observation inspired Barry Goldwater to say at the 1964 Republican National
Convention: "Extremism in the defense of liberty is no vice. And . . . moderation in the
pursuit of justice is no virtue." Goldwater's line, delivered so confidently at the time of his
presidential nomination, went on to doom his chances at winning the election.

MONEY [Wise]

(see also MONEY [Wry & Witty] and SUCCESS and
SUCCESS & FAILURE and WEALTH)

Money speaks sense in a language all nations understand.

—APHRA BEHN

The love of money is the root of all evil.

—THE BIBLE, 1 TIMOTHY 6:10

**Money is a protection, a cloak;
it can buy one quiet, and some sort of dignity.**

—WILLA CATHER

**To fulfill a dream, to be allowed to sweat over lonely labor,
to be given a chance to create, is the meat and potatoes of life.
The money is the gravy.
As everyone else, I love to dunk my crust in it.
But alone, it is not a diet designed to keep body and soul together.**

—BETTE DAVIS

**Money, which represents the prose of life,
and which is hardly spoken of in parlors without an apology,
is, in its effects and laws, as beautiful as roses.**

—RALPH WALDO EMERSON

Money is a singular thing.
It ranks with love as man's greatest source of joy.
And with death as his greatest source of anxiety.

—JOHN KENNETH GALBRAITH

If you make money your god,
it will plague you like the devil.

—PROVERB (ENGLISH)[*]

Money is human happiness in the abstract.

—ARTHUR SCHOPENHAUER

The price we have to pay for money is paid in liberty.

—ROBERT LOUIS STEVENSON

When it is a question of money,
everybody is of the same religion.

—VOLTAIRE

---

[*] Almost all Internet sites mistakenly attribute this observation to Henry Fielding (1707–1754). In 1824, Thomas Fielding (no relation) included the saying in his *Select Proverbs of All Nations*. When subsequent reference works included the proverb, they followed the common practice of the time by attributing it simply to "Fielding." Most readers naturally assumed that Henry Fielding was the author, and thus began his association with an observation he never authored. The error stubbornly continues to the present day.

MONEY [Wry & Witty]

(see also MONEY [Wise] and SUCCESS and SUCCESS &
FAILURE and WEALTH)

Money is the root of all evil,
and yet it is such a useful root that we cannot get on without it
any more than we can without potatoes.

—LOUISA MAY ALCOTT

That money talks
I'll not deny,
I heard it once,
it said goodbye.

—RICHARD ARMOUR

Money cannot buy
The fuel of love
But is excellent kindling.

—W. H. AUDEN

We all need money, but there are degrees of desperation.

—ANTHONY BURGESS

Money doesn't talk, it swears.

—BOB DYLAN

Money often costs too much.

—RALPH WALDO EMERSON

**Money's a horrid thing to follow,
but a charming thing to meet.**

—HENRY JAMES

**Always try to rub up against money,
for if you rub up against money long enough,
some of it may rub off on you.**

—DAMON RUNYON

**Unexpected money is a delight.
The same sum is a bitterness when you expected more.**

—MARK TWAIN

**Money—pardon my expression—money is like manure;
it's not worth a thing unless it's spread around
encouraging young things to grow.**

—THORNTON WILDER[*]

---

[*] The words come from Mrs. Dolly Levi in Wilder's *The Matchmaker* (1954), a play that inspired the 1964 Broadway musical *Hello, Dolly!* Wilder was clearly inspired by Francis Bacon, who wrote in a 1625 essay, "Money is like muck, not good except it be spread."

MOTHERS & MOTHERHOOD

(see also BABIES and CHILDHOOD and CHILDREN and
FAMILY and LOVE and MARRIAGE)

What fabrications they are, mothers.
Scarecrows, wax dolls for us to stick pins into, crude diagrams.
We deny them an existence of their own,
we make them up to suit ourselves—
our own hungers, our own wishes, our own deficiencies.

—MARGARET ATWOOD

Mothering has left me with stretch marks.
I have been stretched beyond what I could have imagined.

—KATHY CALLAHAN

There is no other closeness in human life like
the closeness between a mother and her baby—
chronologically, physically, and spiritually
they are just a few heartbeats away from being the same person.

—SUSAN CHEEVER

A mother is not a person to lean on,
but a person to make leaning unnecessary.

—DOROTHY CANFIELD FISHER

Blaming mother is just a negative way of clinging to her still.

—NANCY FRIDAY

After my mother's death, I began to see her as she had really been. . . .
It was less like losing someone than discovering someone.

—NANCY HALE

Feeling inadequate is an occupational hazard of motherhood.

—HARRIET LERNER

Probably there is nothing in human nature more resonant with charges
than the flow of energy between two biologically alike bodies,
one of which has lain in amniotic bliss inside the other,
one of which has labored to give birth to the other.
The materials are here for the deepest mutuality
and the most painful estrangement.

—ADRIENNE RICH

For the mother is, and must be, whether she knows it or not,
the greatest, strongest, and most lasting teacher her children have.

—HANNAH WHITALL SMITH

Mother is the name for God in the lips and hearts of little children.

—WILLIAM MAKEPEACE THACKERAY

MOTIVATION

(see also AIMS & AIMING and AMBITION and DREAMS
[Aspirational] and GOALS and PURPOSE and SUCCESS)

All that we do is done with an eye to something else.

—ARISTOTLE

**Motivation is a fire from within.
If someone else tries to light that fire under you,
chances are it will burn very briefly.**

—STEPHEN R. COVEY

**We know nothing about motivation.
All we can do is write books about it.**

—PETER F. DRUCKER

**Motivation is not a thinking word;
it's a feeling word.**

—JOHN KOTTER

**We should often feel ashamed of our best actions
if the world could see all of the motives which produced them.**

—FRANÇOIS, DUC DE LA ROCHEFOUCAULD

There are two basic motivating forces: fear and love.
When we are afraid, we pull back from life.
When we are in love, we open to all that life has to offer
with passion, excitement, and acceptance.

—JOHN LENNON

There are only two forces that unite men—fear and interest.

—NAPOLEON BONAPARTE

There is no such thing as an exact synonym
and no such thing as an unmixed motive.

—KATHERINE ANNE PORTER

Too great a preoccupation with motives
(especially one's own motives)
is liable to lead to too little concern for consequences.

—KATHARINE WHITEHORN

Motivation is the fuel necessary to keep the human engine running.

—ZIG ZIGLAR

MUSIC

(see also ART and BLUES and CREATIVITY and
IMAGINATION and JAZZ)

Music washes away from the soul the dust of everyday life.

—BERTHOLD AUERBACH[*]

**Great music is that which penetrates the ear with facility
and quits the memory with difficulty.
Magical music never leaves the memory.**

—THOMAS BEECHAM

Music is the mediator between the spiritual and the sensual life.

—LUDWIG VAN BEETHOVEN

**Who hears music, feels his solitude
Peopled at once.**

—ROBERT BROWNING

Music is a means of rapid transportation.

—JOHN CAGE

---

[*]   On most Internet sites, an almost identical version of this thought—but about *art* as
opposed to music—is mistakenly attributed to Pablo Picasso.

Music has charms to soothe a savage breast,
To soften rocks, or bend a knotted oak.

—WILLIAM CONGREVE*

Music is only love looking for words.

—LAWRENCE DURRELL

Music expresses that which cannot be said
and on which it is impossible to be silent.

—VICTOR HUGO

After silence that which comes nearest
to expressing the inexpressible is music.

—ALDOUS HUXLEY

If music be the food of love, play on.

—WILLIAM SHAKESPEARE

---

* When this passage is cited these days, *savage beast* has almost completely supplanted
savage breast (I provide an explanation for the dropped *r* in *DMDMQ*). *Hath* is also often
mistakenly used instead of *has*).

NATURE

(see also ANIMALS and BEAUTY and FLOWERS and
GARDENS & GARDENING)

Nature is often hidden, sometimes overcome, seldom extinguished.

—FRANCIS BACON (1561–1626)

**I love to think of nature as an unlimited broadcasting system
through which God speaks to us every hour, if we will only tune Him in.**

—GEORGE WASHINGTON CARVER

**Americans are nature-lovers:
but they only admit of nature proofed and corrected by man.**

—SIMONE DE BEAUVOIR

**We do not see nature with our eyes,
but with our understandings and our hearts.**

—WILLIAM HAZLITT

**You may drive out nature with a pitchfork,
but she will always return.**

—HORACE

**In nature there are neither rewards nor punishments—
there are consequences.**

—ROBERT G. INGERSOLL

Nature distributes her favors unequally.

—GEORGE SAND

I love Nature partly *because* she is not man,
but a retreat from him.
None of his institutions control or pervade her.
There a different kind of right prevails.

—HENRY DAVID THOREAU

Adapt or perish, now as ever,
is Nature's inexorable imperative.

—H. G. WELLS

Nature never did betray
The heart that loved her.

—WILLIAM WORDSWORTH

NEUROTICS

(see also FANATICISM and ILLNESS and ILLUSION and
MIND and SELF-DECEPTION)

The neurotic is nailed to the cross of his fiction.

—ALFRED ADLER

A mistake which is commonly made about neurotics
is to suppose that they are interesting.
It is not interesting to be always unhappy, engrossed with oneself,
malignant and ungrateful, and never quite in touch with reality.
—CYRIL CONNOLLY

The true believer is in a high degree
protected against the danger of certain neurotic afflictions;
by accepting the universal neurosis
he is spared the task of forming a personal neurosis.
—SIGMUND FREUD

They complain of their illness but exploit it with all of their strength;
and if someone tries to take it away from them they defend it
like the proverbial lioness with her young.
—SIGMUND FREUD, ON NEUROTICS

Neurosis can be understood best as the battle
between two tendencies within an individual.
—ERICH FROMM

The neurotic . . . feels caught in a cellar with many doors,
and whichever door he opens leads only into new darkness.
And all the time he knows that others are walking outside in sunshine.
—KAREN HORNEY

Every person, to the extent that he is neurotic,
is like an airplane directed by remote control.

—KAREN HORNEY

Neurosis is always a substitute for legitimate suffering.

—CARL JUNG

Everything we think of as great has come to us from neurotics.
It is they and they alone who found religions and create great works of art.
The world will never realize how much it owes to them
and what they have suffered in order to bestow their gifts on it.

—MARCEL PROUST

A neurosis is a secret you don't know you're keeping.

—KENNETH TYNAN

NOVELISTS

(see also AUTHORS and BOOKS and FICTION and
LITERATURE and NOVELS and READING and WRITERS
and WRITERS—ON THEMSELVES & THEIR WORK and
WRITING and WRITING ADVICE)

With a novelist, like a surgeon,
you have to get a feeling that you've fallen into good hands—
someone from whom you can accept the anesthetic with confidence.

—SAUL BELLOW

When you're a novelist,
you're writing a play but you're acting all the parts,
you're controlling the lights and the scenery and the whole business,
and it's your show.

—ROBERTSON DAVIES

Life, of course, is the basic raw material of all art,
but no artist is so close to his raw material as the novelist.

—ELIZABETH A. DREW

There are many reasons why novelists write, but they all have
one thing in common—a need to create an alternative world.

—JOHN FOWLES

The economy of a novelist is a little like that of a careful housewife,
who is unwilling to throw away anything that might perhaps serve its turn.
Or perhaps the comparison is closer to the Chinese cook
who leaves hardly any part of the duck unserved.

—GRAHAM GREENE

The novelist screws up his courage in order to
invest another two or three years in another attempt
to float a boat of original design upon an invented ocean.

—EDWARD HOAGLAND

A novelist is, like all mortals, more fully at home
on the surface of the present than in the ooze of the past.

—VLADIMIR NABOKOV

In the compact between novelist and reader,
the novelist promises to lie, and the reader promises to allow it.

—CYNTHIA OZICK

I am looking for the novelists whose writing
is an extension of their intellect
rather than an extension of their neurosis.

—TOM ROBBINS

NOVELS

(see also AUTHORS and BOOKS and FICTION and
LITERATURE and NOVELISTS and READING and
WRITERS and WRITERS—ON THEMSELVES & THEIR
WORK and WRITING and WRITING ADVICE)

A novel is never anything but a philosophy put into images.

—ALBERT CAMUS

One doesn't "get" an "idea" for a novel.
The "idea" more or less "gets" you.
It uses you as a kind of culture, the way a pearl uses an oyster.

—DIANA CHANG

A good novel tells us the truth about its hero;
but a bad novel tells us the truth about its author.

—G. K. CHESTERTON

A novel, in the end, is a container,
a shape which you are trying to pour your story into.

—HELEN DUNMORE

Writing a novel is like making love,
but it's also like having a tooth pulled.
Pleasure and pain.
Sometimes it's like making love while having a tooth pulled.

—DEAN KOONTZ

The return to a favorite novel is generally tied up with changes in oneself
that must be counted as improvements, but have the feel of losses.
It is like going back to a favorite house, country, person;
nothing is where it belongs, including one's heart.

—MARY MCCARTHY

A novel . . . is the smallest number of characters
in the least number of situations
necessary to precipitate a given crisis.

—FRANK O'CONNOR

A great novel is a kind of conversion experience.
We come away from it changed.

—KATHERINE PATERSON

A novel is a mirror which passes over a highway.
Sometimes it reflects to your eyes the blue of the skies,
at others the churned-up mud of the road.

—STENDHAL (MARIE-HENRI BEYLE)

OBSTACLES

(see also ADVERSITY and DIFFICULTIES and PROBLEMS
and TROUBLE)

We combat obstacles in order to get repose, and,
when got, the repose is unsupportable.

—HENRY BROOKS ADAMS

Obstacles are those frightful things
you see when you take your eyes off the goal.

—AUTHOR UNKNOWN[*]

If there are obstacles,
the shortest line between two points may be the crooked line.

—BERTOLT BRECHT

Every obstacle yields to stern resolve.

—LEONARDO DA VINCI

---

[*] After first appearing in the early 1940s, this saying—with slight variations—has been attributed to the English writer Hannah More, the American industrialist Henry Ford, the mail-order guru E. Joseph Cossman, and the rocker David Byrne of the Talking Heads.

It still holds true that man is most uniquely human
when he turns obstacles into opportunities.

—ERIC HOFFER

Life is like walking along a crowded street—there always
seem to be fewer obstacles to getting along on the opposite pavement—
and yet, if one crosses over, matters are rarely mended.

—T. H. HUXLEY

The block of granite which was an obstacle on the pathway of the weak,
becomes a stepping-stone on the pathway of the strong.

—G. H. LEWES[*]

The greater the obstacle, the greater the glory in overcoming it;
and difficulties are but the maids of honor to set off the virtue.

—MOLIÈRE

My life seems like one long obstacle course,
with me as the chief obstacle.

—JACK PAAR

He is the best sailor who can steer within the fewest points of the wind,
and extract a motive power out of the greatest obstacles.

—HENRY DAVID THOREAU

[*]   Almost all Internet sites mistakenly attribute this observation to Thomas Carlyle.

PAIN

(see also ILLNESS and PLEASURE and PLEASURE &
PAIN and SORROW and SUFFERING)

It is easy for the one who stands outside
The prison-wall of pain to exhort and teach the one
Who suffers.

—AESCHYLUS

Isn't the fear of pain next brother to pain itself?

—ENID BAGNOLD

Pain is always new to the sufferer,
but loses its originality for those around him.

—ALPHONSE DAUDET

There is much pain that is quite noiseless;
and vibrations that make human agonies are often a mere whisper
in the roar of hurrying existence.

—GEORGE ELIOT

He has seen but half the universe
who never has been shown the house of pain.

—RALPH WALDO EMERSON

Life's sharpest rapture is surcease of pain.

—EMMA LAZARUS

There are ships sailing to many ports,
but not a single one goes where life is not painful.

—FERNANDO PESSOA

In the country of pain we are each alone.

—MAY SARTON

Nothing begins, and nothing ends,
That is not paid with moan;
For we are born in others' pain,
And perish in our own.

—FRANCIS THOMPSON

The Fellowship of Those who Bear the Mark of Pain.
Who are the members of this Fellowship?
Those who have learnt by experience
what physical pain and bodily anguish mean,
belong together all the world over;
they are united by a secret bond.

—ALBERT SCHWEITZER

PARENTS & PARENTHOOD

(see also BABIES and CHILDREN and FAMILY and
MOTHERS & MOTHERHOOD)

All parents damage their children. It cannot be helped.
Youth, like pristine glass, absorbs the prints of its handlers.
Some parents smudge, others crack, a few shatter childhoods completely
into jagged little pieces, beyond repair.

—MITCH ALBOM

Children rarely want to know who their parents were
before they were parents, and when age
finally stirs their curiosity there is no parent left to tell them.

—RUSSELL BAKER

It's frightening to think that you mark your children
merely by being yourself.

—SIMONE DE BEAUVOIR

Romance fails us and so do friendships—
but the relationship of parent and child
remains indelible and indestructible, the strongest relationship on earth.
There is no call coming from those living
as insistent, permanent, and penetrating
as the silent voice of our parents from the country of the dead.

—THEODORE REIK

There is no magic on earth strong enough
to wipe out the legacies of one's parents.

—SALMAN RUSHDIE

Parents teach in the toughest school in the world—
The School for Making People.
You are the board of education,
the principal, the classroom teacher, and the janitor.

—VIRGINIA SATIR

Parentage is a very important profession;
but no test of fitness for it is ever imposed in the interest of the children.

—GEORGE BERNARD SHAW

In automobile terms, the child supplies the power
but the parents have to do the steering.

—DR. BENJAMIN SPOCK

Despite the increasing complexity of the task,
parenthood remains the greatest single preserve of the amateur.

—ALVIN TOFFLER

Parents are the bones on which children sharpen their teeth.

—PETER USTINOV

PASSION

(see also ENTHUSIASM and LOVE and SEX and ZEAL)

**Without passion man is a mere latent force and possibility,
like the flint which awaits the shock of the iron
before it can give forth its spark.**

—HENRI FRÉDÉRIC AMIEL

Only passions, great passions, can elevate the soul to great things.

—DENIS DIDEROT

Passion, though a bad regulator, is a powerful spring.

—RALPH WALDO EMERSON

If passion drives, let reason hold the reins.

—BENJAMIN FRANKLIN

A man in passion rides a horse that runs away with him.

—THOMAS FULLER, MD

The passions are the only orators which always persuade.

—FRANÇOIS, DUC DE LA ROCHEFOUCAULD

**Be still when you have nothing to say; when genuine passion
moves you, say what you've got to say, and say it hot.**

—D. H. LAWRENCE

We welcome passion, for the mind is briefly let off duty.

—MIGNON MCLAUGHLIN

Passion makes the best observations
and draws the most wretched conclusions.

—JEAN PAUL RICHTER

It is the soul's duty to be loyal to its own desires.
It must abandon itself to its master passion.

—REBECCA WEST

PAST

(see also FUTURE and HISTORY and MEMORY and TIME)

A long past vividly remembered is like a heavy garment
that clings to your limbs when you would run.

—MARY ANTIN

One faces the future with one's past.

—PEARL S. BUCK

In the carriages of the past you can't go anywhere.

—MAXIM GORKY

The past is a foreign country; they do things differently there.

—L. P. HARTLEY

You can live in the past, but there is no future in it.

—KALMAN PACKOUZ

Those who cannot remember the past are condemned to repeat it.

—GEORGE SANTAYANA

The past is the only dead thing that smells sweet.

—EDWARD THOMAS[*]

The story and study of the past, both recent and distant,
will not reveal the future, but it flashes beacon lights along the way
and it is a useful nostrum against despair.

—BARBARA W. TUCHMAN

The past is really almost as much
a work of the imagination as the future.

—JESSAMYN WEST

Each had his past shut in him
like the leaves of a book known to him by heart;
and his friends could only read the title.

—VIRGINIA WOOLF

* Numerous Internet sites mistakenly attribute this quotation to Cyril Connolly.

PLADY

(see also CHILDHOOD and JOY and SPORT and WORK)

It is a happy talent to know how to play.

—RALPH WALDO EMERSON

**The man who does not play
has lost forever the child who lived in him,
and he will certainly miss him.**

—PABLO NERUDA

In our play we reveal what kind of people we are.

—OVID

Play is the real work of childhood.

—FRED ROGERS

Deep meaning oft lies hid in childish play.

—JOHANN FRIEDRICH VON SCHILLER

**If all the year were playing holidays,
To sport would be as tedious as to work.**

—WILLIAM SHAKESPEARE

**Find your own play, your own self-renewing compulsion,
and you will become the person you are meant to be.**

—GEORGE SHEEHAN

If necessity is the mother of invention, play is the father.

—ROGER VON OECH

**This is the real secret of life—to be completely engaged
with what you are doing in the here and now.
And instead of calling it work, realize that it is play.**

—ALAN WATTS

There is for many a poverty of play.

—D. W. WINNICOTT

PLEASURE

(see also HAPPINESS and LAUGHTER and PAIN and
PLEASURE & PAIN)

When Pleasure is at the bar the jury is not impartial.

—ARISTOTLE

**The more he plumbed the depths of sensual pleasure,
the more he emerged with grit rather than pearls.**

—HONORÉ DE BALZAC[*]

---

[*] In recent years, this passage from Balzac's *The Girl with the Golden Eyes* (1835) has
become popular in what looks like a very liberal translation: "In diving to the bottom of
pleasures, we bring up more gravel than pearls."

Debauchee, *n.* One who has so earnestly pursued pleasure
that he has had the misfortune to overtake it.

—AMBROSE BIERCE*

Pleasure's a sin, and sometimes sin's a pleasure.

—GEORGE NOEL GORDON, LORD BYRON

Do not bite at the bait of pleasure,
till you know there is no hook beneath it.

—THOMAS JEFFERSON

Pleasure is very seldom found where it is sought.
Our brightest blazes of gladness
are commonly kindled by unexpected sparks.

—SAMUEL JOHNSON

Most men pursue pleasure with such breathless haste
that they hurry past it.

—SØREN KIERKEGAARD

It's true Heaven forbids some pleasures,
but a compromise can usually be found.

—MOLIÈRE

---

* The word *debauchee* has become almost obsolete, but not the word from which it derives.
Debauchery is defined as "extreme indulgence in sensual pleasures; dissipation."

When the cup of any sensual pleasure is drained to the bottom,
there is always poison in the dregs.

—JANE PORTER

That man is richest whose pleasures are the cheapest.

—HENRY DAVID THOREAU

PLEASURE & PAIN

(see also HAPPINESS and LAUGHTER and PAIN and
PLEASURE)

In educating the young we use pleasure and pain
as rudders to steer their course.

—ARISTOTLE

When pain is over,
the remembrance of it often becomes a pleasure.

—JANE AUSTEN

Nature has placed mankind under the governance
of two sovereign masters, *pain* and *pleasure.*

—JEREMY BENTHAM

There is a pleasure in poetic pains
Which only poets know.

—WILLIAM COWPER

Pain wastes the body;
pleasures, the understanding.

—BENJAMIN FRANKLIN

Pleasure is oft a visitant; but pain
Clings cruelly to us.

—JOHN KEATS

Pain insists upon being attended to.
God whispers to us in our pleasures,
speaks in our conscience, but shouts in our pains.

—C. S. LEWIS

Every nerve that can thrill with pleasure can also agonize with pain.

—HORACE MANN

It is not shameful for man to succumb under pain,
and it is shameful for him to succumb under pleasure.

—BLAISE PASCAL

There is room in the halls of pleasure
For a large and lordly train,
But one by one we must all file on
Through the narrow isles of pain.

—ELLA WHEELER WILCOX

POEM

(see also LANGUAGE and POETRY and POETS and
WRITERS and WRITING)

A poem is less a thing than any other work of art.

—HANNAH ARENDT

The poet marries the language,
and out of this marriage the poem is born.

—W. H. AUDEN

Every good poem, in fact, is a bridge built from the known,
familiar side of life over into the unknown.

—C. DAY-LEWIS

A good poem is like a bouillon cube.
It's concentrated, you carry it around with you,
and it nourishes you when you need it.

—RITA DOVE

A poem begins with a lump in the throat;
a home-sickness or a love-sickness.
It is a reaching-out toward expression; an effort to find fulfillment.
A complete poem is one where an emotion has found its thought
and the thought has found the words.

—ROBERT FROST

What are poems but words
Set edgewise up like children's blocks
To build a structure no one can inhabit.

—AMY LOWELL

In a poem,
the words should be as pleasing to the ear
as the meaning is to the mind.

—MARIANNE MOORE

Touched by poetry, language is more fully language
and at the same time is no longer language: it is a poem.

—OCTAVIO PAZ

A poem releases itself, secretes itself slowly,
sometimes almost poisonously, into the mind of the reader.

—MARK STRAND

And in the end, the poem is not a thing we see—
it is, rather, a light by which we may see—and what we see is life.

—ROBERT PENN WARREN

POETRY

(see also LANGUAGE and POEM and POETS and WRITERS
and WRITING)

Poetry is life distilled.

—GWENDOLYN BROOKS

A vein of Poetry exists in the hearts of all men.

—THOMAS CARLYLE

If I read a book and it makes my whole body so cold
no fire can ever warm me, I know that is poetry.
If I feel physically as if the top of my head were taken off,
I know that is poetry.

—EMILY DICKINSON

Poetry is the purest of the language arts.
It's the tightest cage,
and if you can get to sing in that cage it's really really wonderful.

—RITA DOVE

Poetry is a way of taking life by the throat.

—ROBERT FROST

By poetry we mean the art of employing words
in such a manner as to produce an illusion on the imagination,
the art of doing by means of words
what the painter does by means of colors.

—THOMAS BABINGTON MACAULAY

Poetry is either language lit up by life
or life lit up by language.

—PETER PORTER

Breathe-in, experience,
breathe-out, poetry.

—MURIEL RUKEYSER

Poetry is the opening and closing of a door,
leaving those who look through
to guess about what is seen during a moment.

—CARL SANDBURG

Poetry lifts the veil from the hidden beauty of the world,
and makes familiar objects be as if they were not familiar.

—PERCY BYSSHE SHELLEY

POETS

(see also LANGUAGE and POEM and POETRY and
WRITERS and WRITING)

A poet is, before anything else,
a person who is passionately in love with language.

—W. H. AUDEN

Poets and painters are outside the class system,
or rather they constitute a special class of their own,
like the circus people and the gypsies.

—GERALD BRENAN

Take a commonplace, clean it and polish it,
light it so that it produces the same effect of youth and freshness
and originality and spontaneity as it did originally,
and you have done a poet's job.

—JEAN COCTEAU

They are masters of us ordinary men in knowledge of the mind
because they drink at streams
which we have not yet made accessible to science.

—SIGMUND FREUD, ON POETS

To be a poet is a condition rather than a profession.

—ROBERT GRAVES

Poets are the leaven in the lump of civilization.

—ELIZABETH JANEWAY

A good poet is someone who manages,
in a lifetime of standing out in thunderstorms,
to be struck by lightning five or six times;
a dozen or two dozen times and he is great.

—RANDALL JARRELL

A poet must be a psychologist, but a secret one:
he should know and feel the roots of phenomena
but present only the phenomena themselves—
in full bloom or as they fade away.

—IVAN TURGENEV

A poet's autobiography is his poetry.
Anything else can be only a footnote.

—YEVGENY YEVTUSHENKO

For me, a poet is someone who is "in contact."
Someone through whom a current is passing.

—MARGUERITE YOURCENAR

POLITICIANS

(see also POLITICS and POLITICS & RELIGION)

Politicians are like diapers.
They should be changed frequently, and for the same reason.

—AUTHOR UNKNOWN*

A group of politicians deciding to dump a President because
his morals are bad is like the Mafia getting together
to bump off the Godfather for not going to church on Sunday.

—RUSSELL BAKER

Politics . . . is run, for the most part, by Madison Avenue advertising firms,
who sell politicians to the public
the way they sell bars of soap or cans of beer.

—HELEN CALDICOTT

In order to become the master, the politician poses as the servant.

—CHARLES DE GAULLE

Politicians, like prostitutes, are held in contempt.
But what man does not run to them when he needs their services?

—BRENDAN FRANCIS (EDWARD F. MURPHY)

---

*   This saying is often attributed to Robin Williams, or to Barry Levinson, who gave the
words to Williams's character Tom Dobbs—the comic turned presidential candidate—in
the 2006 film *Man of the Year*.

They are the same all over.
They promise to build a bridge even when there is no river.
—NIKITA KHRUSHCHEV, ON POLITICIANS

Politicians are like monkeys.
The higher they climb, the more revolting are the parts they expose.
—GWILYM LLOYD GEORGE

Natural politicians are skilled actors, recreating reality,
adjusting and ad-libbing, synthesizing the words, ideas, and feelings of others,
slipping into different roles in different scenes,
saying the same thing over and over again
and making it seem like they are saying it for the first time.
—DAVID MARANISS

The politician . . . is trained in the art of inexactitude.
His words tend to be blunt or rounded, because if they have a cutting edge
they may return later to wound him.
—EDWARD R. MURROW

Politicians make good company for a while, just as children do—
their self-enjoyment is contagious.
But they soon exhaust their favorite subjects—themselves.
—GARRY WILLS

POLITICS

(see also POLITICIANS and POLITICS & RELIGION)

Modern politics is, at bottom, a struggle not of men but of forces.

—HENRY BROOKS ADAMS

Politics is a blood sport.

—ANEURIN BEVAN

**Politics, *n.* A strife of interests masquerading as a contest of principles.
The conduct of public affairs for private advantage.**

—AMBROSE BIERCE

The pursuit of politics is religion, morality, and poetry all in one.

—GERMAINE DE STAËL

**Politics is not the art of the possible.
It consists in choosing between the disastrous and the unpalatable.**

—JOHN KENNETH GALBRAITH[*]

**There is no sea more dangerous than the ocean of practical politics—
none in which there is more need of good pilotage
and of a single, unfaltering purpose when the waves rise again.**

—T. H. HUXLEY

---

[*]   In expressing this thought to President John F. Kennedy in a 1962 letter, Galbraith was
piggybacking on German chancellor Otto von Bismarck's 1867 remark, "Politics is the art
of the possible."

Politics is war without bloodshed,
while war is politics with bloodshed.

—MAO ZEDONG

I've always thought that the American eagle
needed a left wing and a right wing.
The right wing would see to it that
economic interests had their legitimate concerns addressed.
The left wing would see to it that
ordinary people were included in the bargain.
Both would keep the great bird on course.
But with two right wings or two left wings,
it's no longer an eagle and it's going to crash.

—BILL MOYERS

The whole art of politics consists in
directing rationally the irrationalities of man.

—REINHOLD NIEBUHR

Politics is supposed to be the second oldest profession.
I have come to realize that it bears a very close resemblance to the first.

—RONALD REAGAN

POLITICS & RELIGION

(see also POLITICIANS and POLITICS)

Politics and religion mixed is the headiest cocktail ever invented.

—NORAH BENTINCK

Religion is organized to satisfy and guide the soul—
politics does the same thing for the body.

—JOYCE CARY

Patriotism is in political life what faith is in religion.

—JOHN DALBERG (LORD ACTON)

The garb of religion is the best cloak for power.

—WILLIAM HAZLITT[*]

It is a truism that almost any sect, cult, or religion will
legislate its creed into law if it acquires the political power to do so.

—ROBERT A. HEINLEIN

When religion and politics travel in the same cart,
the riders believe nothing can stand in their way.

—FRANK HERBERT

---

[*]   Hazlitt offered this thought in an 1819 essay; his observation might have stimulated
      Aldous Huxley, who, a century and a half later, wrote, "Idealism is the noble toga that
      political gentlemen drape over their will to power."

Politics is the science of domination,
and the persons in the process of enlargement and illumination
are notoriously difficult to control.
Therefore, to protect its vested interests,
politics usurped religion a very long time ago.

—TOM ROBBINS

Politics is a game of compromise . . . faith isn't.

—CAL THOMAS

How are we to disentangle religion from politics in a revolution?
Religion may form the outlook of an individual.
It may serve as an ideological intoxicant for a crowd.

—HUGH TREVOR-ROPER

Politics in America is the binding secular religion.

—THEODORE H. WHITE

POSSESSIONS

(see also MONEY and SUCCESS and WEALTH)

Possessions delude the human heart into believing
that they provide security and a worry-free existence,
but in truth they are the very cause of worry.

—DIETRICH BONHOEFFER

He who possesses most must be most afraid of loss.

—LEONARDO DA VINCI

Possessions possess.

—PAUL ELDRIDGE

Most people seek after what they do not possess
and are thus enslaved by the very things they want to acquire.

—ANWAR EL-SADAT

Things are in the saddle,
And ride mankind.

—RALPH WALDO EMERSON

In our rich consumers' civilization
we spin cocoons around ourselves
and get possessed by our possessions.

—MAX LERNER

An object in possession seldom retains
the same charm that it had in pursuit.

—PLINY THE YOUNGER

It is preoccupation with possession, more than anything else,
that prevents men from living freely and nobly.

—BERTRAND RUSSELL

Many possessions, if they do not make a man better,
are at least expected to make his children happier;
and this pathetic hope is behind many exertions.

—GEORGE SANTAYANA

Many wealthy people are little more than janitors of their possessions.

—FRANK LLOYD WRIGHT

POTENTIAL

(see also AIMS & AIMING and ASPIRATION and DREAMS
[Aspirational] and GOALS and VISION)

Potential has a shelf-life.

—MARGARET ATWOOD

Few men during their lifetime
come anywhere near exhausting the resources dwelling within them.
There are deep wells of strength that are never used.

—RICHARD E. BYRD

Man's main task in life is to give birth to himself,
to become what he potentially is.

—ERICH FROMM

Most people live . . . in a very restricted circle of their potential being.
They *make use* of a very small portion of their possible consciousness . . .
much like a man who, out of his whole bodily organism,
should get into a habit of using and moving only his little finger.

—WILLIAM JAMES

If you deliberately plan to be less than you are capable of being,
then I warn you that you'll be deeply unhappy for the rest of your life.

—ABRAHAM MASLOW

If any organism fails to fulfill its potentialities, it becomes sick,
just as your legs would wither if you never walked . . .
your whole organism would be the weaker.

—ROLLO MAY

We are all such a waste of our potential,
like three-way lamps using one-way bulbs.

—MIGNON MCLAUGHLIN

The struggle is to synchronize the potential being with the actual being,
to make a fruitful liaison between
the man of yesterday and the man of tomorrow.

—HENRY MILLER

There are so many things we are capable of, that we could be or do.
The potentialities are so great that we never,
any of us, are more than one-fourth fulfilled.

—KATHERINE ANNE PORTER

There's no heavier burden than a great potential!

—CHARLES M. SCHULZ

POWER

(see also AMBITION and LEADERS & LEADERSHIP and
POLITICIANS and POLITICS and POLITICS & RELIGION)

The jaws of power are always opened to devour,
and her arm is always stretched out, if possible,
to destroy the freedom of thinking, speaking, and writing.

—JOHN ADAMS

Those who have been once intoxicated with power . . .
can never willingly abandon it.

—EDMUND BURKE

Power tends to corrupt and absolute power corrupts absolutely.
Great men are almost always bad men.

—JOHN DALBERG (LORD ACTON)[*]

The real cause, the effective one, that makes men lose power
is that they have become unworthy to exercise it.

—ALEXIS DE TOCQUEVILLE

[*] "Lord Acton's dictum" may be history's most famous quotation on the *power corrupts*
theme, though it certainly isn't the first: more than a century earlier, English statesman
William Pitt (1708–78) said, "Unlimited power is apt to corrupt the minds of those who
possess it."

Given a little power over another,
little natures swell to hideous proportions.

—AMELIA EARHART

Power is pleasure; and pleasure sweetens pain.

—WILLIAM HAZLITT

Most people can bear adversity.
But if you wish to know what a man really is, give him power.
This is the supreme test.

—ROBERT G. INGERSOLL[*]

Those who have more power are liable to sin more;
no theorem in geometry is more certain than this.

—GOTTFRIED WILHELM VON LEIBNIZ

Power is sweet, and when you are a little clerk
you love its sweetness quite as much as if you were an emperor,
and maybe you love it a good deal more.

—OUIDA (MARIA LOUISE RAMÉ)

Power takes as ingratitude the writhing of its victims.

—RABINDRANATH TAGORE

[*] Ingersoll was thinking about Abraham Lincoln when he wrote this in 1885. Given the careless way quotations are presented on the Internet, it's not surprising that numerous sites attribute the saying directly to Lincoln.

PRAISE

(see also COMPLIMENTS and CRITICISM and FLATTERY)

Accepting praise that is not our due
is not much better than to be a receiver of stolen goods.

—JOSH BILLINGS (HENRY WHEELER SHAW)

Praise out of season, or tactlessly bestowed,
can freeze the heart as much as blame.

—PEARL S. BUCK

If each of us were to confess his most secret desire,
the one that inspires all his deeds and designs, he would say,
"I want to be praised."

—E. M. CIORAN

Nothing so soon the drooping Spirits can raise,
As Praises from the Men, whom all Men Praise.

—ABRAHAM COWLEY

What every genuine philosopher (every genuine man, in fact)
craves most is *praise*—
although the philosophers generally call it "recognition."

—WILLIAM JAMES

The applause of a single human being is of a great consequence.

—SAMUEL JOHNSON

People can be induced to swallow anything,
provided it is sufficiently seasoned with praise.

—MOLIÈRE

Even in the best, most friendly, and simple relations of life,
praise and commendation are essential,
just as grease is necessary to wheels that they may run smoothly.

—LEO TOLSTOY

One cares so little for the style in which one's praises are written.

—EDITH WHARTON

The love of praise, howe'er conceal'd by art,
Reigns more or less, and glows in ev'ry heart.

—EDWARD YOUNG (1683–1765)

PRAYER

(see also SOLITUDE and WISHES & WISHING)

To pray is to pay attention to something or someone other than oneself.
Whenever a man so concentrates his attention—
on a landscape, a poem, a geometrical problem, an idol, or the True God—
that he completely forgets his own ego and desires, he is praying.

—W. H. AUDEN

Nothing is so at odds with prayer as vanity.

—DIETRICH BONHOEFFER

A prayer in its simplest definition is merely a wish turned Godward.

—PHILLIPS BROOKS

When thou prayest, rather let thy heart be without words,
than thy words without a heart.

—JOHN BUNYAN

If the only prayer you say in your entire life
is "Thank You," that would suffice.

—MEISTER ECKHART

Your cravings as a human animal do not become a prayer
just because it is God whom you ask to attend to them.

—DAG HAMMARSKJÖLD

One single grateful thought raised to heaven is the most perfect prayer.

—G. E. LESSING[*]

Often when I pray I wonder if I am not
posting letters to a non-existent address.

—C. S. LEWIS

[*]   See the similar observation by Victor Hugo in THOUGHT.

Whatever a man prays for, he prays for a miracle.
Every prayer reduces itself to this:
"Great God, grant that twice two be not four."

—IVAN TURGENEV

You can't pray a lie.

—MARK TWAIN

PROBLEMS

(see also ADVERSITY and DIFFICULTIES and
OBSTACLES and SUFFERING and TROUBLE)

There is no such thing as a problem without a gift for you in its hands.
You seek problems because you need their gifts.

—RICHARD BACH

We are all faced with a series of great opportunities—
brilliantly disguised as insoluble problems.

—JOHN W. GARDNER

Problems worthy of attack
prove their worth by hitting back.

—PIET HEIN

Problems are only opportunities in work clothes.

—HENRY KAISER

There is at bottom only one problem in the world,
and this is its name.
How does one break through?
How does one get into the open?
How does one burst the cocoon and become a butterfly?

—THOMAS MANN

When the only tool you have is a hammer,
it is tempting to treat everything as if it were a nail.

—ABRAHAM MASLOW[*]

There is always a well-known solution to every human problem—
neat, plausible, and wrong.

—H. L. MENCKEN

Problems are to the mind what exercise is to the muscles,
they toughen and make strong.
Problems make one better able to cope with life.

—NORMAN VINCENT PEALE

There is no problem that doesn't have within it
the seeds of its own solution.

—ALEXANDRA STODDARD

---

[*] This is one of Maslow's most famous observations, offered in a number of slightly varying ways over the years—but never with the phrase *treat every problem as a nail*, as it is commonly presented on most Internet sites.

Don't get involved in partial problems,
but always take flight to where there is
a free view over the whole *single* great problem,
even if this view is still not a clear one.

—LUDWIG WITTGENSTEIN

PURPOSE

(see also AIMS & AIMING and ASPIRATION and DREAMS
[Aspirational] and GOALS)

Until thought is linked with purpose
there is no intelligent accomplishment.

—JAMES ALLEN

The very first condition of lasting happiness is that a life
should be full of purpose, aiming at something outside self.

—HUGO BLACK

The man without a purpose is like a ship without a rudder.

—THOMAS CARLYLE

We need not only a purpose in life to give meaning to our existence
but also something to give meaning to our suffering.

—ERIC HOFFER

Many persons have a wrong idea of what constitutes true happiness.
It is not attained through self-gratification
but through fidelity to a worthy purpose.

—HELEN KELLER

The living self has one purpose only:
to come into its own fullness of being, as a tree comes into full blossom,
or a bird into spring beauty, or a tiger into luster.

—D. H. LAWRENCE

He who has a *why* to live for can bear with almost any *how*.

—FRIEDRICH NIETZSCHE

To want to be what one *can* be is purpose in life.

—CYNTHIA OZICK

This is the true joy in life,
the being used for a purpose recognized by yourself as a mighty one;
the being thoroughly worn out before you are thrown on the scrap heap;
the being a force of Nature instead of
a feverish selfish little clod of ailments and grievances
complaining that the world will not devote itself to making you happy.

—GEORGE BERNARD SHAW

Nothing contributes so much to tranquilize the mind as a steady purpose—
a point on which the soul may fix its intellectual eye.

—MARY SHELLEY

QUARRELS

(see also ANGER and FAMILY [Not-So-Positive] and
FRIENDSHIP and RELATIONSHIPS)

The quarrels of friends are the opportunities of foes.

—AESOP

During a quarrel, to have said too little may be mended;
to have said too much, not always.

—MINNA ANTRIM

A quarrel between friends, when made up, adds a new tie to friendship;
as experience shows that the callosity formed round a broken bone
makes it stronger than before.

—SAINT FRANCIS DE SALES[*]

We are never so much disposed to quarrel with others
as when we are dissatisfied with ourselves.

—WILLIAM HAZLITT

It takes in reality only one to make a quarrel.
It is useless for the sheep to pass resolutions in favor of vegetarianism,
while the wolf remains of a different opinion.

—WILLIAM RALPH INGE

---

[*] *Callosity* means "the condition of being callused" and refers to the hardened tissue that
develops around a fractured bone as it heals.

An association of men who will not quarrel with one another
is a thing which never yet existed,
from the greatest confederacy of nations
down to a town meeting or a vestry.

—THOMAS JEFFERSON

A quarrel is quickly settled when deserted by one party;
there is no battle unless there be two.

—LUCIUS ANNAEUS SENECA (SENECA THE YOUNGER)

The test of a man or woman's breeding is how they behave in a quarrel.
Anybody can behave well when things are going smoothly.

—GEORGE BERNARD SHAW

Weakness on both sides is, as we know, the motto of all quarrels.

—VOLTAIRE

We make out of the quarrel with others, rhetoric,
but of the quarrel with ourselves, poetry.

—WILLIAM BUTLER YEATS

QUESTIONS

(see also ANSWERS and CURIOSITY and DISCOVERY and
QUESTIONS & ANSWERS and RESEARCH)

Once you start asking questions, innocence is gone.

—MARY ASTOR

A sudden, bold, and unexpected question
doth many times surprise a man and lay him open.

—FRANCIS BACON (1561–1626)

The questions which one asks oneself begin,
at last, to illuminate the world,
and become one's key to the experience of others.

—JAMES BALDWIN

The noblest question in the world is *What Good may I do in it?*

—BENJAMIN FRANKLIN

To ask the right question is already half the solution of a problem.

—CARL JUNG

If we would have new knowledge,
we must get us a whole world of new questions.

—SUSANNE K. LANGER

The words "question" and "quest" are cognates.
Only through inquiry can we discover truth.

—CARL SAGAN[*]

There are no ugly questions except those clothed in condescension.

—JOHN STEINBECK

You start a question, and it's like starting a stone.
You sit quietly on top of a hill; and the stone goes, starting others.

—ROBERT LOUIS STEVENSON

Truth walks toward us on the path of our questions.

—JACQUELINE WINSPEAR

QUESTIONS & ANSWERS

(see also ANSWERS and CURIOSITY and DISCOVERY and
QUESTIONS and RESEARCH)

Questions are dangerous, for they have answers.

—JACQUELINE CAREY

---

[*] In linguistics, cognates are words that have a common etymology, and therefore may be said to belong to the same family. *The American Heritage Dictionary* has this lovely metaphorical definition: "Related in origin, as certain words in genetically related languages descended from the same ancestral root."

A good question is never answered.
It is not a bolt to be tightened into place but a seed to be planted
and to bear more seed
toward the hope of greening the landscape of idea.

—JOHN CIARDI

A timid question will always receive a confident answer.

—CHARLES JOHN DARLING

When we have arrived at the question, the answer is already near.

—RALPH WALDO EMERSON

A wise man's question contains half the answer.

—SOLOMON IBN GABIROL

Questions show the mind's range, and answers its subtlety.

—JOSEPH JOUBERT

If they can get you asking the wrong questions,
they don't have to worry about the answers.

—THOMAS PYNCHON

We make our world significant by the courage of our questions
and by the depth of our answers.

—CARL SAGAN

Good questions outrank easy answers.

—PAUL A. SAMUELSON

Questions are never indiscreet. Answers sometimes are.

—OSCAR WILDE

QUOTATIONS

(see also APHORISMS and LANGUAGE and WRITERS and
WRITING)

I pick up favorite quotations,
and store them in my mind as ready armor,
offensive or defensive,
amid the struggle of this turbulent existence.

—ROBERT BURNS

A quotation, like a pun, should come unsought and then be welcomed
only for some propriety or felicity justifying the intrusion.

—ROBERT WILLIAM CHAPMAN

To be apt in quotation is a splendid and dangerous gift.
Splendid, because it ornaments a man's speech with other men's jewels;
dangerous, for the same reason.

—ROBERTSON DAVIES

Whenever we would prepare the mind by a forcible appeal,
an opening quotation is a symphony preluding on the chords
whose tones we are about to harmonize.

—ISAAC D'ISRAELI

A quotation in a speech, article, or book
is like a rifle in the hands of an infantryman.
It speaks with authority.

—BRENDAN FRANCIS (EDWARD F. MURPHY)

We speak a language that draws on quotations.
They are telegraphic, a form of shorthand.
We use them to lend point and luster to what we say.

—JUSTIN KAPLAN

Quotes are the mental furniture of my life.
From certain angles my inner landscape resembles a gallery
hung with half-recalled citations, the rags and tag-ends
of a lifetime of reading and listening.

—GEOFFREY O'BRIEN

A good quotation must be a complete entity.
It must be like a headline—sharp, clear, whole.

—AYN RAND

A fine quotation is a diamond on the finger of a man of wit,
and a pebble in the hand of a fool.

—JOSEPH ROUX

I think of quotes as mini–instruction manuals for the soul.

—CHERYL STRAYED

READING

(see also BOOKS and FICTION and LEARNING and
LITERATURE and NOVELS and WRITERS and
WRITING)

Reading is to the mind what exercise is to the body.

—JOSEPH ADDISON

The best moments in reading are when you come across something—
a thought, a feeling, a way of looking at things—
which you had thought special and particular to you.
Now here it is, set down by someone else,
a person you have never met, someone even who is long dead.
And it is as if a hand has come out and taken yours.

—ALAN BENNETT

To describe my scarce leisure time in today's terms,
I always default to reading.

—JIMMY BUFFETT

Reading is not an operation performed on something inert
but a relationship entered into with another vital being.

—CLIFTON FADIMAN

What is reading but silent conversation?
—WALTER SAVAGE LANDOR

**To acquire the habit of reading is to construct for yourself
a refuge from almost all of the miseries of life.**
—W. SOMERSET MAUGHAM

**I don't think we should read for instruction
but to give our souls a chance to luxuriate.**
—HENRY MILLER

**Study has been for me the sovereign remedy against
all the disappointments of life.
I have never known any trouble that an hour's reading would not dissipate.**
—MONTESQUIEU

**It is the sole means by which we slip, involuntarily,
often helplessly, into another's skin; another's voice; another's soul.**
—JOYCE CAROL OATES, ON READING

***Reading* is equivalent to thinking with someone else's head
instead of with one's own.**
—ARTHUR SCHOPENHAUER

RELATIONSHIPS

(see also FRIENDSHIP and LONELINESS and LOVE and
MALE-FEMALE DYNAMICS and MARRIAGE and MEN &
WOMEN)

Almost all of our relationships begin and most of them continue
as forms of mutual exploitation, a mental or physical barter,
to be terminated when one or both parties run out of goods.

—W. H. AUDEN

My attachment has neither the blindness of the beginning—
nor the microscopic accuracy of the close of such liaisons.

—GEORGE NOEL GORDON, LORD BYRON[*]

The formula for achieving a successful relationship is simple:
you should treat all disasters as if they were trivialities
but never treat a triviality as if it were a disaster.

—QUENTIN CRISP

There is no way to take the danger out of human relationships.

—BARBARA GRIZZUTI HARRISON

---

[*] In an 1820 letter to a friend, Byron was describing his relationship with his lover, the
Countess Teresa Guicciolo. In doing so, he provided a glimpse into his view of romantic
relationships in general.

Underground issues from one relationship or context
invariably fuel our fires in another.

—HARRIET LERNER

A good relationship has a pattern like a dance
and is built on some of the same rules.
The partners do not need to hold on tightly,
because they move confidently in the same pattern.

—ANNE MORROW LINDBERGH

In all proper relationships there is no sacrifice of anyone to anyone.

—AYN RAND

Man is a knot, a web, a mesh into which relationships are tied.

—ANTOINE DE SAINT-EXUPÉRY

Human relations just are not fixed in their orbits like the planets—
they're more like galaxies, changing all the time,
exploding into light for years, then dying away.

—MAY SARTON

Assumptions are the termites of relationships.

—HENRY WINKLER

RESEARCH

(see also CURIOSITY and DISCOVERY and FACTS
and KNOWLEDGE and LEARNING and SCIENCE &
SCIENTISTS)

Research is the process of going up alleys to see if they are blind.

—MARSTON BATES

In research the front line is almost always in a fog.

—FRANCIS CRICK

When curiosity turns to serious matters, it's called research.

—MARIE VON EBNER-ESCHENBACH

**The way to do research is to attack the facts
at the point of greatest astonishment.**

—CELIA GREEN

Research has been defined as guerrilla warfare on the unknown.

—ALAN GREGG

**The subject matter of research is no longer nature in itself,
but nature subjected to human questioning.**

—KARL HEISENBERG

Research is formalized curiosity.
It is poking and prying with a purpose.

—ZORA NEALE HURSTON

Research means going out into the unknown
with the hope of finding something new to bring home.

—ALBERT SZENT-GYÖRGI

Blind alleys and garden paths leading nowhere
are the principal hazards in research.

—LEWIS THOMAS

The outcome of any serious research can only be
to make two questions grow where only one grew before.

—THORSTEIN VEBLEN

RESENTMENT

(see also ENVY and JEALOUSY)

Hanging on to resentment is
letting someone you despise live rent-free in your head.

—AUTHOR UNKNOWN[*]

---

[*] This observation is often mistakenly attributed to Ann Landers.

Resentments, carried too far, expose us
to a fate analogous to that of the fish-hawk,
when he strikes his talons too deep into a fish beyond his capacity to lift,
and is carried under and drowned by it.

—CHRISTIAN NESTELL BOVEE

Resentment is like taking poison and hoping it'll kill someone else.

—ALAN BRANDT[*]

Resentment is an extremely bitter diet, and eventually poisonous.
I have no desire to make my own toxins.

—NEIL KINNOCK

Resentment is an evil so costly to our peace that we
should find it more cheap to forgive.

—HANNAH MORE

Nothing on earth consumes a man more quickly
than the passion of resentment.

—FRIEDRICH NIETZSCHE

Resentment isn't a magnetic personal style.

—PEGGY NOONAN

---

[*]   First offered in 1995, Brandt's thought morphed into a modern proverb: "Resentment is like taking poison and waiting for the other person to die." Variations have been offered by Rita Mae Brown, Malachy McCourt, Susan Cheever, and others.

Resentment is a communicable disease and should be quarantined.

—CYNTHIA OZICK

Resentment or grudges do no harm
to the person against whom you hold these feelings,
but every day and every night of your life, they are eating at you.

—NORMAN VINCENT PEALE

To show resentment at a reproach
is to acknowledge that one may have deserved it.

—TACITUS

RISK & RISK-TAKING

(see also COURAGE and COWARDICE and FEAR and
HEROES & HEROISM)

And the day came when the risk to remain closed in a bud
became more painful than the risk it took to blossom.

—ELIZABETH APPELL[*]

To conquer without risk is to triumph without glory.

—PIERRE CORNEILLE

---

[*] Almost all Internet sites mistakenly attribute this quotation to the celebrated diarist
Anaïs Nin.

To a certain extent,
a little blindness is necessary when you undertake a risk.

—BILL GATES

The man who knows it can't be done counts the risk, not the reward.

—ELBERT HUBBARD

It is only by risking our persons
from one hour to another that we live at all.
And often enough our faith beforehand in an uncertified result
is the only thing that makes the result come true.

—WILLIAM JAMES

All inquiries carry with them some element of risk.

—CARL SAGAN

One hour of life, crowded to the full with glorious action,
and filled with noble risks, is worth whole years of
those mean observances of paltry decorum, in which men
steal through existence, like sluggish waters through a marsh.

—WALTER SCOTT

Everything is sweetened by risk.

—ALEXANDER SMITH

A lot of people approach risk as if it's the enemy,
when it is really fortune's accomplice.
A risk you take may seem ridiculous to other people,
but risk isn't random or rash when it's a necessity.

—STING

What you risk reveals what you value.

—JEANETTE WINTERSON

ROMANCE & ROMANTICS

(see also KISSES & KISSING and LOVE and MALE-
FEMALE DYNAMICS and PASSION and RELATIONSHIPS
and SEX)

In a great romance,
each person basically plays a part that the other really likes.

—ELIZABETH ASHLEY

The essence of romantic love is that wonderful beginning,
after which sadness and impossibility may become the rule.

—ANITA BROOKNER

I have always been suspicious of romantic love.
It looks too much like a narcissism shared by two.

—RITA MAE BROWN

Romance has been elegantly defined
as the offspring of fiction and love.

—ISAAC D'ISRAELI

Romance dies hard, because its very nature is to want to live.

—ANDRE DUBUS

And what's romance?
Usually, a nice little tale where you have everything As You Like It,
where rain never wets your jacket and gnats never bite your nose
and it's always daisy-time.

—D. H. LAWRENCE

The curse of the romantic is a greed for dreams,
an intensity of expectation that, in the end, diminishes the reality.

—MARYA MANNES

Romances in general are calculated rather to fire the imagination
than to inform the judgment.

—SAMUEL RICHARDSON

Love is a reality which is born in the fairy region of romance.

—CHARLES MAURICE DE TALLEYRAND

The very essence of romance is uncertainty.

—OSCAR WILDE

SATIRE

(see also CRITICISM and CRITICS and WIT and WIT & HUMOR)

**Satire is dependent on strong beliefs,
and on strong beliefs wounded.**

—ANITA BROOKNER

**The difference between satire and humor is that
the satirist shoots to kill while the humorist brings his prey back alive—
often to release him again for another chance.**

—PETER DE VRIES

**A satirist is a man whose flesh creeps so
at the ugly and the savage and the incongruous aspects of society
that he has to express them as brutally and nakedly as possible to get relief.
He seeks to put his grisly obsession into expressive form
the way a bacteriologist seeks to isolate a virus.**

—JOHN DOS PASSOS

**Satire should, like a polish'd razor keen,
Wound with a touch, that's scarcely felt or seen.**

—MARY WORTLEY MONTAGU

Satire is focused bitterness.

—LEO ROSTEN

Satire is a sort of glass, wherein beholders
do generally discover everybody's face but their own.

—JONATHAN SWIFT[*]

The satirist who writes nothing but satire
should write but little—or it will seem that
his satire springs rather from his own caustic nature
than from the sins of the world in which he lives.

—ANTHONY TROLLOPE

Criticizing a political satirist for being unfair
is like criticizing a 260-pound noseguard for being physical.

—GARRY TRUDEAU

Satire is a wrapping of exaggeration around a core of reality.

—BARBARA W. TUCHMAN

A satirist is a man profoundly revolted
by the society in which he lives.
His rage takes the form of wit, ridicule, mockery.

—GORE VIDAL

[*]   *Glass* was the common term for a mirror in the early eighteenth century.

SCIENCE & SCIENTISTS

(see also CURIOSITY and DISCOVERY and FACTS and
KNOWLEDGE and LEARNING and RESEARCH)

When I find myself in the company of scientists,
I feel like a shabby curate who has strayed by mistake
into a drawing room full of dukes.

—W. H. AUDEN

That is the essence of science: ask an impertinent question,
and you are on the way to a pertinent answer.

—JACOB BRONOWSKI

What is a scientist after all?
It is a curious man looking through a keyhole,
the keyhole of nature, trying to know what's going on.

—JACQUES COUSTEAU[*]

A scientist in his laboratory is not only a technician:
he is also a child placed before natural phenomena
which impress him like a fairy tale.

—MARIE CURIE

Equipped with his five senses, man explores the universe
around him and calls the adventure Science.

—EDWIN HUBBLE

---

[*] Arthur Koestler may have been inspired by this line when, in *The Roots of Coincidence*
(1972), he described scientists as "Peeping Toms at the keyhole of eternity."

The great tragedy of Science—
the slaying of a beautiful hypothesis by an ugly fact.

—T. H. HUXLEY

Reason, Observation, and Experience—the Holy Trinity of Science.

—ROBERT G. INGERSOLL

Science has made us gods even before we are worthy of being men.

—JEAN ROSTAND

Modern science has been a voyage into the unknown,
with a lesson in humility waiting at every stop.

—CARL SAGAN

The ideal scientist thinks like a poet
and only later works like a bookkeeper.

—EDWARD O. WILSON

SELF

(see also AUTHENTICITY and INDIVIDUALISM and
INTEGRITY)

The center of the universe is still the self.

—HENRI FRÉDÉRIC AMIEL

Resolve to be thyself; and know, that he
Who finds himself, loses his misery.

—MATTHEW ARNOLD

There is no such flatterer as is a man's self.

—FRANCIS BACON (1561–1626)

We are all serving a life-sentence in the dungeon of self.

—CYRIL CONNOLLY[*]

Maybe being oneself is always an acquired taste.

—PATRICIA HAMPL

There's only one corner of the universe you can be certain
of improving, and that's your own self.

—ALDOUS HUXLEY

The greatest hazard of all, losing one's self, can occur
very quietly in the world, as if it were nothing at all.
No other loss can occur so quietly; any other loss—
an arm, a leg, five dollars, a wife, etc.—is sure to be noticed.

—SØREN KIERKEGAARD

[*] Connolly was likely inspired by the following passage from Nathaniel Hawthorne's *The House of the Seven Gables* (1851): "What other dungeon is so dark as one's own heart? What jailer so inexorable as one's self!"

The self holds both a hell and a heaven.

—LEWIS MUMFORD

**The self is merely the lens through which we see others and the world,
and if this lens is not clear of distortions, we cannot perceive others.**

—ANAÏS NIN

**People often say that this or that person has not yet found himself.
But the self is not something one finds, it is something one creates.**

—THOMAS SZASZ

SELF-DECEPTION

(see also ERROR and ILLUSION and MEMORY and TRUTH
and TRUTH & ERROR)

The man who suspects his own tediousness is yet to be born.

—THOMAS BAILEY ALDRICH

**O wad some Pow'r the giftie gie us
To see oursels as others see us!
It would frae mony a blunder free us,
And foolish notion.**

—ROBERT BURNS[*]

---

[*] From "To a Louse" (1786), this is the origin of the expression "the power to see ourselves as others see us." If God could give us such a gift, Burns was suggesting, it would free us from all kinds of blunders and foolish notions.

Self-deception once yielded to,
all other deceptions follow naturally more and more.

—THOMAS CARLYLE

We are most deeply asleep at the switch
when we fancy we control any switches at all.

—ANNIE DILLARD

No estimate is more in danger of erroneous calculation
than those by which a man computes the force of his own genius.

—SAMUEL JOHNSON

Every stink that fights the ventilator thinks it is Don Quixote.

—STANISLAW JERZY LEC

Men have an extraordinarily erroneous opinion of their position in nature;
and the error is ineradicable.

—W. SOMERSET MAUGHAM

The ingenuity of self-deception is inexhaustible.

—HANNAH MORE

The most common sort of lie is the one uttered to one's self.

—FRIEDRICH NIETZSCHE

We do not deal much in fact when we are contemplating ourselves.

—MARK TWAIN

SELF-PITY

(see also COWARDICE and DIFFICULTIES and SORROW
and SUFFERING)

Self-pity in its early stage is as snug as a feather mattress.
Only when it hardens does it become uncomfortable.

—MAYA ANGELOU

Self-pity is, perhaps, the least becoming of all emotions,
and we often indulge in it only because we are too exhausted to resist.

—IVY BAKER PRIEST

Self-pity dries up our sympathy for others.

—MASON COOLEY

Never feel self-pity, the most destructive emotion there is.
How awful to be caught up in the terrible squirrel cage of self.

—MILLICENT FENWICK

Self-pity is the worst possible emotion anyone can have.
And the most destructive. It destroys everything around it, except itself.

—STEPHEN FRY

Self-pity is easily the most destructive
of the non-pharmaceutical narcotics;
it is addictive, gives momentary pleasure,
and separates the victim from reality.

—JOHN W. GARDNER

I never saw a wild thing
Sorry for itself.
A small bird will drop frozen dead from a bough
Without ever having felt sorry for itself.

—D. H. LAWRENCE

You can never win when you wear the ugly cloak of self-pity,
and the sour sound of whining
will certainly frighten away any opportunity for success.

—OG MANDINO

All depression has its roots in self-pity,
and all self-pity is rooted in people taking themselves too seriously.

—TOM ROBBINS

Shall a man go and hang himself
because he belongs to the race of pygmies,
and not be the biggest pygmy that he can?

—HENRY DAVID THOREAU

SEX [Wise]

(see also KISSES & KISSING and LOVE and MEN &
WOMEN and PASSION and ROMANCE & ROMANTICS and
SEX [Wry & Witty])

Love is music, and sex is only the instrument.

—ISABEL ALLENDE

Sex finds us out. Sex sees through us.
That's why it's so shattering. It strips us of appearances.

—DON DELILLO

The sexual embrace can only be compared with music and with prayer.

—HAVELOCK ELLIS

It is a crossing of a Rubicon in life history.

—PAUL H. GEPHARD, ON ONE'S FIRST SEXUAL INTERCOURSE[*]

---

[*] In 49 BC, when Julius Caesar defied the Roman Senate's orders by crossing the Rubicon river to attack Pompey, he said, "The die is cast." Ever since, *crossing a Rubicon* has been a popular metaphor for an action from which there is no turning back.

Sex is just another form of talk,
where you act the words instead of saying them.

—D. H. LAWRENCE

You mustn't force sex to do the work of love
or love to do the work of sex.

—MARY MCCARTHY

Sex—in actual life—touches the heavens
only when it simultaneously touches the gutter and the mud.

—GEORGE JEAN NATHAN

Sexual union is a holy moment
in which a part of Heaven flows into the Earth.

—JAMES REDFIELD

Sex is a conversation carried out by other means.

—PETER USTINOV[*]

Sex and religion are bordering states.
They use the same vocabulary, share like ecstasies,
and often serve as a substitute for one another.

—JESSAMYN WEST

[*] Ustinov is playing off an observation by Karl von Clausewitz, to be found in WAR.

SEX [Wry & Witty]

(see also KISSES & KISSING and LOVE and MEN &
WOMEN and PASSION and ROMANCE & ROMANTICS and
SEX [Wise])

Sex is the great amateur art.

—DAVID CORT

**For flavor, Instant Sex will never supersede
the stuff you had to peel and cook.**

—QUENTIN CRISP

Sex is identical to comedy in that it involves timing.

—PHYLLIS DILLER

**In a business society, the role of sex can be summed up
in five pitiful little words. There is money in it.**

—MARGARET HALSEY

**I was wondering today what the religion of the country is—
and all I could come up with was sex.**

—CLARE BOOTHE LUCE

It is true I swim in a perpetual sea of sex
but the actual excursions are fairly limited.

—HENRY MILLER

Sex is like art.
Most of it is pretty bad,
and the good stuff is out of your price range.

—SCOTT ROEBEN

Sex is every man's loco spot.

—DOROTHY L. SAYERS

Sex is an emotion in motion.

—MAE WEST

Sex is the Tabasco sauce
which an adolescent national palate
sprinkles on every course in the menu.

—MARY DAY WINN

SILENCE

(see also COMMUNICATION and CONVERSATION and
LISTENING and SOLITUDE and SPEECH)

Thought works in silence, so does virtue.
One might erect statues to silence.

—THOMAS CARLYLE

Silence is the unbearable repartee.

—G. K. CHESTERTON

The silence that accepts merit
as the most natural thing in the world
is the highest applause.

—RALPH WALDO EMERSON

There is an eloquent silence:
it serves sometimes to approve, sometimes to condemn.

—FRANÇOIS, DUC DE LA ROCHEFOUCAULD

Sometimes you have to be silent to be heard.

—STANISLAW JERZY LEC

Silence is one of the great arts of conversation.

—HANNAH MORE

True silence is the rest of the mind;
it is to the spirit, what sleep is to the body,
nourishment and refreshment.

—WILLIAM PENN

A part of all art is to make silence speak.
The things left out in painting, the note withheld in music,
the void in architecture—
all are as necessary and as active as the utterance itself.

—FREYA STARK

The cruelest lies are often told in silence.

—ROBERT LOUIS STEVENSON

To sin by silence when we should protest,
Makes cowards of men.

—ELLA WHEELER WILCOX

SIN

(see also EVIL and ERROR and VICE and VICE & VIRTUE)

All sin tends to be addictive,
and the terminal point of addiction is what is called damnation.

—W. H. AUDEN

One leak will sink a ship: and one sin will destroy a sinner.

—JOHN BUNYAN

Fashions in sin change.

—LILLIAN HELLMAN

We are not punished for our sins, but by them.

—ELBERT HUBBARD

Sin is a queer thing.
It isn't the breaking of divine commandments.
It is the breaking of one's own integrity.

—D. H. LAWRENCE

There's only one real sin,
and that is to persuade oneself that the second-best
is anything but the second-best.

—DORIS LESSING

Sin looks much more terrible to those who look at it
than to those who do it.

—OLIVE SCHREINER

After the first blush of sin comes its indifference.

—HENRY DAVID THOREAU

All sins are attempts to fill voids.

—SIMONE WEIL

There is no sin except stupidity.

—OSCAR WILDE

SLEEP

(see also DREAMS [Nocturnal])

Sleep is forgiveness. The night absolves.
Darkness wipes the slate clean, not spotless to be sure,
but clean enough for another day's chalking.

—FREDERICK BUECHNER

Sleep and waking states are like separate countries with a common border.
We cross over twice daily,
remembering one world and forgetting the other,
inadvertently tracking invisible residues from one into the other.

—KAT DUFF

Finish each day before you begin the next,
and interpose a solid wall of sleep between the two.

—RALPH WALDO EMERSON

When every inch of the world is known,
sleep may be the only wilderness that we have left.

—LOUISE ERDRICH

Sleep is when all the unsorted stuff comes flying out
as from a dustbin upset in a high wind.

—WILLIAM GOLDING

Sleep is the best meditation.

—TENZIN GYATSO, THE FOURTEENTH DALAI LAMA

That we are not much sicker and much madder than we are is due
exclusively to that most blessed and blessing of all natural graces, sleep.

—ALDOUS HUXLEY

And if tonight my soul may find her peace
In sleep, and sink in good oblivion,
And in the morning wake like a new-opened flower
Then I have been dipped again in God, and new-created.

—D. H. LAWRENCE

It is a common experience that a problem difficult at night
is resolved in the morning after the committee of sleep has worked on it.

—JOHN STEINBECK

Sleeplessness is a desert without vegetation or inhabitants.

—JESSAMYN WEST

SOLITUDE

(see also LONELINESS and SILENCE)

Solitude is that human situation in which I keep myself company.

—HANNAH ARENDT

I love people. I love my family, my children . . .
but inside myself is a place where I live all alone
and that's where you renew your springs that never dry up.

—PEARL S. BUCK

To a heart formed for friendship and affection
the charms of solitude are very short-lived.

—FANNY BURNEY

There are days when solitude, for someone my age,
is a heady wine which intoxicates you with freedom,
others when it is a bitter tonic,
and still others when it is a poison that
makes you beat your head against the wall.

—COLETTE (SIDONIE-GABRIELLE COLETTE)

These are the voices which we hear in solitude,
but they grow faint and inaudible as we enter into the world.

—RALPH WALDO EMERSON

Solitude is as needful to the imagination
as society is wholesome for the character.

—JAMES RUSSELL LOWELL

Solitude gives birth to the original in us,
to beauty unfamiliar and perilous—to poetry.
But also, it gives birth to the opposite:
to the perverse, the illicit, the absurd.

—THOMAS MANN

One can acquire everything in solitude except character.

—STENDHAL (MARIE-HENRI BEYLE)

I never found the companion that was so companionable as solitude.

—HENRY DAVID THOREAU

Our language has wisely sensed these two sides of man's being alone.
It has created the word "loneliness" to express the pain of being alone.
And it has created the word "solitude" to express the glory of being alone.

—PAUL TILLICH

SORROW

(see also GRIEF & GRIEVING and PAIN and SUFFERING)

There is something pleasurable in calm remembrance of a past sorrow.

—MARCUS TULLIUS CICERO

All sorrows can be borne if you put them into a story
or tell a story about them.

—ISAK DINESEN (KAREN BLIXEN)

Sorrow has its reward.
It never leaves us where it found us.

—MARY BAKER EDDY

I have been in Sorrow's kitchen and licked out all the pots.
Then I have stood on the peaky mountain wrapped in rainbows,
with a harp and a sword in my hands.

—ZORA NEALE HURSTON

The sorrow for the dead is the only sorrow
from which we refuse to be divorced.
Every other wound, we seek to heal—every other affliction to forget;
but this wound we consider it a duty to keep open—
this affliction we cherish and brood over in solitude.

—WASHINGTON IRVING

In this sad world of ours, sorrow comes to all;
and, to the young, it comes with bitterest agony,
because it takes them unawares.

—ABRAHAM LINCOLN

Believe me, every heart has his secret sorrows
which the world knows not,
and oftentimes we call a man cold, when he is only sad.

—HENRY WADSWORTH LONGFELLOW[*]

Sorrow is so easy to express and yet so hard to tell.

—JONI MITCHELL

When sorrows come, they come not single spies,
But in battalions.

—WILLIAM SHAKESPEARE

Where there is sorrow there is holy ground.

—OSCAR WILDE

SPEECH

(see also COMMUNICATION and CONVERSATION and
LANGUAGE and UNDERSTANDING)

Eloquent speech is not from lip to ear,
but rather from heart to heart.

—WILLIAM JENNINGS BRYAN

---

[*] Many Internet sites and published reference works mistakenly contain the phrase "every man" instead of "every heart."

I learn immediately from any speaker how much he has already lived,
through the poverty or the splendor of his speech.

—RALPH WALDO EMERSON

The true use of speech is not so much
to express our wants as to conceal them.

—OLIVER GOLDSMITH

Speak clearly, if you speak at all;
Carve every word before you let it fall.

—OLIVER WENDELL HOLMES SR.

It is amazing how much a thought expands
and refines by being put into speech:
I should think it could hardly know itself.

—L. E. LANDON

Lucidity of speech is unquestionably
one of the surest tests of mental precision.

—DAVID LLOYD GEORGE

Speech belongs half to the speaker, half to the listener.

—MICHEL DE MONTAIGNE

Speech is a kind of action.

—SOCRATES

All speech, written or spoken, is a dead language,
until it finds a willing and prepared hearer.

—ROBERT LOUIS STEVENSON

Speech is a mirror of the soul; as a man speaks, so is he.

—PUBLILIUS SYRUS

SPORT

(see also DEFEAT and FAILURE and PLAY and VICTORY
and VICTORY & DEFEAT)

In America, it is sport that is the opiate of the masses.

—RUSSELL BAKER

Sport is something that does not matter,
but is performed as if it did.
In that contradiction lies its beauty.

—SIMON BARNES

Sports do not build character. They reveal it.

—HEYWOOD HALE BROUN

What I know most surely about morality
and the duty of man I owe to sport.

—ALBERT CAMUS

Sports is the toy department of life.

—JIMMY CANNON

Giving your body a chance to exult, however you choose to do it,
is the essence of sport.

—ROBIN CHOTZINOFF

Everything about sport is derived from the hunt:
there is no sport in existence that does not base itself either on
the chase or on aiming, the two key elements of primeval hunting.

—DESMOND MORRIS

Serious sport has nothing to do with fair play.
It is bound up with hatred, jealousy, boastfulness,
disregard of all rules and sadistic pleasure in witnessing violence:
in other words, it is war minus the shooting.

—GEORGE ORWELL

Beauty is not the goal of competitive sports,
but high-level sports are a prime venue for the expression of human beauty.
The relation is roughly that of courage to war.

—DAVID FOSTER WALLACE

Greek philosophers considered sport
a religious and civic—in a word, moral—undertaking.
Sport, they said, is morally serious because mankind's noblest aim
is the loving contemplation of worthy things, such as beauty or courage.

—GEORGE F. WILL

STRUGGLE

(see also ADVERSITY and DIFFICULTIES and PAIN and
PROBLEMS and SUFFERING)

The struggle itself toward the heights
is enough to fill a man's heart.
One must imagine Sisyphus happy.

—ALBERT CAMUS[*]

It's better to lose some of the battles in the struggles for your dreams
than to be defeated without ever knowing what you're fighting for.

—PAULO COELHO

One day, in retrospect, the years of struggle
will strike you as the most beautiful.

—SIGMUND FREUD

It is wrong to expect a reward for your struggles.
The reward is the act of struggle itself, not what you win.

—PHIL OCHS

The struggle alone pleases us, not the victory. . . .
We never seek things for themselves, but for the search.

—BLAISE PASCAL

---

[*]   These are the concluding words of Camus's famous philosophical essay *The Myth of Sisyphus* (1942).

We take no delight in existence except when
we are struggling for something.

—ARTHUR SCHOPENHAUER

The battle of life is,
in most cases, fought uphill;
and to win it without a struggle were,
perhaps, to win it without honor.

—SAMUEL SMILES

I've never forgotten for long at a time that living is struggle.
I know that every good and excellent thing in the world stands
moment by moment on the razor-edge of danger and must be
fought for——whether it's a field, or a home, or a country.

—THORNTON WILDER

Once you fully apprehend the vacuity of a life without struggle
you are equipped with the basic means of salvation.

—TENNESSEE WILLIAMS

Nothing, I am sure, calls forth the faculties
so much as the being obliged to struggle with the world.

—MARY WOLLSTONECRAFT

STUPIDITY

(see also FOLLY and FOOLS & FOOLISHNESS and
IGNORANCE)

Stupidity is the same as evil if you judge by the results.

—MARGARET ATWOOD

Readiness to answer all questions is the infallible sign of stupidity.

—SAUL BELLOW

**What distresses me is to see that human genius has limits
and human stupidity none.**

—ALEXANDRE DUMAS, FILS[*]

Nature delights in punishing stupid people.

—RALPH WALDO EMERSON

Stupidity's the deliberate cultivation of ignorance.

—WILLIAM GADDIS

**We never really know what stupidity is
until we have experimented on ourselves.**

—PAUL GAUGUIN

---

[*] Written around 1865, this is history's first observation suggesting that, when compared
with genius (or intelligence), stupidity has no limits—a sentiment repeated by many,
many others in subsequent years.

A sinner can reform, but stupid is forever.

—ALAN JAY LERNER[*]

A stupid person's notions and feelings
may confidently be inferred from those which prevail
in the circle by which the person is surrounded.

—JOHN STUART MILL

The fundamental cause of the trouble is that in the modern world
the stupid are cocksure while the intelligent are full of doubt.

—BERTRAND RUSSELL

Against stupidity the gods
Themselves contend in vain.

—FRIEDRICH VON SCHILLER

SUCCESS

(see also DEFEAT and FAILURE and SUCCESS & FAILURE
and VICTORY and VICTORY & DEFEAT)

Success is sweet, the sweeter if long delayed
and attained through manifold struggles and defeats.

—A. BRONSON ALCOTT

---

[*] A 1969 *Washington Post* article attributes this quotation to Lerner. He appears to be the
original author of the saying "stupid is forever," now a modern proverb.

Success is full of promise till men get it;
and then it is a last year's nest from which the bird has flown.

—HENRY WARD BEECHER

Success took me to her bosom like a maternal boa constrictor.

—NOËL COWARD

Success is counted sweetest
By those who ne'er succeed.

—EMILY DICKINSON

Success is a lousy teacher.
It seduces smart people into thinking they can't lose.

—BILL GATES

Once we find the fruits of success,
the taste is nothing like what we had anticipated.

—WILLIAM RALPH INGE

Every success is usually an admission ticket to a new set of decisions.

—HENRY KISSINGER

There is no deodorant like success.

—ELIZABETH TAYLOR

I have learned that success is to be measured not so much
by the position that one has reached in life
as by the obstacles which he has overcome while trying to succeed.

—BOOKER T. WASHINGTON

One day it happens. Success happens and it catches you by surprise.
One day you are a signature, next day, you are an autograph.

—BILLY WILDER

SUCCESS & FAILURE

(see also DEFEAT and FAILURE and SUCCESS and
VICTORY and VICTORY & DEFEAT)

We mount to heaven
mostly on the ruins of our cherished schemes,
finding our failures were successes.

—A. BRONSON ALCOTT

Nothing fails like success because we don't learn from it.
We learn only from failure.

—KENNETH E. BOULDING

A minute's success pays the failure of years.

—ROBERT BROWNING

Failure is the condiment that gives success its flavor.

—TRUMAN CAPOTE

Success is more dangerous than failure,
the ripples break over a wider coastline.

—GRAHAM GREENE

Failure is the foundation of success,
and the means by which it is achieved.
Success is the lurking place of failure;
but who can tell when the turning-place will come?

—LAO-TZU

Pursue failure.
Failure is success's only launching pad.

—TOM PETERS

Success is a public affair. Failure is a private funeral.

—ROSALIND RUSSELL

Success and failure—we think of them as opposites, but they're really not.
They're companions—the hero and the sidekick.

—LAURENCE SHAMES

Success is never final and failure is never fatal.

—GEORGE F. TILTON

SUFFERING

(see also ADVERSITY and DIFFICULTIES and ILLNESS
and PAIN and PROBLEMS and TROUBLE)

**When suffering knocks at your door and you say there is no seat for him,
he tells you not to worry because he has brought his own stool.**

—CHINUA ACHEBE

**You desire to know the art of living, my friend?
It is contained in one phrase: make use of suffering.**

—HENRI FRÉDÉRIC AMIEL

Suffering isn't ennobling, recovery is.

—CHRISTIAAN BARNARD

**Out of suffering have emerged the strongest souls;
the most massive characters are seamed with scars.**

—E. H. CHAPIN[*]

**Deep, unspeakable suffering may well be called a baptism,
a regeneration, the initiation into a new state.**

—GEORGE ELIOT

---

[*]   This quotation, but with *seared* instead of *seamed*, was mistakenly attributed to Kahlil
Gibran in *The Treasured Writings of Kahlil Gibran* (1995). Ever since, almost all quotation
anthologies have repeated the error.

The task is to *use* our suffering
and to use it so well that we can use it up.

—ALFRED KAZIN

I do not believe that sheer suffering teaches.
If suffering alone taught, all the world would be wise,
since everyone suffers.
To suffering must be added mourning, understanding, patience, love,
openness, and the willingness to remain vulnerable.

—ANNE MORROW LINDBERGH

The scene of suffering is a scene of joy when the suffering is past;
and the silent reminiscence of hardships departed,
is sweeter than the presence of delight

—HERMAN MELVILLE

Suffering is universal,
suffering is that which unites all us living beings together;
it is the universal or divine blood that flows through us all.

—MIGUEL DE UNAMUNO

Suffering is also one of the ways of knowing you're alive.

—JESSAMYN WEST

TACT

(see also COMMUNICATION and KINDNESS and
RELATIONSHIPS)

**The austere principles of tact
tell the tongue to keep away from the aching thought.**

—ELIZABETH BIBESCO

**Silence is not always tact,
and it is tact that is golden, not silence.**

—SAMUEL BUTLER (1835–1902)

Tact consists in knowing how far to go in going too far.

—JEAN COCTEAU

Tact is good taste in action.

—DIANE DE POITIERS

**Don't flatter yourselves that friendship
authorizes you to say disagreeable things to your intimates.
On the contrary, the nearer you come into relation with a person,
the more necessary do tact and courtesy become.**

—OLIVER WENDELL HOLMES SR.

Tact is after all a kind of mind-reading.

—SARAH ORNE JEWETT

In the battle of existence, Talent is the punch;
Tact is the clever footwork.

—WILSON MIZNER

Tact is not only kindness, but kindness skillfully extended.

—J. G. RANDALL

Although tact is a virtue, it is very closely allied to certain vices;
the line between tact and hypocrisy is a very narrow one.
I think the distinction comes in the motive.

—BERTRAND RUSSELL

Tact does for life just what lubricating oil does for machinery.
It makes the wheels run smoothly, and without it
there is a great deal of friction and the possibility of a breakdown.

—LAURA INGALLS WILDER

TALENT

(see also ABILITY and DISCIPLINE and EXCELLENCE and
GENIUS and MEDIOCRITY and TALENT & GENIUS)

Talent is like electricity.
We don't understand electricity. We use it.

—MAYA ANGELOU

Talented people almost always know full well
the excellence that is in them.

—CHARLOTTE BRONTË

Ideas are a capital that bears interest only in the hands of talent.

—ANTOINE DE RIVAROL

A true talent delights the possessor first.

—RALPH WALDO EMERSON

If you have a talent, use it in every way possible.
Don't hoard it. Don't dole it out like a miser.
Spend it lavishly like a millionaire intent on going broke.

—BRENDAN FRANCIS (EDWARD F. MURPHY)

Well-matured and well-disciplined talent is always sure of a market,
provided it exerts itself;
but it must not cower at home and expect to be sought for.

—WASHINGTON IRVING

Great talents are the most lovely
and often the most dangerous fruits on the tree of humanity.
They hang upon the most slender twigs that are easily snapped off.

—CARL JUNG

You cannot define talent.
All you can do is build the greenhouse and see if it grows.

—WILLIAM P. STEVEN

Talent is cheap; dedication is expensive.

—IRVING STONE

If a man has a talent and cannot use it, he has failed.
If he has a talent and uses only half of it, he has partly failed.
If he has a talent and learns somehow to use the whole of it,
he has gloriously succeeded,
and won a satisfaction and a triumph few men ever know.

—THOMAS WOLFE

TALENT & GENIUS

(see also ABILITY and DISCIPLINE and EXCELLENCE and
GENIUS and MEDIOCRITY and TALENT)

To do easily what is difficult for others is the mark of talent.
To do what is impossible for talent is the mark of genius.

—HENRI FRÉDÉRIC AMIEL

Genius makes its observations in shorthand;
talent writes them out at length.

—CHRISTIAN NESTELL BOVEE

Mediocrity knows nothing higher than itself;
but talent instantly recognizes genius.

—ARTHUR CONAN DOYLE

Genius is the gold in the mine;
talent is the miner who works and brings it out.

—MARGUERITE GARDINER (LADY BLESSINGTON)

Talent is a docile creature.
It bows its head meekly while the world slips the collar over it. . . .
But genius is always impatient of its harness;
its wild blood makes it hard to train.

—OLIVER WENDELL HOLMES SR.

The discovery of truth by slow, progressive meditation is talent.
Intuition of the truth, not preceded by perceptible meditation, is genius.

—JOHANN KASPAR LAVATER

Talent is that which is in a man's power;
genius is that in whose power a man is.

—JAMES RUSSELL LOWELL

Talent is a tenant in the house owned by genius.

—AUSTIN O'MALLEY

Talent is like the marksman who hits a target which others cannot reach;
genius is like the marksman who hits a target . . . others cannot even see.

—ARTHUR SCHOPENHAUER[*]

---

[*] This is a faithful translation of the original thought; almost all Internet quotation sites
now present a briefer and more liberal rendering: "Talent hits a target no one else can hit.
Genius hits a target no one else can see."

Genius is talent exercised with courage.

—LUDWIG WITTGENSTEIN

TEACHERS & TEACHING

(see also CURIOSITY and DISCOVERY and EDUCATION
and KNOWLEDGE and LEARNING)

A teacher affects eternity;
he can never tell where his influence stops.

—HENRY BROOKS ADAMS

Have you ever really had a teacher?
One who saw you as a raw but precious thing,
a jewel that, with wisdom, could be polished to a proud shine?

—MITCH ALBOM

The whole art of teaching is only the art of
awakening the natural curiosity of young minds
for the purpose of satisfying it afterwards.

—ANATOLE FRANCE

Good teaching is one-fourth preparation and three-fourths theater.

—GAIL GODWIN

To teach is to learn twice.

—JOSEPH JOUBERT

A teacher who is attempting to teach
without inspiring the pupil with a desire to learn,
is hammering on cold iron.

—HORACE MANN

We teachers can only help the work going on,
as servants wait upon a master.

—MARIA MONTESSORI

Teaching is an act of love,
a spiritual cohabitation,
one of the few sacred relationships left
in a crass secular world.

—THEODORE ROETHKE

The art of teaching is the art of assisting discovery to take place.

—MARK VAN DOREN

Teaching is the royal road to learning.

—JESSAMYN WEST

TECHNOLOGY

(see also COMPUTERS and INTERNET & WORLD WIDE
WEB and SCIENCE & SCIENTISTS and TELEVISION)

Technology, like art,
is a soaring exercise of the human imagination.

—DANIEL BELL

Any sufficiently advanced technology
is indistinguishable from magic.

—ARTHUR C. CLARKE

Shortly after the turn of the [20th] century,
America marshaled her resources,
contracted painfully, and gave birth to the New Technology.
The father was a corporation,
and the New Technology grew up in the Corporate image.

—ALICE EMBREE

Technology . . . the knack of so arranging the world
that we need not experience it.

—MAX FRISCH

The acceleration of technological progress has created
an urgent need for a counter ballast—for high-touch experience.

—JOHN NAISBITT

We live in a society exquisitely dependent on science and technology,
in which hardly anyone knows anything about science and technology.
This is a clear prescription for disaster.

—CARL SAGAN

Technology . . . is a queer thing.
It brings you great gifts with one hand,
and it stabs you in the back with the other.

—C. P. SNOW

That great, growling engine of change—technology.

—ALVIN TOFFLER

Technology doesn't just do things for us.
It does things to us,
changing not just what we do but who we are.

—SHERRY TURKLE

The most profound technologies are those that disappear.
They weave themselves into the fabric of everyday life
until they are indistinguishable from it.

—MARK WEISER

TELEVISION

(see also COMMUNICATION and INTERNET & WORLD
WIDE WEB and TECHNOLOGY)

It is our latest medium—we call it a medium because nothing's well done.

—GOODMAN ACE, A 1953 REMARK ABOUT TELEVISION

The illusion of companionship sits waiting in the television set.
We keep our televisions on . . . an average of more than seven hours a day.
For background. For company.

—LOUISE BERNIKOW

Some television programs are so much chewing gum for the eyes.

—JOHN MASON BROWN, QUOTING HIS SON'S FRIEND

Television's perfect.
You turn a few knobs . . . and lean back and drain your mind of all thought. . .
You don't have to concentrate . . . to react . . . to remember.
You don't miss your brain because you don't need it.

—RAYMOND CHANDLER

Television is not the truth. Television's a goddamned amusement park.
Television is a circus, a carnival, a traveling troupe of
acrobats, storytellers, dancers, singers, jugglers,
sideshow freaks, lion tamers, and football players.
We're in the boredom-killing business.

—PADDY CHAYEFSKY

It is a medium of entertainment which permits
millions of people to listen to the same joke at the same time,
and yet remain lonesome.

—T. S. ELIOT, ON TELEVISION

Television is an invention that permits you to be entertained in your
living room by people you wouldn't have in your home.

—DAVID FROST

I wish all televisions would come with
a warning from the Surgeon General:
"Overuse of this medium may hinder the development of healthy
interpersonal relationships, retard the growth of neural connections,
diminish creativity, and foster poor family communication."

—MARY HEER-FORSBERG

In television, images are projected at you.
You are the screen.

—MARSHALL MCLUHAN

Television was not intended to make humans vacuous;
but it is an emanation of their vacuity.

—MALCOLM MUGGERIDGE

TEMPTATION

(see also SIN and VICE and VICE & VIRTUE and VIRTUE)

**Watch and pray, that ye enter not into temptation:
the spirit indeed is willing, but the flesh is weak.**

—THE BIBLE, MATTHEW 26:41[*]

**It is good to be without vices,
but it is not good to be without temptations.**

—WALTER BAGEHOT

Temptations are enemies outside the castle seeking entrance.

—HENRY WARD BEECHER

**We've all of us got to meet the devil alone.
Temptation is a lonely business.**

—MARGARET DELAND

**As the Sandwich Islander believes
that the strength and valor of the enemy he kills passes into himself,
so we gain the strength of the temptation we resist.**

—RALPH WALDO EMERSON

[*]   This is the origin of the popular proverb "The spirit is willing, but the flesh is weak."

Integrity which has been attacked by no temptation can at best
be considered but as gold not yet brought to the test,
of which therefore the true value cannot be assigned.

—SAMUEL JOHNSON

"Every man has his price." This is not true.
But for every man there exists a bait which he cannot resist swallowing.

—FRIEDRICH NIETZSCHE

Where there is no temptation, there is no virtue.

—AGNES REPPLIER

Temptation almost always assails us at the point
where we thought no defense necessary.

—ELIZABETH ELTON SMITH

I can resist everything except temptation.

—OSCAR WILDE

THINKING & THINKERS

(see also BRAIN and IDEAS and MIND and THOUGHT)

To think and to be fully alive are the same.

—HANNAH ARENDT

Every thinker puts some portion of an apparently stable world in peril
and no one can wholly predict what will emerge in its place.

—JOHN DEWEY

Thinking in its lower grades is comparable to paper money,
and in its higher forms it is a kind of poetry.

—HAVELOCK ELLIS

Beware when the great God lets loose a thinker on this planet.
Then all things are at risk.

—RALPH WALDO EMERSON

A moment's thinking is an hour in words.

—THOMAS HOOD

Thinking is the endeavor to capture reality by the means of ideas.

—JOSÉ ORTEGA Y GASSET

Man is only a reed, the weakest in nature, but he is a thinking reed.

—BLAISE PASCAL

People get wisdom from thinking, not from learning.

—LAURA RIDING

When the mind is thinking, is it simply talking to itself,
asking questions and answering them, and saying yes or no.

—SOCRATES

To have ideas is to gather flowers.
To think is to weave them into garlands.

—ANNE SOPHIE SWETCHINE

THOUGHT

(see also ACTION and BRAIN and IDEAS and MIND and
THINKING & THINKERS)

If we were all on trial for our thoughts,
we would all be hanged.

—MARGARET ATWOOD

Such as are your habitual thoughts,
such also will be the character of your mind;
for the soul is dyed by the thoughts.

—MARCUS AURELIUS

Thought once awakened does not again slumber.

—THOMAS CARLYLE[*]

One great thought breathed into a man may regenerate him.

—WILLIAM ELLERY CHANNING

---

[*]   Zora Neale Hurston was almost certainly inspired by this Carlyle observation when she
wrote in *Moses: Man of the Mountain* (1939): "Once you wake up thought in a man, you
can never put it to sleep again."

The revelation of Thought takes men out of servitude into Freedom.

—RALPH WALDO EMERSON

Conversation is the legs on which thought walks;
and writing, the wings by which it flies.

—MARGUERITE GARDINER (LADY BLESSINGTON)

There are thoughts which are prayers.
There are moments when, whatever the posture of the body,
the soul is on its knees.

—VICTOR HUGO[*]

Thoughts, like fleas, jump from man to man.
But they don't bite everybody.

—STANISLAW JERZY LEC

Associate reverently and as much as you can with your loftiest thoughts.

—HENRY DAVID THOREAU

Life does not consist mainly—or even largely—
of facts and happenings.
It consists mainly of the storm of thoughts
that is forever blowing through one's mind.

—MARK TWAIN

[*]   See the similar observation by G. E. Lessing in PRAYER.

TIME

(see also AGE & AGING and FUTURE and PAST)

Time is a dressmaker specializing in alterations.

—FAITH BALDWIN

**Time is a great teacher,
but unfortunately it kills all its pupils.**

—HECTOR BERLIOZ

Time is the reef upon which all of our frail mystic ships are wrecked.

—NOËL COWARD

**Time will explain it all.
He is a talker, and needs no questioning before he speaks.**

—EURIPIDES

**Dost thou love life?
Then do not squander time,
for that's the stuff life is made of.**

—BENJAMIN FRANKLIN

Time, the subtle thief of youth.

—JOHN MILTON

Time is the coin of your life.
You spend it.
Do not allow others to spend it for you.

—CARL SANDBURG

Time is but the stream I go a-fishing in.
I drink at it; but while I drink
I see the sandy bottom and detect how shallow it is.

—HENRY DAVID THOREAU

I wasted time, and now doth time waste me.

—WILLIAM SHAKESPEARE

The innocent and the beautiful
Have no enemy but time.

—WILLIAM BUTLER YEATS

TRAVEL

(see also ADVENTURE and CURIOSITY and DISCOVERY)

Travel, in the younger sort, is a part of education;
in the elder, a part of experience.

—FRANCIS BACON (1561–1626)

Certainly, travel is more than the seeing of sights;
it is a change that goes on,
deep and permanent, in the ideas of living.

—MIRIAM BEARD

The whole object of travel is not to set foot on foreign land;
it is at last to set foot on one's own country as a foreign land.

—G. K. CHESTERTON

To lose your prejudices you must travel.

—MARLENE DIETRICH

Some travelers are drawn forward by a goal lying before them
in the way iron is drawn to the magnet.
Others are driven on by a force lying behind them.
In such a way the bowstring makes the arrow fly.

—ISAK DINESEN (KAREN BLIXEN)

Travel can be one of the most rewarding forms of introspection.

—LAWRENCE DURRELL

Though we travel the world over to find the beautiful,
we must carry it with us, or we find it not.

—RALPH WALDO EMERSON

We travel to learn; and I have never been in any country
where they did not do something better than we do it,
think some thoughts better than we think,
catch some inspiration from heights above our own.

—MARIA MITCHELL

Travel is fatal to prejudice, bigotry, and narrow-mindedness,
and many of our people need it sorely on these accounts.

—MARK TWAIN

We travel not to discover new lands or new people, but new selves . . .
the textbook to be studied is you, yourself,
not the country through which you travel.

—JESSAMYN WEST

TROUBLE

(see also ADVERSITY and DIFFICULTIES and
OBSTACLES and PROBLEMS and SUFFERING)

To run away from trouble is a form of cowardice.

—ARISTOTLE

The art of living lies less in eliminating our troubles
than in growing with them.

—BERNARD M. BARUCH

The methods by which men
have met and conquered trouble, or been slain by it,
are the same in every age. Some have floated on the sea,
and trouble carried them on its surface as the sea carries cork.
Some have sunk at once to the bottom as foundering ships sink.
Some have run away from their own thoughts.
Some have coiled themselves up into a stoical indifference.
Some have braved the trouble, and defied it.
Some have carried it as a tree does a wound,
until by new wood it can overgrow and cover the old gash.

—HENRY WARD BEECHER

The way out of trouble is never as simple as the way in.

—EDGAR WATSON HOWE

Do you not see how necessary a world of pains and troubles
is to school an intelligence and make it a soul?

—JOHN KEATS

Borrow trouble for yourself, if that's your nature,
but don't lend it to your neighbors.

—RUDYARD KIPLING

Expect trouble as an inevitable part of life and, when it comes,
hold your head high, look it squarely in the eye and say,
"I will be bigger than you. You cannot defeat me."

—ANN LANDERS

Every good thing that comes is accompanied by trouble.

—MAXWELL PERKINS

Whether 'tis nobler in the mind to suffer
The slings and arrows of outrageous fortune,
Or to take arms against a sea of troubles,
And by opposing end them?

—WILLIAM SHAKESPEARE

Half the trouble in life is caused by pretending there isn't any.

—EDITH WHARTON

TRUTH

(see also ERROR and TRUTH & ERROR)

Every truth has two sides;
it is well to look at both before we commit ourselves to either.

—AESOP

Ye shall know the truth, and the truth shall make you free.

—THE BIBLE, JOHN 8:32[*]

---

[*] Few passages in history are more widely quoted—or more widely tweaked. The best
spin-off comes from Herbert Agar's *A Time For Greatness* (1942): "The truth which makes
men free is for the most part the truth which men prefer not to hear."

There are two kinds of truth:
the truth that lights the way and the truth that warms the heart.
The first of these is science, and the second is art.

—RAYMOND CHANDLER

Truth is a river that is always splitting up into arms that reunite.
Islanded between the arms
the inhabitants argue for a lifetime as to which is the main river.

—CYRIL CONNOLLY

Whoever undertakes to set himself up as judge in the field of Truth
and Knowledge is shipwrecked by the laughter of the gods.

—ALBERT EINSTEIN

Wherever the truth is injured, defend it.

—RALPH WALDO EMERSON

Who speaks the truth stabs Falsehood to the heart.

—JAMES RUSSELL LOWELL

Truth often suffers more by the heat of its defenders
than from the arguments of its opposers.

—WILLIAM PENN

The truth knocks on the door
and you say, "Go away, I'm looking for the truth,"
and so it goes away. Puzzling.

—ROBERT M. PIRSIG

The best mind-altering drug is truth.

—JANE WAGNER

TRUTH & ERROR

(see also ERROR and FOLLY and MISTAKES and TRUTH)

An error is the more dangerous in proportion to
the degree of truth which it contains.

—HENRI FRÉDÉRIC AMIEL

Truth emerges more readily from error than confusion.

—FRANCIS BACON (1561–1626)

It seems, indeed, a necessary weakness of our mind
to be able to reach truth
only across a multitude of errors and obstacles.

—CLAUDE BERNARD

There is no such source of error as the pursuit of absolute truth.

—SAMUEL BUTLER (1835–1902)

Error is to truth as sleep is to waking.
I have observed that one turns,
as if refreshed, from error back to truth.

—JOHANN WOLFGANG VON GOETHE

To rise from error to truth is rare and beautiful.

—VICTOR HUGO

The study of error is not only in the highest degree prophylactic,
but it serves as a stimulating introduction to the study of truth.

—WALTER LIPPMANN

It is one thing to show a man that he is in an error,
and another to put him in possession of the truth.

—JOHN LOCKE

It is error only, and not truth, that shrinks from inquiry.

—THOMAS PAINE

Truth burns up error.

—SOJOURNER TRUTH

UNDERSTANDING

(see also DISCOVERY and KNOWLEDGE and LEARNING
and UNDERSTANDING OTHERS and WISDOM)

If you only hear one side of the story,
you have no understanding at all.

—CHINUA ACHEBE

I shall light a candle of understanding in thine heart,
which shall not be put out.

—APOCRYPHA, 2 ESDRAS 14:25

I'm not a speed reader.
I'm a speed understander.

—ISAAC ASIMOV

The human understanding is like a false mirror which . . . distorts and
discolors the nature of things by mingling its own nature with it.

—FRANCIS BACON (1561–1626)

The goal of education is disciplined understanding.

—JEROME S. BRUNER

Nothing in life is to be feared. It is only to be understood.

—MARIE CURIE

We can sometimes love what we do not understand,
but it is impossible completely to understand what we do not love.

—ANNA JAMESON

Shallow understanding from people of good will is more frustrating
than absolute misunderstanding from people of ill will.

—MARTIN LUTHER KING JR.

No one has ever taken the trouble to stretch
and carry his understanding as far as it could go.

—FRANÇOIS, DUC DE LA ROCHEFOUCAULD

It is difficult to get a man to understand something,
when his salary depends upon his not understanding it.

—UPTON SINCLAIR

UNDERSTANDING OTHERS

(see also COMMUNICATION and LISTENING and
RELATIONSHIPS and UNDERSTANDING)

To be misunderstood even by those whom one loves
is the cross and bitterness of life.

—HENRI FRÉDÉRIC AMIEL

The heart of another is a dark forest, always,
no matter how close it has been to one's own.

—WILLA CATHER

All persons are puzzles until at last we find
in some word or act the key to the man, to the woman;
straightway all their past words and actions lie in light before us.

—RALPH WALDO EMERSON

We do know that no one gets wise enough
to really understand the heart of another,
though it is the task of our life to try.

—LOUISE ERDRICH

In the sick room, ten cents' worth of human understanding
equals ten dollars' worth of medical science.

—MARTIN H. FISCHER

If one does not understand a person, one tends to regard him as a fool.

—CARL JUNG

You never really understand a person
until you consider things from his point of view—
until you climb into his skin and walk around in it.

—HARPER LEE

You have to be grown up, really grown up,
not merely in years, to understand your parents.

—DORIS LESSING

How can you expect a man who's warm to understand one who's cold?

—ALEXANDER SOLZHENITSYN

I wonder if we are all wrong about each other,
if we are just composing unwritten novels about the people we meet?

—REBECCA WEST

VANITY

(see also HUMILITY and SELF-DECEPTION and VICE and
VICE & VIRTUE)

A desire to be observed, considered, esteemed,
praised, beloved, and admired by his fellows
is one of the earliest as well as the keenest dispositions
discovered in the heart of man.

—JOHN ADAMS

Vanity working on a weak head produces every sort of mischief.

—JANE AUSTEN

Nothing is so agonizing to the fine skin of vanity
as the application of a rough truth!

—EDWARD GEORGE BULWER-LYTTON

Vanity plays lurid tricks with our memory.

—JOSEPH CONRAD

The most violent passions sometimes leave us at rest,
but vanity agitates us constantly.

—FRANÇOIS, DUC DE LA ROCHEFOUCAULD

There is scarcely any fault in another which offends us more than vanity,
though perhaps there is none that really injures us so little.

—HANNAH MORE

Everyone has his vanity, and each one's vanity
is his forgetting that there are others with an equal soul.

—FERNANDO PESSOA

Vanity dies hard; in some obstinate cases it outlives the man.

—ROBERT LOUIS STEVENSON

Let us thank God for imparting to us, poor weak mortals,
the inestimable blessing of vanity.
How many half-witted votaries of the arts—
poets, painters, actors, musicians—
live upon this food, and scarcely any other!

—WILLIAM MAKEPEACE THACKERAY

There are no grades of vanity,
there are only grades of ability in concealing it.

—MARK TWAIN

VICE

(see also CONSCIENCE and EVIL and SIN and VICE &
VIRTUE and VIRTUE)

It is only in some corner of the brain
which we leave empty that Vice can obtain a lodging.

—EDWARD GEORGE BULWER-LYTTON

So in the wicked there's no vice
Of which the saints have not a spice.

—SAMUEL BUTLER (1613–1680)

Half the vices which the world condemns most loudly
have seeds of good in them
and require moderate use rather than total abstinence.

—SAMUEL BUTLER (1835–1902)

Vice knows she's ugly,
so puts on her Mask.

—BENJAMIN FRANKLIN*

The vices of the rich and great are mistaken for errors,
and those of the poor and lowly for crimes.

—MARGUERITE GARDINER (LADY BLESSINGTON)

When our vices leave us,
we flatter ourselves that we leave them.

—FRANÇOIS, DUC DE LA ROCHEFOUCAULD

* This thought from a 1746 issue of *Poor Richard's Almanack* was almost certainly "borrowed" from Thomas Fuller, who wrote in *Gnomologia* (1732): "Vice would be frightful if
it did not wear a mask."

Astronomy was born of superstition;
eloquence of ambition, hatred, falsehood, and flattery;
geometry of avarice;
physics of an idle curiosity;
and even moral philosophy of human pride.
Thus the arts and sciences owe their birth to our vices.

—JEAN-JACQUES ROUSSEAU

Some, either from being glued to vice by a natural attachment,
or from long habit,
no longer recognize its ugliness.

—MICHEL DE MONTAIGNE

The gods are just, and of our pleasant vices
Make instruments to plague us.

—WILLIAM SHAKESPEARE

I haven't a particle of confidence in a man
who has no redeeming petty vices.

—MARK TWAIN[*]

[*] This observation from *Sketches New and Old* (1875) likely inspired Oscar Wilde to say of a colleague, "He hasn't a single redeeming vice." The Wilde quotation has now become more familiar than Twain's original thought on the subject.

VICE & VIRTUE

(see also CONSCIENCE and EVIL and SIN and VICE and
VIRTUE)

We are more apt to catch the vices of others than their virtues,
as disease is far more contagious than health.

—CHARLES CALEB COLTON

There are some faults so nearly allied to excellence
that we can scarce weed out the vice without eradicating the virtue.

—OLIVER GOLDSMITH

There are amiable vices and obnoxious virtues.

—WILLIAM HAZLITT

Virtue by calculation is the virtue of vice.

—JOSEPH JOUBERT

I prefer an accommodating vice to an obstinate virtue.

—MOLIÈRE

Sometimes Virtue starves, while Vice is fed.

—ALEXANDER POPE

Our virtues and vices couple with one another,
and get children that resemble both of their parents.

—GEORGE SAVILE (LORD HALIFAX)

Vices creep into our hearts under the name of virtues.

—LUCIUS ANNAEUS SENECA (SENECA THE YOUNGER)

There is no vice so simple but assumes
Some mark of virtue on his outward parts.

—WILLIAM SHAKESPEARE

There is never an instant's truce between virtue and vice.

—HENRY DAVID THOREAU

VICTORY

(see also DEFEAT and FAILURE and SUCCESS and
VICTORY & DEFEAT)

Victory is by nature haughty and insolent.

—MARCUS TULLIUS CICERO

The god of Victory is said to be one-handed,
but Peace gives victory to both sides.

—RALPH WALDO EMERSON

All victories breed hate,
and that over your superior is foolish or fatal.

—BALTASAR GRACIÁN

Victory is not won in miles but in inches.
Win a little now, hold your ground, and later win a little more.

—LOUIS L'AMOUR

Upon the fields of friendly strife
Are sown the seeds
That, upon other fields, on other days
Will bear the fruits of victory.

—DOUGLAS MACARTHUR[*]

The moment of greatest peril is the moment of victory.

—NAPOLEON BONAPARTE

The moment of victory is much too short to live for that and nothing else.

—MARTINA NAVRATILOVA

It is no doubt a good thing to conquer on the field of battle,
but it needs greater wisdom and greater skill to make use of victory.

—POLYBIUS (SECOND CENTURY BC)

[*] While serving as Superintendent of the U. S. Military Academy at West Point (1919–22), MacArthur initiated many reforms, including mandatory participation in sports activities. He wrote this poem as a rationale and had the words carved on stone portals over the entrance to the school's gymnasium. They continue to be seen there today.

Another such victory and we are undone.

—PYRRHUS (THIRD CENTURY BC)[*]

There is no pain in the wound received in the moment of victory.

—PUBLILIUS SYRUS

VICTORY & DEFEAT

(see also DEFEAT and FAILURE and SUCCESS and
VICTORY)

**The problems of victory
are more agreeable than those of defeat,
but they are no less difficult.**

—WINSTON CHURCHILL

**Victory has a hundred fathers,
but no one wants to recognize defeat as his own.**

—GALEAZZO CIANO[†]

---

[*] This remark from the emperor of the Greek city-state of Epirus after a 279 BC military triumph over the Romans is the origin of the term *pyrrhic* (*PEER-ick*) *victory,* for a win so costly it is indistinguishable from a defeat.

[†] This 1942 diary entry from Italy's WWII foreign minister ultimately morphed into JFK's famous 1961 remark after the Bay of Pigs invasion: "There's an old saying that victory has a hundred fathers and defeat is an orphan."

If one lives long enough, one sees that
every victory sooner or later turns to defeat.

—SIMONE DE BEAUVOIR

A defeat borne with pride is also a victory.

—MARIE VON EBNER-ESCHENBACH

Victory is sweetest when you've known defeat.

—MALCOLM S. FORBES

The fullness of life is in the hazards of life.
And, at the worst, there is that in us which can turn defeat into victory.

—EDITH HAMILTON

There are defeats more triumphant than victories.

—MICHEL DE MONTAIGNE

More people are ruined by victory, I imagine, than by defeat.

—ELEANOR ROOSEVELT

Far better it is to dare mighty things,
to win glorious triumphs, even though checkered by failure,
than to take rank with those poor spirits
who neither enjoy much nor suffer much,
because they live in the gray twilight that knows not victory nor defeat.

—THEODORE ROOSEVELT

Some are destroyed by defeat, and some made small and mean by victory.
Greatness lives in one who triumphs equally over defeat and victory.

—JOHN STEINBECK

VIRTUE

(see also SIN and VICE and VICE & VIRTUE)

There can be no virtue without temptation;
for virtue is victory over temptation.

—LYMAN ABBOTT

Virtue . . . is a mean state between two vices,
the one of excess and the other of deficiency.

—ARISTOTLE[*]

Virtue is like a rich stone, best plain set.

—FRANCIS BACON (1561–1626)

He is ill clothed that is bare of virtue.

—BENJAMIN FRANKLIN

Virtue would not go nearly so far if vanity did not keep her company.

—FRANÇOIS, DUC DE LA ROCHEFOUCAULD

---

[*] This principle, from *Nicomachean Ethics* (fourth century BC), ultimately became known as the Golden Mean.

One advantage resulting from virtuous actions
is that they elevate the mind
and dispose it to attempt others more virtuous still.

—JEAN-JACQUES ROUSSEAU

Virtue must shape itself in deed.

—ALFRED, LORD TENNYSON[*]

The weakest of all weak things is a virtue
that has not been tested in the fire.

—MARK TWAIN

Few men have virtue to withstand the highest bidder.

—GEORGE WASHINGTON

Virtue is the roughest way,
But proves at night a bed of down.

—HENRY WOTTON

---

[*] This passage, written in 1885, is the most elegant expression of an idea that had been expressed earlier. In William Godwin's 1794 novel *Caleb Williams*, for example, a character says: "Virtue, sir, consists in actions, and not in words."

VISION

(see also AIMS & AIMING and ASPIRATION and DREAMS
[Aspirational] and GOALS and PURPOSE)

Your Vision is the promise of what you shall one day be.

—JAMES ALLEN

**We are all visionaries,
and what we see is our soul in things.**

—HENRI FRÉDÉRIC AMIEL

Where there is no vision, the people perish.

—THE BIBLE, PROVERBS 29:18

**The vision must be followed by the venture.
It is not enough to stare up the steps—we must step up the stairs.**

—VANCE HAVNER

**Cherish your visions and your dreams.
They are the children of your soul,
the blueprints of your ultimate achievements.**

—NAPOLEON HILL

**Man cannot live without some vision of himself.
But still less can he live with a vision
that is not true to his inner experience and inner feeling.**

—D. H. LAWRENCE

Nobody sees with his eyes alone;
we see with our souls.

—HENRY MILLER

Throughout the centuries there were men who took first steps
down new roads armed with nothing but their own vision.

—AYN RAND

A rock pile ceases to be a rock pile
the moment a single man contemplates it,
bearing within him the image of a cathedral.

—ANTOINE DE SAINT-EXUPÉRY

Vision is the art of seeing things invisible.

—JONATHAN SWIFT

WAR

(see also POLITICS and POLITICS & RELIGION and
VICTORY and VICTORY & DEFEAT)

The first casualty of war is truth.

—AUTHOR UNKNOWN[*]

---

[*]   This sentiment has long been mistakenly attributed to Hiram Johnson (1866–1945), a US
senator from California.

We used to wonder where war lived,
what it was that made it so vile.
And now we realize that we know where it lives,
that it is inside ourselves.

—ALBERT CAMUS

War is the continuation of politics by other means.

—KARL VON CLAUSEWITZ[*]

I look upon the whole world as my fatherland,
and every war has to me the horror of a family feud.

—HELEN KELLER

Wars are poor chisels for carving out peaceful tomorrows.

—MARTIN LUTHER KING JR.

The most persistent sound which reverberates
through man's history is the beating of war drums.

—ARTHUR KOESTLER

All war is a symptom of man's failure as a thinking animal.

—JOHN STEINBECK

---

[*] This is how the quotation is typically presented—even in many respected reference works—but Ralph Keyes says in *The Quote Verifier* (2006) that Clausewitz meant "*policy* by other means," not *politics*.

War is the unfolding of miscalculations.

—BARBARA W. TUCHMAN

**Before a war military science seems a real science, like astronomy;
but after a war it seems more like astrology.**

—REBECCA WEST

War is fear cloaked in courage.

—WILLIAM C. WESTMORELAND

WEALTH

(see also MONEY [Wise] and MONEY [Wry & Witty] and
SUCCESS)

**If we command our wealth, we shall be rich and free:
if our wealth commands us, we are poor indeed.**

—EDMUND BURKE

**It is only when the rich are sick
that they fully feel the impotence of wealth.**

—CHARLES CALEB COLTON

Without the rich heart, wealth is an ugly beggar.

—RALPH WALDO EMERSON

Wealth is not without its advantages,
and the case to the contrary, although it has often been made,
has never proved widely persuasive.

—JOHN KENNETH GALBRAITH

What a ready passport wealth gives its possessor
to the good opinions of this world!

—SARA JOSEPHA HALE

Wherever there is excessive wealth,
there is also in the train of it excessive poverty;
as, where the sun is brightest, the shade is deepest.

—WALTER SAVAGE LANDOR

Wealth has never the value to its possessor
as it is supposed to have by an avaricious admirer.

—ANTHONY LISLE

Superfluous wealth can buy superfluities only.
Money is not required to buy one necessary of the soul.

—HENRY DAVID THOREAU[*]

Wealth is the product of man's capacity to think.

—AYN RAND

---

[*] Most Internet sites mistakenly present this quotation as if it were phrased "one necessity of the soul."

It isn't what a man has that constitutes wealth.
No—it is to be *satisfied* with what one has; that is wealth.

—MARK TWAIN

WISDOM

(see also FOLLY and FOOLS & FOOLISHNESS and
KNOWLEDGE and LEARNING)

Mixing one's wines may be a mistake,
but old and new wisdom mix admirably.

—BERTOLT BRECHT

Wisdom consists of the anticipation of consequences.

—NORMAN COUSINS

All human wisdom is summed up in these two words—*Wait and Hope.*

—ALEXANDRE DUMAS, PÈRE

The art of being wise is the art of knowing what to overlook.

—WILLIAM JAMES

Wisdom is to the soul what health is to the body.

—FRANÇOIS, DUC DE LA ROCHEFOUCAULD

Humanity has to travel a hard road to wisdom,
and it has to travel it with bleeding feet.

—NELLIE MCCLUNG

The growth of wisdom may be gauged
exactly by the diminution of ill temper.

—FRIEDRICH NIETZSCHE

We do not receive wisdom,
we must discover it for ourselves,
after a journey through the wilderness
which no one else can make for us,
which no one can spare us.

—MARCEL PROUST

It is characteristic of wisdom not to do desperate things.

—HENRY DAVID THOREAU

Wisdom is ofttimes nearer when we stoop
Than when we soar.

—WILLIAM WORDSWORTH

WISHES & WISHING

(see also ASPIRATION and DREAMS [Aspirational] and
GOALS and HOPE)

Destiny has two ways of crushing us—
by refusing our wishes and by fulfilling them.

—HENRI FRÉDÉRIC AMIEL

When you love someone all your saved-up wishes start coming out.

—ELIZABETH BOWEN

It seems to me we can never give up longing and wishing
while we are thoroughly alive.
There are certain things we feel to be beautiful and good,
and we *must* hunger after them.

—GEORGE ELIOT

If man could have half his wishes, he would double his troubles.

—BENJAMIN FRANKLIN

Always leave something to wish for;
otherwise you will be miserable from your very happiness.

—BALTASAR GRACIÁN

In real life wishing, divorced from willing, is sterile and begets nothing.

—CYNTHIA OZICK

If wishes were horses, beggars would ride.

—PROVERB (ENGLISH)

**It seems to me that the most universal revolutionary wish
now or ever is a wish for heaven,
a wish by a human being to be honored by angels
for something other than beauty or usefulness.**

—KURT VONNEGUT JR.

**I mistrust the judgment of every man in a case
in which his own wishes are concerned.**

—ARTHUR WELLESLEY (DUKE OF WELLINGTON)

**Like our shadows,
Our wishes lengthen as our sun declines.**

—EDWARD YOUNG (1683–1765)

WIT

(see also HUMOR and [Sense of] HUMOR and LAUGHTER
and SATIRE and WIT & HUMOR)

**Wit is a treacherous dart.
It is perhaps the only weapon with which it is possible
to stab oneself in one's own back.**

—GEOFFREY BOCCA

Wit is like caviar; it should be savored in small elegant proportions,
and not spread about like marmalade.

—NOËL COWARD

Wit is the salt of conversation, not the food.

—WILLIAM HAZLITT

The greatest fault of a penetrating wit is to go beyond the mark.

—FRANÇOIS, DUC DE LA ROCHEFOUCAULD

Wit has a deadly aim and it is possible
to prick a large pretense with a small pin.

—MARYA MANNES

Impropriety is the soul of wit.

—W. SOMERSET MAUGHAM[*]

There is no possibility of being witty without a little ill-nature;
the malice in a good thing is the barb that makes it stick.

—RICHARD BRINSLEY SHERIDAN

It is with wits as with razors,
which are never so apt to cut those they are employed on
as when they have lost their edge.

—JONATHAN SWIFT

---

[*] Maugham is playing off the classic line from Polonius in Shakespeare's *Hamlet*: "Brevity is the soul of wit."

Somebody has said, "Wit is the sudden marriage of ideas which,
before their union, were not perceived to have any relation."

—MARK TWAIN[*]

Wit is the only wall
Between us and the dark.

—MARK VAN DOREN

WIT & HUMOR

(see also HUMOR and [Sense of] HUMOR and LAUGHTER
and SATIRE and WIT)

There is this difference between wit and humor:
wit makes you think, humor makes you laugh.

—JOSH BILLINGS (HENRY WHEELER SHAW)

Humor comes from self-confidence.
There's an aggressive element to wit.

—RITA MAE BROWN

---

[*]   The thought being recalled by Twain was an 1803 Sydney Smith observation: "The pleasure arising from wit proceeds from our surprise at suddenly discovering two things to be
similar, in which we suspected no similarity."

Humor inspires sympathetic, good-natured laughter
and is favored by the "healing power" gang.
Wit goes for the jugular, not the jocular.

—FLORENCE KING

Humor is of the heart, and has its tears;
but wit is of the head, and has only smiles—
and the majority of those are bitter.

—L. E. LANDON

Don't try for wit. Settle for humor. You'll last longer.

—ELSA MAXWELL

Humor does not include sarcasm, invalid irony,
sardonicism, or any other form of cruelty.
When these things are raised to a high point they can become wit.

—JAMES THURBER

Wit penetrates; humor envelops.
Wit is a function of verbal intelligence;
humor is imagination operating on good nature.

—PEGGY NOONAN

There's a hell of a distance between wisecracking and wit.
Wit has truth in it; wisecracking is simply calisthenics with words.

—DOROTHY PARKER

Wit is born of conscious effort;
humor, of the allotted ironies of fate.
Wit can be expressed only in language;
humor can be developed sufficiently in situation.

—AGNES REPPLIER

Wit and Humor—if any difference it is in duration—
lightning and electric light.
Same material, apparently;
but one is vivid, brief, and can do damage.

—MARK TWAIN

WORDS

(see also IDEAS and LANGUAGE and SPEECH and
THOUGHT and WRITERS and WRITING)

By words the mind is winged.

—ARISTOPHANES

All words are pegs to hang ideas on.

—HENRY WARD BEECHER

Words easy to be understood do often hit the mark,
when high and learned ones do only pierce the air.

—JOHN BUNYAN

One must be drenched in words, literally soaked in them,
to have the right ones form themselves
into the proper patterns at the right moment.

—HART CRANE

Words are like leaves, some wither every year,
And every year a younger race succeeds.

—HORACE

Words are, of course, the most powerful drug used by mankind.

—RUDYARD KIPLING

The beautiful word begets the beautiful deed.

—THOMAS MANN

Apt words have pow'r to swage
The tumors of a troubled mind,
And are as balm to fester'd wounds.

—JOHN MILTON

A word is the carving and coloring of a thought,
and gives it permanence.

—OSBERT SITWELL

For words, like Nature, half reveal
And half conceal the Soul within.

—ALFRED, LORD TENNYSON

WORK

(see also AMBITION and MONEY and SUCCESS and
SUCCESS & FAILURE and WEALTH)

To find joy in work is to discover the fountain of youth.

—PEARL S. BUCK

Every man's work, whether it be literature or music or pictures
or architecture or anything else, is always a portrait of himself.

—SAMUEL BUTLER (1835–1902)

Work is the grand cure of all the maladies
and miseries that ever beset mankind.

—THOMAS CARLYLE

I don't like work—no man does—but I like
what is in the work—the chance to find yourself.

—JOSEPH CONRAD

I look on that man as happy, who, when there is
a question of success, looks into his work for a reply.

—RALPH WALDO EMERSON

Work expands so as to fill the time available for its completion.

—C. NORTHCOTE PARKINSON[*]

---

[*]   Originally written in 1955, this observation went on to achieve quotation immortality as
     Parkinson's Law.

The passions that motivate you may change,
but it is your work in life that is the ultimate seduction.

—PABLO PICASSO

Far and away the best prize that life offers
is the chance to work hard at work worth doing.

—THEODORE ROOSEVELT

If a man love the labor of any trade,
apart from any question of success or fame, the gods have called him.

—ROBERT LOUIS STEVENSON

The greatest analgesic, soporific, stimulant, tranquilizer,
narcotic, and to some extent even antibiotic—in short, the closest thing
to a genuine panacea—known to medical science is work.

—THOMAS SZASZ

WRITERS

(see also AUTHORS and BOOKS and BOOKSTORES
and LITERATURE and NOVELS and READING and
WRITERS—ON THEMSELVES and WRITING)

The writer of good will carries a lamp to illuminate the dark corners.
Only that, nothing more—a tiny beam of light
to show some hidden aspect of reality.

—ISABEL ALLENDE

The responsibility of a writer
is to excavate the experience of the people who produced him.

—JAMES BALDWIN

A writer is a reader moved to emulation.

—SAUL BELLOW

A great writer creates a world of his own
and his readers are proud to live in it.
A lesser writer may entice them in for a moment,
but soon he will watch them filing out.

—CYRIL CONNOLLY

The writer is an explorer.
Every step is an advance into a new land.

—RALPH WALDO EMERSON

It is splendid to be a great writer,
to put men into the frying pan of your words
and make them pop like chestnuts.

—GUSTAVE FLAUBERT

Thought flies and words go on foot.
Therein lies all the drama of the writer.

—JULIEN GREEN

We never know how much has been missing from our lives
until a true writer comes along.

—ALFRED KAZIN

Writers do not live one life, they live two.
There is the living and then there is the writing.
There is the second tasting.

—ANAÏS NIN

A writer out of loneliness is trying to communicate
like a distant star sending signals . . .
he seeks to establish a relationship.

—JOHN STEINBECK

WRITERS—ON THEMSELVES & THEIR WORK

(see also AUTHORS and BOOKS and BOOKSTORES and
LITERATURE and NOVELS and READING and WRITERS
and WRITING and WRITING ADVICE)

It has always been my ambition to die in harness
with my head face down on a keyboard
and my nose caught between two of the keys.

—ISAAC ASIMOV

I am a galley slave to pen and ink.

—HONORÉ DE BALZAC

My stories have led me through my life.
They shout, I follow. They run up and bite me on the leg—
I respond by writing down everything that goes on during the bite.
When I finish, the idea lets go.

—RAY BRADBURY

I can't write without a reader.
It's precisely like a kiss—you can't do it alone.

—JOHN CHEEVER

Medicine is my lawful wife and literature is my mistress.
When I get tired of one, I spend the night with the other.

—ANTON CHEKHOV[*]

A day when I do not write tastes of ashes.

—SIMONE DE BEAUVOIR

I look at my books the way parents look at their children.
The fact that one becomes more successful than the other
doesn't make them love the less successful one any less.

—ALEX HALEY

---

[*] Chekhov was a practicing physician as well as a writer. He began writing in his spare time while in medical school, and he juggled both careers until his premature death at age forty-four (from complications related to tuberculosis).

I live with the people I create
and it has always made my essential loneliness less keen.

—CARSON MCCULLERS

I have never written a book that was not
born out of a question I needed to answer for myself.

—MAY SARTON

There is no doubt that I have lots of words inside me;
but at moments, like rush-hour traffic at the mouth of a tunnel, they jam.

—JOHN UPDIKE

WRITING

(see also AUTHORS and BOOKS and LITERATURE and
NOVELISTS and NOVELS and WRITERS and WRITERS—
ON THEMSELVES & THEIR WORK and WRITING
ADVICE)

It is easy to write a check if you have enough money in the bank,
and writing comes more easily if you have something to say.

—SHOLEM ASCH

Writing is to descend like a miner to the depths of the mine
with a lamp on your forehead,
a light whose dubious brightness falsifies everything,
whose wick is in permanent danger of explosion, whose blinking
illumination in the coal dust exhausts and corrodes your eyes.

—BLAISE CENDRARS

Writing a book is an adventure.
To begin with it is a toy, then an amusement.
Then it becomes a mistress, and then it becomes a master,
and then it becomes a tyrant and, in the last stage,
just as you are about to be reconciled to your servitude,
you kill the monster and fling him to the public.

—WINSTON CHURCHILL

Writing is like driving at night.
You can see only as far as the headlights,
but you can make the whole trip that way.

—E. L. DOCTOROW

Writing is not an amusing occupation.
It is a combination of ditch-digging,
mountain-climbing, treadmill, and childbirth.
Writing may be interesting, absorbing, exhilarating, racking, relieving.
But amusing? Never!

— EDNA FERBER

Writing books is the closest men ever come to childbearing.

—NORMAN MAILER

True ease in writing comes from art, not chance,
As those move easiest who have learned to dance.

—ALEXANDER POPE

Writing a column is easy. You just sit at your typewriter
until little drops of blood appear on your forehead.

—WALTER "RED" SMITH[*]

Writing is, for most, laborious and slow.
The mind travels faster than the pen; consequently,
writing becomes a question of learning to make occasional wing shots,
bringing down the bird of thought as it flashes by.

—E. B. WHITE

Writing is thinking on paper.

—WILLIAM K. ZINSSER

WRITING ADVICE

(see also ADVICE and AUTHORS and BOOKS and FICTION
and LITERATURE and NOVELS and WRITERS and
WRITING)

You are working in clay, not marble, on paper, not eternal bronze;
let that first sentence be as stupid as it wishes.

—JACQUES BARZUN

[*] Smith offered various versions of this thought in his career, the earliest in 1949. He may
have been inspired by a similar metaphor from fellow sportswriter Paul Gallico, who
wrote in *Confessions of a Story Writer* (1946): "It is only when you open your veins and
bleed onto the page a little that you establish contact with your reader."

Dear authors! Suit your topics to your strength,
And ponder well your subject, and its length;
Nor lift your load, before you're quite aware
What weight your shoulders will, or will not, bear.

—GEORGE NOEL GORDON, LORD BYRON

One of the few things I know about writing is this:
spend it all, shoot it, play it, lose it, all, right away, every time.
Do not hoard what seems good for a later place in the book,
or for another book; give it, give it all, give it now.

—ANNIE DILLARD

Cut out all those exclamation marks.
An exclamation mark is like laughing at your own joke.

—F. SCOTT FITZGERALD

Be still when you have nothing to say;
when genuine passion moves you, say what you've got to say, and say it hot.

—D. H. LAWRENCE

You expect far too much of a first sentence.
Think of it as analogous to a good country breakfast:
What we want is something simple, but nourishing to the imagination.
Hold the philosophy, hold the adjectives,
just give us a plain subject and verb,
and perhaps a wholesome, nonfattening adverb or two.

—LARRY MCMURTRY

If you here require a practical rule of me,
I will present you with this:
"Whenever you feel an impulse to perpetrate a piece
of exceptionally fine writing, obey it—wholeheartedly—
and delete it before sending your manuscript to press.
Murder your darlings."

—ARTHUR QUILLER-COUCH [*]

Vigorous writing is concise.
A sentence should contain no unnecessary words,
a paragraph no unnecessary sentences,
for the same reason that a drawing should have no unnecessary lines
and a machine no unnecessary parts.

—WILLIAM STRUNK JR.

A sentence should read as if its author,
had he held a plough instead of a pen,
could have drawn a furrow deep and straight to the end.

—HENRY DAVID THOREAU

Only write when your pillow is on fire.

—ELIE WIESEL

[*]   Quiller-Couch, who offered this advice in *On The Art of Writing* (1916), was almost
certainly familiar with a similar remark made by Samuel Johnson in 1773. Discussing
a contemporary writer known for his verbosity, Johnson said he would benefit from the
words of "an old college tutor" who had advised: "Read over your compositions, and
wherever you meet with a passage which you think is particularly fine, strike it out."

YEARS

(see also AGE & AGING and MATURITY and TIME and
YOUTH & AGE)

Years teach us more than books.

—BERTHOLD AUERBACH

Who expects small things to survive
when even the largest get lost?
People forget years and remember moments.

—ANN BEATTIE

Years steal
Fire from the mind as vigor from the limb.

—GEORGE NOEL GORDON, LORD BYRON

I could not prove that years had feet—
Yet confident they run.

—EMILY DICKINSON

The years teach much which the days never know.

—RALPH WALDO EMERSON

There are years that ask questions and years that answer.

—ZORA NEALE HURSTON

Our years
Glide silently away.

—HORACE

Years are only garments,
and you either wear them with style all your life,
or else you go dowdy to the grave.

—DOROTHY PARKER

I have wrung the color from the years,
And I have seen the red blood flow and tears,
And I have seen gold come and love pass by.

—FRANCIS POLLOCK

Years following years steal something every day;
At last they steal us from ourselves away.

—ALEXANDER POPE

YOUTH

(see also ADOLESCENCE and AGE & AGING and
CHILDREN and CHILDHOOD and YOUTH & AGE)

The young are permanently in a state resembling intoxication.

—ARISTOTLE

Youth has the resilience to absorb disaster
and weave it into the pattern of its life,
no matter how anguishing the thorn that penetrates its flesh.

—SHOLEM ASCH

Youth is like spring, an overpraised season—
delightful if it happen to be a favored one,
but in practice very rarely favored and more remarkable,
as a general rule, for biting east winds than genial breezes.

—SAMUEL BUTLER (1835–1902)

The two things that nearly all of us
have thoroughly and really been through are childhood and youth.
And though we would not have them back again on any account,
we feel that they are both beautiful, because we have drunk them dry.

—G. K. CHESTERTON

Youth is a marvelous garment.

—IRIS MURDOCH

It is not possible for civilization to flow backward
while there is youth in the world.

—HELEN KELLER

Youth is the seed-time of good habits, as well in nations as in individuals.

—THOMAS PAINE

In early youth, as we contemplate our coming life,
we are like children in a theater before the curtain is raised,
sitting there in high spirits and eagerly waiting for the play to begin.
—ARTHUR SCHOPENHAUER

Don't laugh at a youth for his affectations;
he is only trying on one face after another to find a face of his own.
—LOGAN PEARSALL SMITH

The deepest definition of Youth is Life as yet untouched by tragedy.
—ALFRED NORTH WHITEHEAD

YOUTH & AGE

(see also ADOLESCENCE and AGE & AGING and
CHILDHOOD and MATURITY and YOUTH)

The arrogance of age must submit to be taught by youth.
—EDMUND BURKE

The excesses of our youth are drafts upon our old age,
payable with interest, about thirty years after date.
—CHARLES CALEB COLTON

Say "no" to the fountain of youth and turn on the fountain of age.
—BETTY FRIEDAN

Youth lives on hope, old age on remembrance.

—GEORGE HERBERT

So different are the colors of life
as we look forward to the future, or backward to the past . . .
that the conversation of the old and young
ends generally with contempt or pity on either side.

—SAMUEL JOHNSON

Youth is the gift of nature, but age is a work of art.

—GARSON KANIN

Youth wrenches the scepter from old age,
and sets the crown on its own head before it is entitled to it.

—HENRY WADSWORTH LONGFELLOW

Old age is ready to undertake tasks
that youth shirked because they would take too long.

—W. SOMERSET MAUGHAM

The denunciation of the young
is a necessary part of the hygiene of older people,
and greatly assists the circulation of their blood.

—LOGAN PEARSALL SMITH

It is so easy for a middle-aged person,
in the presence of youth, to be deluded about his own age.
The young faces are so exactly like the one
he saw in his own mirror—only day before yesterday, it seems.
The young, on the other hand, look into visages dull-eyed,
long-toothed, wattle-necked, and chop-fallen, something
they have never been and which they cannot imagine ever being.

—JESSAMYN WEST

ZEAL

(see also ENTHUSIASM and FANATICISM and
MODERATION and PASSION)

Zeal should not outrun discretion.

—AESOP

Zeal, *n.* A certain nervous disorder afflicting the young and inexperienced.
A passion that goeth before a sprawl.

—AMBROSE BIERCE[*]

The greatest dangers to liberty lurk in insidious encroachment
by men of zeal, well-meaning but without understanding.

—LOUIS BRANDEIS

---

[*] Bierce is playing off "Pride goeth before a fall," an English proverb derived from the biblical passage: "Pride goeth before destruction, and a haughty spirit before a fall" (*Book of Proverbs*, 16:18)

All zeal for a reform that gives offense
To peace and charity, is mere pretense.

—WILLIAM COWPER

Zeal without knowledge is the sister of folly.

—JOHN DAVIES

Because zeal is an ardent and vehement love,
it requires guidance; otherwise it can become excessive.

—SAINT FRANCIS DE SALES

Zeal is a volcano, on the peak of which
the grass of indecisiveness does not grow.

—KAHLIL GIBRAN

There is a holy mistaken zeal in politics, as well as in religion.
By persuading others, we convince ourselves.

—JUNIUS

Zeal without knowledge is fire without light.

—PROVERB (ENGLISH)

Zeal is only fit for wise men;
but it is chiefly in fashion among fools.

—JOHN TILLOTSON

acknowledgments

My deepest gratitude goes to my wife, Katherine Robinson, a partner in every aspect of my life, including my book-writing efforts.

I'm also deeply grateful to my agent, George Greenfield of *CreativeWell, Inc.*, and Hannah Robinson, my HarperCollins editor. This book would never have come to fruition without them.

Richard Nordquist has been a continual source of encouragement and a first-rate reactor to every idea I've asked him to consider. The same can be said for Leonard Roy Frank, who passed away while I was working on this project.

Dan Hart and David Hartson, two of my oldest and dearest friends, provided support, encouragement, and a fresh perspective every step of the way. Thanks also to Don Hauptman for his regular *Donvelopes*. And finally, Linnda Durré, Tom Howe, and Carolanne Reynolds deserve proofreading medals and editing awards for meticulously poring over first-draft material.

Whenever I was stymied in my quotation-verification efforts, I took comfort in knowing that three of the world's great quotation sleuths had my back: Ralph Keyes, author of *The Quote Verifier* (2006), Garson O'Toole, also known as The Quote Investigator (www.quoteinvestigator.com), and Barry Popik of The Big Apple website (www.barrypopik.com).

A book like this would have been impossible without the efforts of innumerable quotation collectors who've preceded me over the centuries. In this project, though, I also benefited enormously from the work of three current quotation anthologists: Rosalie Maggio of the "Quotations by Women" website (www.quotationsbywomen.com), Fred R. Shapiro, editor of the *Yale Book of Quotations* (2006), and G. Armour Van Horn of the "Quotes of the Day" website (www.qotd.org).

Several thousand subscribers to my weekly e-newsletter—far too numerous to list here—have cheered me on for years and alerted me to many of the quotations that ultimately found their way into this book. My heartfelt thanks to all of them.

Author Index

Author Index { *463* }

Author Index { *470* }

Author Index { *472* }

Author Index { 473 }

Author Index { 477 }

about the author

DR. MARDY GROTHE is a retired psychologist, management consultant, and platform speaker, the author of six word and language books, and the creator of *Dr. Mardy's Dictionary of Metaphorical Quotations (DMDMQ)*, the world's largest online database of metaphorical quotations. Dr. Mardy—as he is known to his many fans around the globe—is one of America's most beloved quotation anthologists. He lives in North Carolina with his wife, Katherine Robinson.

WWW.DRMARDY.COM

ALSO BY
DR. MARDY GROTHE

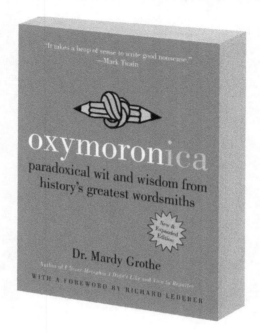

oxymoronica

Paradoxical Wit and Wisdom from History's Greatest Wordsmiths

Available in Paperback and Ebook

"Truly the most comprehensible collection of contradictions around."
— Erin McKean, former editor of the *New Oxford American*
***Dictionary* and founder of Wordnik**

For over a decade Dr. Mardy Grothe has delighted readers with this
collection of 1,400 of the most provocative quotations of all time.